INTO THE LABYRINTH
THE UNITED STATES AND THE MIDDLE EAST
1945–1993

America in Crisis

A series of books on American Diplomatic History

EDITOR: Robert A. Divine

INTO THE LABYRINTH
THE UNITED STATES AND THE MIDDLE EAST
1945–1993

H. W. Brands
Professor of History
Texas A&M University

McGraw-Hill, Inc.

New York   St. Louis   San Francisco   Auckland   Bogotá   Caracas
Lisbon   London   Madrid   Mexico City   Milan   Montreal   New Delhi
San Juan   Singapore   Sydney   Tokyo   Toronto

INTO THE LABYRINTH
THE UNITED STATES AND THE MIDDLE EAST, 1945–1993

This book is printed on recycled paper containing a minimum of 50% total recycled fiber with 10% postconsumer de-inked fiber.

1 2 3 4 5 6 7 8 9 0   DOH   DOH   9 0 9 8 7 6 5 4 3

ISBN 0-07-007188-8

This book was set in Caledonia by The Clarinda Company.
The editor was Peter Labella;
the production supervisor was Richard A. Ausburn.
The cover was designed by Nicholas Krenitsky.
R. R. Donnelley & Sons Company was printer and binder.

Library of Congress Cataloging-in-Publication Data

Brands, H. W.
    Into the labyrinth: the United States and the Middle East,
    1945–1993 / H. W. Brands.
        p.   cm.
    Includes bibliographical references and index.
    ISBN 0-07-007188-8
        1. Middle East—Foreign relations—United States.   2. United
    States—Foreign relations—Middle East.   I. Title.
    DS63.2.U5B73   1994
    327.73056—dc20   93-28110

About the Author

H. W. Brands grew up in Oregon before earning history degrees at Stanford University and the University of Texas at Austin. He has taught at the University of Texas, Vanderbilt University, and Texas A & M University. He is the author of nine books on American history and international relations. Recent titles include *The Devil We Knew: Americans and the Cold War* and *The United States in the World: A History of American International Relations.*

Contents

Foreword

"The United States always wins the war and loses the peace," runs a persistent popular complaint. Neither part of the statement is accurate. The United States barely escaped the War of 1812 with its territory intact, and in Korea in the 1950s the nation was forced to settle for a stalemate on the battlefield. At Paris in 1782, and again in 1898, American negotiators drove hard bargains to win notable diplomatic victories. Yet the myth persists, along with the equally erroneous American belief that we are a peaceful people. Our history is studded with conflict and violence. From the Revolution to the Cold War, Americans have been willing to fight for their interests, their beliefs, and their ambitions. The United States has gone to war for many objectives—for independence in 1775, for honor and trade in 1812, for territory in 1846, for humanity and empire in 1898, for neutral rights in 1917, and for national security in 1941. Since 1945 the nation has been engaged in two wars in Asia, a relatively brief but bloody struggle in Korea, and a longer and even more tragic encounter in Vietnam. And most recently, Americans fought for both oil and the Wilsonian principle of collective security in the Persian Gulf War.

In this volume of the America in Crisis series, Professor H. W. Brands provides a comprehensive and balanced overview of American policy in the Middle East since 1945. Defining the region broadly, he covers both familiar topics such as the dangerous Suez crisis of 1956, the embarrassing Iranian hostage episode, and the triumphant Gulf War, as well as less well-known incidents like the Cyprus crisis and the civil war in Yemen in the 1960s. The result is a book that not only relates the Middle East to the broader issues of the Cold War but also illuminates the specific dilemmas confronting American diplomats in a strange and exotic part of the world. By bringing his account down to Desert Storm, he is able to show how even the end of the Cold War did not resolve the difficulties this region posed for American interests. The vast oil reserves of the Persian Gulf as well as the long-standing American commitment to the survival of Israel transcended the power struggle between the United States and the Soviet Union. In describing the last half-century of American experience in the Middle East, Professor Brands offers insight and perspective on the issues the United States still faces in the troubled area.

Robert A. Divine

Preface

Shortly before World War II began, a writer in *Harper's* magazine surveyed American relations with the various peoples and regions of the world. Arriving at the Middle East, he declared, "Our relations with these people are not important." Several months later, an American diplomat drew an assignment to the Middle East and prepared for a boring turn of duty. An associate commiserated, saying of the area, "Nothing ever happens there." As late as 1943, an American government official who displeased President Franklin Roosevelt was exiled to Iraq, on the reasoning that he could hardly cause trouble in such an insignificant, out-of-the-way place.

Half a century later, it requires a stretch of the historical imagination to fathom such opinions. Since 1945, no portion of the planet has been at the center of more momentous events than the Middle East. Hardly a year has passed without a war somewhere in the neighborhood, without a revolution or a couple of coups, without an embargo of oil, without airplane hijackings or hostage-takings. And for much of the period from 1945 until the 1990s, every time a crisis roiled the region, the world held its breath to see how this latest nail-biter would affect the superpowers, and whether this one might be the long-feared trigger to touch off World War III.

Americans, despite their pre-1945 lack of interest in the Middle East, soon came to recognize the region's importance. World War II wrought a revolution in American foreign policy, with Pearl Harbor and its aftermath thoroughly discrediting the isolationists who had kept the United States on the sidelines of world affairs during the 1930s. By 1945, most Americans, and nearly all American policy makers, believed that the United States must take an active part in keeping the peace in areas previously beyond the pale of official American concern. The Middle East, where peace chronically needed keeping, was one of those areas.

Three factors, in particular, drew American attention to the Middle East: oil, the Soviet Union, and Israel. Oil preoccupied American policy makers during the decades after 1945, for the reason that

American petroleum demand, and that of the United States' allies, outstripped Western petroleum production. The Middle East was the world's largest source of exportable oil; therefore, the Middle East was vital to the prosperity and security of the Western alliance. World oil prices jumped with every jolt to the Middle Eastern status quo; each jump threatened the United States and its trading partners with inflation, recession, or both. The mere thought of a cutoff of Middle Eastern oil gave American leaders nightmares. Although the United States might survive a petroleum blockade, relying on its own resources and alternative suppliers, the Europeans and Japanese, both of whom were more dependent on Middle Eastern oil than the United States, would be terribly tempted to come to terms with the blockaders. What such temptations might do to the Western alliance was anyone's guess. None of the guesses afforded encouragement.

If oil preoccupied American leaders, the Soviet Union—the second cause of American interest in the Middle East—obsessed them. From the late 1940s until the late 1980s, Americans worried about the Soviet Union more than they have ever worried about any other foreign foe. And with good cause: never has any other country possessed the power to wipe out American civilization within a matter of hours. In reality, few American leaders expected a bolt from the blue; instead, they feared a gradual expansion of Soviet influence in regions that mattered to the welfare of the West—regions such as the Middle East. For four decades after World War II, American officials worked strenuously to keep the Soviets out of the Middle East. Washington never succeeded entirely, but each advance by the Kremlin simply caused American leaders to work all the harder. Not until the self-liquidation of the Soviet Union in the early 1990s did American leaders allow themselves to relax.

Concerns about oil and the Soviet Union pulled Americans in the same direction: stymieing Soviet adventurism in the Middle East helped guarantee Western access to oil, while Middle Eastern oil helped guarantee the Western economic, military, and political power that stymied Soviet adventurism. By contrast, the third factor that made the Middle East so important to Americans—Israel—pulled them in the opposite direction. Nearly all the oil of the Middle East lay beneath the soil of Israel's enemies; by supporting Israel, the United States tended to alienate the West's oil suppliers. Likewise, by backing the Israelis, Washington encouraged several of Israel's enemies to look to Moscow for support. Nonetheless, the American people and the administrations of nine American presidents (if not always the State Department and other Washington bureaus) consistently judged the Zionist dream of a Jewish homeland in Palestine worthy of American assistance. Sometimes the assistance took diplomatic and political form; sometimes it came in the harder currency of dollars and weapons. But it rarely faltered, and never for long.

These three factors—oil, the Soviet Union, and Israel—as well as some lesser concerns, propelled the United States into the affairs of the Middle East to an extent most Americans of the pre-1945 era could hardly have imagined. American involvement didn't happen all at once; it developed over nearly half a century. Nor did it happen according to any preconceived plan. To a greater extent than American dealings with some other parts of the world, American relations with the Middle East were frequently reactive, consisting of ad hoc responses to regional crises. The three strongest influences on American policies—oil, the Soviet Union, and Israel—were simply that: influences. They disposed Americans to act in certain ways, but they didn't entirely determine American actions. Coming to grips with the Middle East defied easy formulas.

By whatever means accomplished, the cumulative change in American relations with the Middle East was breathtaking. In 1945, it never would have occurred to an American president to send 500,000 American soldiers to settle a dispute between two Arab countries, and the American public never would have supported a president who hatched such a crazy scheme. In the early 1990s, not only could an American president order a half million troops to war in the Persian Gulf, but the American public enthusiastically approved his decision to do so. How and why this great change took place is the subject of what follows.

I would like to thank Robert Divine for suggesting the topic of this book, and for commenting on an early version of the manuscript. Nathan Brown, George Washington University, and Howard Jones, University of Alabama, likewise offered valuable suggestions for improvements. Peter Labella, Laura Warner, and the staff at McGraw-Hill made the production process a pleasure.

H. W. Brands

Clement Attlee of Britain, Harry Truman of the United States, and Joseph Stalin of the Soviet Union at the Potsdam conference, August 1945. *(Truman Library / U.S. Army)*

American Secretary of State Dean Acheson and Iranian Prime Minister Muhammad Mossadeq during the Anglo-Iranian oil dispute. *(Truman Library / U.S. Department of State)*

David Ben Gurion of Israel and Dwight Eisenhower in Washington. *(Eisenhower Library / National Park Service)*

Eisenhower and Egypt's Gamal Abdul Nasser at the Waldorf Astoria Hotel in New York, September 1960. *(Eisenhower Library / Nat Fein: New York Herald Tribune)*

**John Kennedy and then Israeli Foreign Minister Golda Meir,
September 1961.** *(Kennedy Library)*

**Israeli Prime Minister Levi Eshkol and Lyndon Johnson after the
June War of 1967.** *(Johnson Library)*

Anwar Sadat of Egypt, Jimmy Carter of the United States, and Menachem Begin of Israel at the Camp David conference. (*Carter Library*)

Carter and the Shah of Iran in Washington. (*Carter Library*)

INTO THE LABYRINTH
THE UNITED STATES AND THE MIDDLE EAST
1945–1993

Chapter 1

First Entanglements: 1945–1948

1. IN THE BEGINNING

Before World War II, the Middle East was about as far away conceptually from the United States as it was possible for an inhabited, civilized region to be. Americans were relatively familiar with East Asia: for a century and a half, American traders had plied the Pacific routes, and for a shorter but not insignificant period, American missionaries had struggled to stem the Niagara of heathen souls plunging from China into the eternal abyss. Americans knew less of India but still something: the transcendentalists of the nineteenth century had fostered a vogue for Indian religions and philosophy. American impressions of Africa were often wrong, but the existence in the United States of several million souls of African descent kept the idea of Africa alive.

American connections to the Middle East were more tenuous. Early explorers of North America had harbored fuzzy notions about discovering the lost tribes of Israel in the American wilderness; Puritans and other empire-of-the-soul builders spoke of raising a new Jerusalem on the Atlantic's western shore; the great majority of Americans who were Christians considered Jesus' homeland holy. But the lost Israelites were never found; the new-Jerusalem language was chiefly allegorical; and not since the Crusades had many Christians thought of the Holy Land as a place they might actually visit. Although American Jews took the idea of Jerusalem more seriously, before the end of the nineteenth century they were only a handful, and, existing in an overwhelmingly Christian and often antisemitic culture, their views carried little weight in American society as a whole.

The great immigration that brought three million Jews from Eastern Europe to the United States between 1880 and 1920 changed the situation somewhat. Not only did their growing numbers raise the visibility in American politics of their concerns, but their arrival coincided with the birth of modern Zionism—the quest for a distinct Jewish homeland, preferably in Palestine—which was itself partly the product of the economic and political forces that triggered the Jewish emigration from Europe. When Zionist founder Theodor Herzl of Hungary died in 1904, mourning swept much of Manhattan's Lower East Side, the home of America's largest Jewish community. American politicians who hoped to draw support in districts containing large numbers of Jews paid increasing attention to what was on those constituents' minds. Other politicians and demagogues who engaged in the older, nativist politics could likewise support the Zionist project as a way of diverting the flow of Jews away from the United States.

As would be true through most of the twentieth century, Jewish voters counted more heavily with the Democratic party than with the Republicans, and when World War I raised the Zionist issue in international politics, Democratic President Woodrow Wilson paid heed. At the behest of Supreme Court Justice and fellow progressive Louis Brandeis, Wilson endorsed the British Balfour Declaration of 1917, the landmark statement affirming that the British government would look favorably on "the establishment in Palestine of a national home for the Jewish people." Amid all the other questions relating to the world war and the subsequent peace settlement, though, Wilson declined to press the issue of a Jewish "national home," whatever that might turn out to be. In particular, he recognized the problems the Zionist program raised for one of his Fourteen Points for peace—the point regarding self-determination—as it applied to the Arabs of Palestine.

Taking advantage of Wilson's diffidence, the U.S. State Department set about circumscribing and generally undermining the president's policy. To a certain extent, the obstructionism of the professional diplomats reflected personal pique: in arranging Wilson's backing for the Balfour Declaration, the Zionists had sidestepped the State Department and gone straight to the White House. Such out-of-channels maneuvering always upsets bureaucrats. To a certain extent, the State Department's resistance revealed antisemitism among the old boys of the department. Most important, it indicated a belief that intruding a new and unsettling element like a Jewish homeland into the Middle East would create many more problems than it would solve, and that associating the United States with such an intrusion would produce endless trouble for Americans. On the oft-proven premise that presidents come and go while bureaucrats remain, the State Department dragged its heels on anything that smacked of implementing the Zionists' goals.

The heel-dragging worked, with the result that for the next generation the United States remained in the background on the Zionist question. Occasionally the diplomats had to deal with other outsiders invading their turf. In 1922, Congress passed a resolution supporting the Balfour Declaration, although—in keeping with the same standoffishness that had caused the Senate to reject the post-World War I peace settlement and membership in the League of Nations—the congressional vote committed the United States to nothing in particular. The revival during the 1920s of the Ku Klux Klan, whose adherents now lumped Jews with blacks, Catholics, feminists, and other radicals as subverters of American values, encouraged a low profile on the part of American Jews; at the same time, however, it demonstrated the desirability of a place Jews could call their own. In 1929, riots at Jerusalem's Western Wall resulted in the deaths of several American Jews and a request by Rabbi Stephen Wise for the State Department's assistance in presenting the Jewish case to an investigative commission of the British government of Palestine. The State Department conspicuously refrained from helping, wanting nothing to do with the matter.

Events of the 1930s thrust the United States slightly further forward. Hitler's pressure on the Jews of Germany inclined many Americans to look more favorably on a Jewish homeland—again if only to prevent the Jews from coming to the United States. When Britain's Peel Commission in 1937 recommended the partition of Palestine and the creation of a Jewish state, American officials waffled, protesting not the Peel report per se but the fact that the British had neglected to consult Washington in advance of its release. This hair-splitting struck the State Department's numerous critics as characteristic of all that was wrong with the United States' handling of the Zionist question. Two years later, when the British government issued an instantly controversial White Paper rejecting the Peel report and advocating strict limits on Jewish immigration to Palestine, Secretary of State Cordell Hull announced that American responsibilities did not include trying to prevent alterations in Britain's governance of Palestine.

Developments of the early 1940s laid the basis for a major change in the United States' Palestine policy, although other developments of the same period prevented the Roosevelt administration from taking immediate action. As the Nazi "final solution" to the Jewish question in Europe assumed its ghastly shape, reports of the extermination program filtered out to Washington. So monstrous were the activities the reports recounted, though, that even American Zionists found the stories hard to credit. In July 1943, a member of the Polish underground who had seen the concentration camp at Belsen for himself, and who had additional firsthand information regarding Auschwitz, Dachau, and Treblinka, informed Supreme Court Justice Felix Frankfurter that nearly two million Jews had already been murdered in Poland and that the Germans intended to kill all the Jews they could get their hands on. Frankfurter didn't believe the account. "I do not have the strength to believe it," he said.[1]

If Frankfurter couldn't believe what was happening to his fellow Jews, Roosevelt had still greater difficulty with the reports. Having served in the Wilson administration during World War I, Roosevelt remembered the exaggerated atrocity stories the British had foisted on the United States at that time; he had no desire to be similarly suckered as president. After the war, when the reports of the murder of the Jews became undeniable, the great crime would impel the American government to press for the creation of a Jewish state. Meanwhile, however, Roosevelt could reasonably argue that the best policy for saving the Jews was one designed to defeat Germany as soon as possible. Such was the tack he took in response to the same account Frankfurter heard. "You tell your leaders in Poland they have a friend in the White House," the president said. "We shall win the war. The guilty will be punished."[2]

Just as World War II increased America's official sensitivity to the Zionist issue, it also elevated Washington's concern regarding Middle Eastern oil. Americans didn't worry about running short of oil themselves; in 1938, the United States produced 60 percent of global output. By comparison, Iran pumped less than 4 percent and Iraq less than 2 percent, while in Saudi Arabia the first commercial production was just coming on line. Within the past decade, East Texas crude had sold for 10 cents per barrel. American oilmen worried more about limiting production than about expanding it.

[1] Peter Grose, *Israel in the Mind of America* (New York, 1983), pp. 132–133.
[2] Idem.

The situation hadn't always been thus. During World War I, when the Allied powers had owed much of their victory to their advantage in oil, American leaders had begun to draw a connection between petroleum and American national security. Simultaneously, the automobile boom was creating a tremendous new demand for oil. In the first two decades of the twentieth century, the number of cars and trucks on American roads jumped nearly a thousandfold, and the American energy economy shifted from one fired by coal to one driven by petroleum. Meanwhile the American oil industry had entered a dry spell between major discoveries. The Spindletop field in southeast Texas had blown in at the turn of the century; wildcatters wouldn't find the huge East Texas field until the 1930s.

With the United States' production predicted to peak and demand outpacing domestic discoveries, Americans started looking abroad for fresh sources of supply. The British and French, however, had started looking sooner and enjoyed a sizable lead in promising places like the Middle East. Nor did they seem willing to relinquish their lead. In 1920, by the so-called San Remo accord, London and Paris agreed on a common front against American entry into Mesopotamia (Iraq). When news of the San Remo pact made its way to the United States, American oil companies, led by Standard Oil of New Jersey, appealed to Washington to lend a hand in cracking the European cartel. Jersey Standard was low on reserves following the 1911 court-ordered breakup of John D. Rockefeller's trust, and so it asked the State and Commerce departments to lean on Britain and France to allow American firms, including especially itself, equal access to Mesopotamian oil.

The British initially responded that the Americans had little cause for complaint. Washington had refused to accept the responsibilities for maintaining world peace inherent in membership in the League of Nations; therefore, Washington shouldn't expect to share in the rewards accruing to members. Ultimately, though, the British and French decided not to alienate the Americans, their principal creditors and their fallback guarantors against a revived Germany and perhaps a belligerent Japan. After haggling for several years, Britain and France in 1928 consented to let American firms join the consortium that controlled petroleum concessions throughout the former Ottoman Empire. (The domain of the consortium was defined by a red line on a French map: hence the name "Red Line agreement" for the deal that specified what members consented to do and refrain from doing.)

Not long after this, new discoveries in the United States and the onset of the depression of the 1930s eased pressure for finding more oil overseas, although activity abroad never ceased. In 1933, Standard Oil of California, a nonparticipant in the Red Line consortium, acquired a concession in Saudi Arabia and created a subsidiary, the California Arabian Standard Oil Company, or Casoc, to exploit it. Casoc subsequently brought in the Texas Company to form what in 1944 would become the Arabian American Oil Company, or Aramco. But Casoc's drillers didn't hit oil in paying quantities until nearly the end of the 1930s, and in the interim, Middle Eastern oil slumbered as an issue in American foreign relations.

The approach of war gradually roused the Roosevelt administration. Accepting, for the sake of diplomacy, if not quite believing, Casoc's dubious argument that Saudi King Ibn Saud had granted concessionary rights to the Americans because he admired their political ideals, and the similarly specious claim that the Germans and Japanese were making significant inroads on the Arabian peninsula, the State Department recommended strengthening American representation at Ibn Saud's court. Roosevelt accepted the recommendation.

The outbreak of fighting in Europe initially stimulated Casoc's sales and production, but after Italy entered the conflict in June 1940 and disrupted tanker traffic in the Mediterranean, the company's revenues started falling. With them, Saud's royalty receipts slumped. Coming atop a drastic decrease in the numbers of pilgrims to Saudi Arabia's holy sites, the shortfall threatened the regime with bankruptcy. Saud turned to Casoc, demanding $6 million to keep his government afloat. Hard up itself, not least from having already advanced the king several million dollars against future royalties, Casoc turned to Washington.

The Roosevelt administration evinced sympathy, less for Casoc than for Saud. Presidential adviser Harry Hopkins suggested using the new Lend-Lease program to prop up Saud's government, although Hopkins recognized that Saud might be a tough sell to Congress, which preferred sending aid to democracies. At first, Roosevelt refused Hopkins's suggestion. The president judged Saudi Arabia's feudal monarchy a little far afield for his political tastes; he chose to funnel aid to Saud through the British, who had been subsidizing the king for years. But after the German attack on the Soviet Union and the Japanese attack on Pearl Harbor, Roosevelt changed his mind. Now that the United States had allied with Stalin, the undemocratic character of Saud's regime wasn't much of a disqualification. In 1943, the president

signed off on a statement asserting that the security of Saudi Arabia
was "vital to the defense of the United States," as the Lend-Lease legislation required, and ordered direct aid to commence.

2. THE COLD WAR BEGINS
IN THE MIDDLE EAST: IRAN, 1946

What was vital about Saudi Arabia, obviously, was its oil. World War II
taught those who fought it a number of lessons, none more important
than the need for petroleum in keeping a modern war machine in the
field. The United States general and supreme allied commander in Europe, Dwight Eisenhower, learned the lesson well and, when he became president, demonstrated extreme sensitivity to anything that
might disrupt access by the United States and its allies to oil.

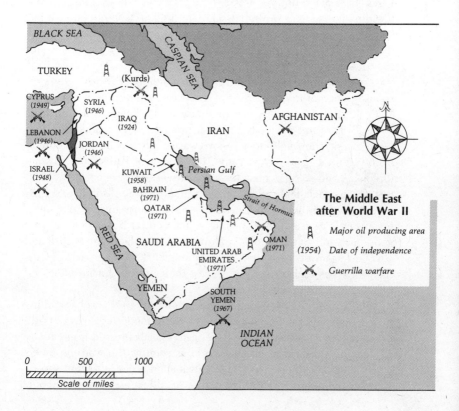

It would stretch the truth, but perhaps not tear it to tatters, to say that World War II was fought over oil. A principal objective of German expansionism was to seize control of the oil fields near the Black and Caspian seas; and it was Japan's desire to break free of dependence on American oil that led Tokyo to thrust toward the Dutch East Indies, thereby prompting the American embargo—of oil, most damagingly—that set in motion the events leading to Pearl Harbor.

It would likewise strain the truth, but not sunder it entirely, to say that the Cold War was fought over oil. A whole constellation of perceptions and interests prompted the United States and the Soviet Union to act as jealously and competitively toward each other as they did during the forty years after 1945. Yet as it involved the Middle East, the Cold War was about oil as much as it was about any other single item. From the American perspective, almost no worse disaster short of nuclear war could befall the "Free World" than for the Soviet Union or some country sympathetic to Moscow's designs to monopolize the oil resources of the Persian Gulf region. Consequently, it became a cardinal feature of American policy—and one that outlasted the Cold War—to prevent the Soviet Union or any potentially unfriendly country from attaining such a monopoly.

American touchiness on the oil issue conditioned Washington's response to one of the first crises of the Cold War, during the winter of 1945–46. Following the German attack on the Soviet Union in June 1941, British and Soviet troops had preemptively invaded Iran. To some extent, the Anglo-Soviet move was simply the latest installment in the Central Asian "great game" that had kept British and Russian diplomats and soldiers busy for a century. A 1907 round of the contest, for instance, had yielded an agreement between Britain and Russia to the effect that northern Iran would be a Russian sphere of influence, southern Iran a British sphere, and central Iran a neutral zone generously left to the Iranians. Thirty-four years later, the British and Russians again decreed the fate of Iran, taking the approach of German forces as their reason, or at least their pretext, for invading and effectively partitioning the country.

The United States, which by the summer of 1941 was bankrolling both Britain and the Soviet Union, found this modern display of traditional imperialism distressing. American officials pressed London and Moscow to promise to evacuate Iran as soon as the wartime emergency reasonably permitted. The British and the Soviets spent several months mumbling excuses why they couldn't accommodate; only after Pearl Harbor brought the United States directly into the war, thereby increasing Washington's leverage, did the two countries agree to evacuate their troops from Iran no later than six months after the fighting's end.

Promises given easily while the Germans were winning the war proved difficult to enforce once the shooting stopped. Part of the difficulty was semantic: *Which* war did the evacuation agreement refer to? The Iranians, who wanted both the British and Soviets out of their country pronto, contended that the European war was the one that mattered, since the German threat was what had triggered the Anglo-Soviet invasion and since, besides, the Soviets were not at war with Japan. The British held that the war was a world war and that they had to stay until the Japanese were defeated. The Soviets, declaring war on Japan at the last moment, in August 1945, argued that whatever the status of the agreement beforehand, this declaration reset the clock.

The Japanese surrender on August 14 placed the deadline, at the latest, at mid-February 1946; but new complications soon arose. The Soviets, flushed with victory and intent on securing the fruits thereof, felt scant inclination to honor a pledge made under the duress of impending doom. Instead, they supported separatists in the region of Azerbaijan, which abutted the Soviet Union, and refused to let the Iranian government move reinforcements to the area. The British insisted on staying as long as the Soviets did, partly as a matter of principle and partly from fear of a Soviet takeover of Iran, which would seriously jeopardize British oil operations, among other interests in the country.

Although American officials eyed still-imperialist Britain with a certain distrust, they worried especially about the Soviets. At a minimum, it seemed, the Kremlin was engineering the creation of a buffer state in Azerbaijan of the kind it was producing in Poland and elsewhere in Eastern Europe; more ambitiously, Moscow might be plotting the conquest of all of Iran, toward the traditional Russian goal of frontage on the Persian Gulf or Indian Ocean.

American worries increased further early in 1946 when, even after the British agreed to a pullout, the Soviets refused to go along. Events not directly related to Iran added to the tension. Talks that were supposed to be leading to a settlement of the German question had bogged down in what looked to many Americans to be Soviet intransigence; at the same time, Moscow was pressuring Turkey over control of the Turkish Straits. On February 9, Soviet Premier Joseph Stalin proclaimed the essential incompatibility of capitalism and communism and declared that the continued existence of the former made war inevitable. Britain's wartime prime minister, Winston Churchill, replied for the West with a speech asserting that an "iron curtain" had descended across Europe, dividing the continent into hostile camps and making anything approaching permanent peace impossible. Stalin, in a rare public interview, countered by saying that Churchill's words amounted to a call to war against the Soviet Union. Within the American bureaucracy, diplomat George Kennan cabled from Moscow the longest telegram in State Department history, describing Stalin's actions as part of a pattern of expansionism that dated from czarist times and required a vigorous American response.

Kennan's warning struck a chord in Washington. The director of the State Department's Middle East division, Loy Henderson, had served with Kennan in Moscow during the 1930s, and both had learned their foreign-service lessons under the tutelage of Robert Kelley, the unremittingly anti-Soviet head of the State Department's Eastern Europe division. From Kelley in Washington, and on their own in Moscow, where they attended the trials that purged the Communist party of Stalin's rivals and marked the full flowering of the Stalinist system, Kennan and Henderson had gained an appreciation of what they considered the malign intentions of the Kremlin. They didn't let themselves be fooled by Stalin's "popular front" policy of the late 1930s, which had Moscow ordering foreign communists to make common cause with liberals against the fascists; nor did they conceive of the wartime alliance with the Soviet Union as anything other than a temporary truce in the Kremlin's battle against the democratic capitalist states.

Henderson interpreted Soviet pressure on Iran in the light of these perceptions and acted accordingly. The Middle East chief directed his staff to prepare a map depicting recent movements of the Red Army in northern Iran and indicating where the Soviet units might be going. Henderson took the map into the office of Secretary of State James Byrnes, where he pointed to three large arrows representing likely Soviet thrusts. One arrow aimed at Turkey and the Turkish Straits; a second headed toward Baghdad and central Iraq; the third targeted the oil fields of the Persian Gulf. Henderson supplemented his visual aids with prose along the lines Kennan had delivered in his long telegram. Byrnes found the presentation compelling; pounding one fist into the other, the secretary of state declared, "Now we'll give it to them with both barrels."[3]

The worries of the State Department were reinforced by the concerns of American military officials. The Pentagon didn't like the idea of Soviet expansion anywhere, but it frowned especially on Soviet expansion into a region that held much of the world's petroleum. Navy Secretary James Forrestal—whose ships would go dead in the water without oil—repeatedly emphasized the necessity of keeping the Soviets away from the Persian Gulf oil fields. Forrestal asserted that Middle Eastern oil was not merely of "substantial interest" to the United States navy but was "one of the great interests of the whole country." Forrestal's associates in the oil business were telling him that American supplies were running down more quickly than most people realized; this made Middle Eastern oil all the more vital. The American government must ensure that the region's oil remain in friendly hands. These definitely didn't include Moscow's.[4]

The Truman administration's reaction to the Soviet pressure on Iran fell short of the double-barreled blast Byrnes called for, but as diplomatic notes go, the letter President Harry Truman ordered Kennan to deliver to the Kremlin was reasonably strong. It indicated clearly that the United States knew what the Soviets were up to in Iran, and it registered the United States' grave concern at the Soviets' failure to honor their part of the evacuation agreement.

The note, in conjunction with some sharp dealing by the Iranian government, produced the desired objective. Iran's representatives promised certain concessions the Soviets had been demanding, including the right to produce oil in northern Iran and permission for the pro-Soviet Iranian Tudeh party to conduct its business unmolested. But the Iranians insisted that these concessions required approval by a new Iranian parliament, which could be elected only after a Soviet withdrawal. Stalin accepted the offer and ordered a pullout—following which the Iranian government dithered until, encouraged by further American support, the parliament rejected crucial aspects of the agreement. With bigger problems by then, the Kremlin refused to make a major case out of the matter.

[3]*Foreign Relations of the United States*, 1946, 7:346.
[4]Daniel Yergin, *Shattered Peace* (Boston, 1977), p. 180.

From the American perspective, the importance of the Iranian affair of 1946 lay in the lesson it apparently taught regarding Moscow's
postwar aims and methods. Unopposed, American officials believed,
the Soviets would press outward all along their borders, especially
into critical regions like the Middle East. Consequently, a firm American response was a necessary condition for a successful defense of
Western interests. For the moment at least, firmness also appeared to
be a sufficient condition. Firmness in Iran had succeeded in warning
the Soviets away, and there seemed little reason to think similar firmness would not succeed elsewhere.

3. PICKING UP WHERE BRITAIN LEFT OFF: THE TRUMAN DOCTRINE

In the case of Iran, the Soviet challenge to perceived American interests took direct form: though opinions might differ regarding the
Kremlin's ultimate aims in Iran, no one could deny the presence of
Red Army troops in that country. Farther west, the challenge came
less starkly. Partly because it did, the American response was less specific and, on account of its lack of specificity, more portentous.

The Russian government had been meddling in the affairs of
Turkey since the time of the Ottomans. From the day Moscow's writ
had touched the Black Sea, czars and subsequently commissars had
looked for means to ease their country's access to the relatively more
open waters of the Mediterranean. Had the Bolsheviks not pulled
Russia out of World War I before the defeat of the Central Powers,
Moscow might have participated in the dismemberment of the Ottoman Empire, with whatever advantages dismemberment may have
yielded in terms of control of the Turkish Straits. But after the Russian defection from the Allies, Moscow could hardly expect favored
treatment at the hands of the British, French, and Americans—who,
in any event, were fully as hostile to the revolutionary new regime in
the Kremlin as it was to them.

World War II left the Soviets in a much stronger position. This
time they had held on until the end, and when the end arrived, their
armies occupied half the European continent. Far from having to accept dictated terms, as had occurred at Brest-Litovsk in 1918,
Moscow could contemplate doing some dictating itself. Stalin had
raised the issue of the Turkish Straits in an October 1944 meeting

with Churchill at Moscow. The Soviet premier complained that the Montreaux Convention of 1936, a pact negotiated among the Black Sea countries as well as outsiders Britain and France, and which guaranteed that Turkey would exercise predominant control over passage through the straits, was anachronistic and unfair. Stalin pointed out that the straits bore much the same relationship to the Soviet Union as Gibraltar and Suez to Britain, and Panama to the United States. In fact, the Soviet Union was in a worse situation than either Britain or America, since alternate sea routes existed around Africa and South America, while no other route led from the Black Sea. Churchill in 1944 wasn't yet convinced of the need to contain Soviet expansion, nor was he sympathetic to the neutral but Axis-leaning Turks, and he evinced a willingness to accommodate Stalin. The British prime minister disavowed the policy of his nineteenth-century predecessors of striving to bottle up Russia and indicated that at the appropriate time Britain would support a revision of the Montreaux treaty.

The question of the Turkish Straits arose again at the February 1945 Yalta conference, where Franklin Roosevelt joined Churchill in accepting the principle of revision; and once more at the Potsdam conference of July 1945, where Truman and Clement Attlee, Churchill's successor, reiterated support for revision.

But by the time the Soviets got around to pressing their claim to revision, the Americans and British were looking at Moscow no longer as an ally in the fight against fascism but as a competitor in the Cold War and a potential enemy in a third world war. In August 1946, the Kremlin delivered a note to Ankara demanding the right to share in the defense of the Turkish Straits, which implied a permanent Soviet presence in Turkey. To increase the pressure on the Turkish government, the Kremlin resurrected Russian claims to portions of eastern Turkey once ruled by the czar.

As in the Iranian case, American officials interpreted the Soviet moves against Turkey as part of a concerted and aggressive campaign of expansion. The State Department warned Truman that a primary objective of the Soviet Union was to gain control of Turkey. Should Moscow succeed in this objective, Loy Henderson continued, the United States would find it extremely difficult, if not impossible, to prevent a Soviet takeover of the entire Middle East.

Truman accepted this analysis of the situation as well as a joint recommendation of the State Department and his top military advisers declaring a need to impress the Soviets with America's resolve. In

August 1946, the president approved a letter to Moscow asserting that control of the Turkish Straits rested with Turkey alone; at the same time, he ordered the dispatch of a naval task force to the vicinity of the straits. Truman understood that this action could lead to an armed confrontation, but he contended that if the Soviets wanted a war, it might as well start soon.

As events proved, the Soviets didn't want a war, at least not then and not over Turkey. They quietly shelved their demand for a base on the straits. But they maintained diplomatic and psychological pressure against the Turks, keeping Ankara on edge and Turkish troops on alert. The experience drained the Turks emotionally and fiscally. By the beginning of 1947, the strain was showing clearly. The American ambassador in Ankara, Edwin Wilson, argued that unless the United States provided substantial assistance to Turkey, the Turks would grow demoralized and broke. To allow such an outcome, with all it might entail for Soviet penetration of the Middle East, would be most unwise.

Circumstances in Turkey took another turn for the worse, or threatened to, in February 1947. In that month, a representative from the British embassy in Washington informed the State Department that Britain was running short of funds with which it had supported the governments of Turkey and Greece. Although the British government sympathized with the plight of the Turks and Greeks and feared for their future under pressure from the Soviets and groups allied with the Soviet Union, it had no financial choice but to cut off aid within six weeks. It hoped the United States government would fill the gap. In light of the importance of Turkey and Greece to the security of the Middle East, it hoped the United States would do so quickly. But whether the United States did or not was a matter for the Americans to decide. Come what may, Britain was pulling out.

At the time of the British *démarche,* the situation next door to Turkey, in Greece, was even more parlous than that in Turkey; and, in the American view, it was no less significant for the future of the Middle East. Few countries had suffered as much as Greece during World War II. Greek partisans fought German occupation forces and collaborators, and the Germans and collaborators exacted ferocious revenge. The end of the world war had afforded scant relief: hardly had the Germans evacuated when Greek monarchists and Greek communists, and lots of other armed persons not so easily identified, turned to fighting each other for control of the country. The British, whose long interest in the Mediterranean had involved them in Greek affairs, backed the currently ruling monarchists. The Soviets, the most obvious potential big brothers of the Greek communists, largely stayed out, partly from the Kremlin's desire to honor a 1944 pledge by Stalin to Churchill to accept British predominance in Greece, and partly from Moscow's distrust of Yugoslavia, whose communist but independent leader Josip Broz Tito *was* helping the Greek communists.

Even with Britain's aid, the Greek government failed to stem the rebellion; and when London decided in early 1947 to yank the plug on aid, the government's fortunes seemed still more in jeopardy. American policy makers had been monitoring the situation in Greece for many months. They worried that the longer the unrest in Greece persisted, the more likely it would be that outside elements would get involved, with hazardous consequences for the stability of the region. As early as November 1945, the State Department's Loy Henderson had asserted, "A weak and chaotic Greece is a constant invitation to its already unfriendly neighbors on the north to take aggressive action and constitutes a menace to international peace and security." A few months later, the American ambassador in Athens, Lincoln MacVeagh, characterized the situation in Greece as "highly flammable" and predicted that unless the United States responded with imagination and energy, the present Greek government would give way to a dictatorship of the right, which in turn "could scarcely fail to produce in due course a Communist dictatorship."

In Washington's judgment, the fate of Greece was closely tied to the fate of Turkey, and both to the fate of the surrounding region. The State Department explained the matter simply: "Greece and Turkey form the sole obstacle to Soviet domination of the Eastern Mediterranean." Should Greece collapse, the Soviets could apply irresistible pressure upon the Turks. Nor were the stakes confined to the neighborhood of the two countries. If Greece and Turkey went down, there could not fail to be "most unfavorable repercussions in all of those areas where political sympathies are balanced precariously in favor of the West and against Soviet communism." The credibility of the democratic countries was at stake.[5]

This double argument for keeping Turkey and Greece out of the communist sphere—that the two countries formed a bulwark against

---

[5]Henderson memo with attachment, Oct. 21, 1946, State Department file 868.00, National Archives, Washington.

Soviet expansionism, and that the world was watching to determine whether the West possessed the will to resist communist subversion—formed the basis of the American response to the British *démarche* of February 1947. Henderson received the British message on a Friday afternoon; throughout the following weekend, officials of the Truman administration worked nearly nonstop preparing the American reply. Early the next week, Undersecretary of State Dean Acheson told the British ambassador that the administration was leaning toward accepting the British proposal, but that convincing Congress to take such a novel step would require time. Could London provide that time, by holding out a bit longer?

The British agreed, on condition that the Americans move quickly. The administration did. The State Department drafted legislation providing $400 million in aid to Turkey and Greece. Some in the department, notably George Kennan, thought the United States ought to focus attention on Greece, which at the moment seemed more seriously threatened than Turkey. Others, particularly Henderson, advocated a broader response, including Iran as well as Greece and Turkey in the aid package.

In terms of the legislation Truman requested of Congress, the president accepted the State Department's recommendation to include only Turkey and Greece in the aid package. But after soundings of congressional leaders, the president decided to wrap the policy of aid to those countries in the broader language of high principle. Truman described the current troubles in the Middle East as the consequence not simply of local political struggles but of a fundamental clash between two ways of life. One way of life, the president said, was based on democratic institutions and personal liberty. The second way of life was based on authoritarianism and terror. The time had come for the American people to throw their weight unmistakably to the side of peoples aspiring to the first. In the sentence that summarized what quickly became known as the Truman Doctrine, the president declared, "I believe that it must be the policy of the United States to support free peoples who are resisting attempted subjugation by armed minorities or by outside pressures."[6]

With this statement, Truman converted a crisis at the edge of the Middle East into a test of the United States' will to resist aggression throughout the world. The president made it sound as though the

[6]*Public Papers of the Presidents,* 1947, pp. 178–179.

congressional decision on the aid package for Turkey and Greece would determine the outcome of the rapidly escalating confrontation with the Soviet Union. A veteran of Congress himself, Truman knew that the senators and representatives would find it easier to defend a vote for peace and anticommunism than to defend a vote for the flawed and unfamiliar governments of Turkey and Greece.

Events proved Truman right. In short order, Congress held hearings on the administration's aid package, debated the issue, and voted it through.

After the commencement of the program of American aid, the insurgency in Greece eventually subsided. To some degree, the Greek government's victory in the civil war resulted from the reinforcement the aid provided; but to a larger extent the victory was due to changing circumstances among Greece's neighbors. In 1948, Yugoslavia and the Soviet Union fell out with each other, principally because Tito refused to toe the Kremlin's line. Now a pariah among communists—including Greek communists, unwisely for them—Tito sought to improve relations with the West. As a first step, he closed his border to the Greek rebels. This eliminated their safe refuge and a major source of supply. When factional squabbling within the rebel ranks added to the strain on the insurgency, the revolt collapsed.

The consequences of the Truman administration's response to the events in Turkey and Greece were global in extent and protracted in duration. The Truman Doctrine amounted to an American declaration of the Cold War, in the forty-year prosecution of which the United States fought two major wars in Asia, otherwise intervened militarily in the Middle East, Central America, and the Caribbean, and engaged in anticommunist paramilitary, political, and economic operations on every continent but Antarctica.

4. PALESTINE AND THE BIRTH OF ISRAEL

By comparison, the consequences of the Truman administration's response to the Palestine crisis of 1947–48 would be more circumscribed geographically, but of even longer duration. The fallout from the administration's decision to support the establishment of a Jewish state in Palestine chiefly affected American relations with the Middle East; yet even after the Soviet Union under Mikhail Gorbachev quit the Cold War, in the late 1980s, the United States remained as enmeshed as ever in Middle Eastern affairs. Although the Persian Gulf War of 1991, the first major armed conflict of the post-Cold War era, did not originate in the Arab-Israeli rivalry, its ramifications inevitably touched that struggle, and considerations relating to the Arab-Israeli issue strongly influenced American actions during and after the war.

Until the spring of 1945, American policy on the Palestine question remained basically unchanged from the beginning of World War II. The Roosevelt administration expressed sympathy for the aspirations of the Zionists, but argued that defeating the fascists took priority. Roosevelt, a chronic procrastinator and an inveterate optimist, believed—or gave the impression of believing—that once the United States and its allies dealt with Hitler and the Japanese, minor problems like Palestine could be solved without great difficulty. Roosevelt told Zionist leader Chaim Weizmann not to worry too much about Arab objections to a Jewish state; a "little baksheesh," the president said, would take care of the Arab complaints. In a discussion specifically of the ruling family of Saudi Arabia, Roosevelt asserted that he could do "anything that needed to be done with Ibn Saud with a few million dollars." Yet just before he died, the president discovered that Saud might be harder to deal with than he had reckoned. Roosevelt described a meeting with the monarch to Rabbi Stephen Wise: "There was nothing I could do with him. We talked for three hours, and I argued with the old fellow up hill and down dale, but he stuck to his guns."[7]

When Truman suddenly became president in April 1945, America's Palestine policy continued to exhibit the ambivalence of the previous three decades. On one hand, many Americans—including, crucially, the new chief executive—admired the determination of the Jews in pursuing their goal of a homeland in Palestine, and believed the United States should do what it reasonably could to help them attain this goal. On the other hand, a majority of the American foreign-policy establishment worried that by supporting the Zionists, the United States would alienate the Arabs, thereby complicating American relations with an already troublesome part of the world.

The end of the war and the onset of hostility between the United States and the Soviet Union brought a third consideration to discussions of the Palestine issue. The crises in Iran and Turkey and Greece indicated, to the satisfaction of American policy makers at any rate,

[7]Grose, op. cit., pp. 139–154.

that the Soviets intended to inject themselves into the Middle East, by fair means or foul. As blocking Moscow's advances in the area became a priority for Washington, American leaders began placing a premium on cultivating friendly, stable regimes in the area. The thrust of the State Department's case against support for the Zionists was that such support would destabilize the Middle East and make the Arabs unfriendly. Pro-Zionists, among the White House staff and elsewhere, countered that Arab friendship was overrated; a friendly Israel would be more important. As for stability, they declared, this was a red herring. The Arabs had never demonstrated an aptitude for stability, and if the creation of a Jewish state made the region less stable, it would be the Arabs, not the Jews, who were to blame.

A final consideration also related to the Soviet Union. As the wartime alliance of the United States, Britain, and the Soviet Union ruptured, the United States and Britain often adopted parallel positions against the Soviets. The Anglo-American "special relationship" reflected a coincidence of views regarding the danger Soviet communism posed to Western institutions and values; but this coincidence was not something American leaders could take for granted, and it was something that had to be cultivated. Whenever possible without doing violence to American interests, American leaders consulted with, and cooperated with, the British. As it related to Palestine, this approach implied an inclination to go along with London in efforts to devise a graceful end to British control of Palestine. Rarely did American policy makers put the matter so plainly, but they understood that it would be foolish to jeopardize cooperation with Britain in Europe, the central theater of the Cold War, to score points in the Middle East. To be sure, on more than one occasion Washington and London found themselves glaring at each other over Middle Eastern issues. But whenever a rift began to appear, both sides acted swiftly to close it.

In the immediate aftermath of the victory in Europe, Jews and Arabs launched intensive lobbying efforts in Washington. The Jews were better organized, had closer ties to the Truman administration, and were quicker off the mark. Representatives of various Jewish groups made frequent visits to the White House and the State Department; at the former, they gained a sympathetic hearing most frequently from David Niles, a presidential aide and enthusiastic Zionist, while at the latter they received polite but cool interviews, chiefly with Loy Henderson, who staunchly opposed American support for a Jewish state.

Truman would decide between the two positions, and the battle for the president's mind began as soon as he moved into the Oval Office. Within a week of his swearing in, Truman received a message from the State Department warning him of the hazards of precipitate action regarding the Zionist issue. Well aware that the Zionists would play on the sympathies aroused by the recent and continuing revelations of Jews' horrific brutalization at Nazi hands, the State Department insisted that sympathy, however justified, made a poor foundation for foreign policy. Secretary of State Edward Stettinius, prompted by Henderson, cautioned Truman that the Palestine question was "highly complex" and involved matters that went "far beyond the plight of the Jews in Europe." Stettinius added that there was "continual tenseness" throughout the Middle East as a result of the Palestine question; because the United States had vital concerns in the region, that question "should be handled with the greatest care and with a view to the long-range interests of this country."[8]

Truman was neither the first nor the last president to feel that the foreign-policy bureaucracy was patronizing him, and he resented the treatment. Like many people from the Midwest, Truman distrusted the Ivy League types who had filled American diplomatic posts for generations. He judged them guilty of elitism, not inaccurately. "The difficulty with many career officials in the government," Truman later wrote, "is that they regard themselves as the men who really make policy and run the government. They look upon the elected officials as just temporary occupants." Truman perceived a variety of motives for the State Department's opposition to a pro-Zionist American policy. "There were some men in the State Department who held the view that the Balfour Declaration could not be carried out without offense to the Arabs," Truman said. "Like most of the British diplomats, some of our diplomats also thought that the Arabs, on account of their numbers and because of the fact that they controlled such immense oil resources, should be appeased. I am sorry to say that there were some among them who were also inclined to be anti-Semitic."[9]

Distrustful as he was, Truman felt no compulsion to consult the State Department in advance of every decision. Indeed, with the encouragement of Niles, who feared that the State Department would attempt to obstruct positive steps, Truman went out of his way to

[8]*Foreign Relations*, 1945, 8:704–705.

[9]Harry S. Truman, *Memoirs* (Garden City, N.Y., 1955–1956), 2:161–165.

keep the professional diplomats in the dark. As a consequence, American policy on the Palestine question was often confused. The diplomats, the bearers of responsibility for implementing decisions made by the president, got used to learning of major presidential actions by reading about them in the newspapers.

They encountered such a situation in the summer of 1945, shortly after the Potsdam conference. A reporter asked Truman whether the issue of a Jewish state in Palestine had arisen in the president's discussions with Stalin and Attlee. Truman said he had spoken about the issue with Attlee, and added that the American position on Palestine was to try and get as many Jews into Palestine as possible.

This was news to the State Department. At the moment, the pressing matter regarding Palestine involved the application for immigration visas of some 100,000 European Jews, many of them survivors of the Nazi death camps. Zionists naturally advocated that Britain allow these displaced persons, or DPs, to enter Palestine. The Jewish Agency, the shadow Zionist government of Palestine, elevated advocacy to the level of a demand, insisting that permission be granted at once. Simple humanitarianism, the Zionists claimed, dictated that the DPs receive the opportunity to leave the scene of the heinous crimes recently inflicted upon them and start a new life in a country they might eventually call their own. The unspoken implication of the Zionist demand was that opening Palestine to the DPs would effectively undo the immigration restrictions of the 1939 British White Paper, bolstering the political and military strength of the Zionists on the ground in Palestine in the process.

The Arabs had no difficulty reading the subtext of the Zionist demand, and they mobilized to prevent the entry of the DPs into Palestine. The Arabs contended that letting the DPs into Palestine would inevitably result in the displacement of Palestinian Arabs, and they complained that the Western powers were attempting to assuage their guilty consciences regarding the Nazi holocaust at the expense of the Palestinians. In Palestine itself, Arabs demonstrated violently against this possible reversal of British policy. Meanwhile, ambassadors and other representatives of the several Arab countries urged the great powers not to let London overturn the White Paper. Egypt's Mahmoud Fawzi, for instance, visited the State Department to warn of wide-scale unrest throughout the Arab world if the British renounced what had been established policy for several years. Fawzi added that the wrath of the Arabs would encompass not merely the

British but any country that supported Britain in trampling the rights of the Arabs of Palestine—which, of course, was why he was visiting the U.S. State Department.

If the American government felt caught between the demands of the Zionists and the threats of the Arabs, the British government felt the pinch even more severely. British soldiers were the ones who had to battle rioters and terrorists in Palestine, and British interests in the Middle East were more extensive and more vulnerable than American interests. (This was leaving aside the volatile question of the 90 million Muslims in India, who would protest bitterly against a British delivery of Jerusalem to the Jews.) Since receiving authority over Palestine from the League of Nations at the end of World War I, the British had had their fill of trying to govern the place, which had brought them nothing but headaches. Yet enough remained of the imperialist sense of responsibility for London to try to avoid simply cutting and running. This would open Palestine to a murderous combat between Jews and Arabs. In seeking to arrange an orderly exit, the British looked to Washington for assistance. To some degree, they sincerely desired American help; at least equally, they hoped to spread the blame for whatever debacles awaited their departure.

As governments and people tend to do, the Truman administration tried to grab a share of power regarding Palestine while avoiding a share of responsibility. In the late summer of 1945, Truman wrote to Attlee advocating the admission of the 100,000 DPs as quickly as could be arranged. (State Department officials learned of the existence and contents of the letter only when it made the *Washington Post* ten days afterward.) Yet, as Attlee and other British leaders couldn't resist remarking, at least among themselves, the president declined to offer assistance in quelling the violence the admission of the DPs would be certain to provoke in Palestine. British Foreign Secretary Ernest Bevin found Truman's position infuriating; voicing an opinion shared by many in Britain, Bevin remarked that of course the Americans wanted the Jews allowed into Palestine since they didn't want "too many Jews in New York."[10]

In an effort to convert the Americans from irresponsible kibitzers on Palestine policy making to responsible participants, the Attlee government proposed a joint Anglo-American committee of inquiry into

[10]Wm. Roger Louis, *The British Empire in the Middle East* (Oxford, England, 1984), p. 428.

the question of the DPs and associated topics. Beginning late in 1945 and continuing into the early part of 1946, the committee held hearings in the United States, in Europe, and in the Middle East. In Washington, the six British members and six American members listened to Jewish Zionists, Jewish non-Zionists, Jewish anti-Zionists, non-Jewish Zionists, non-Jewish non-Zionists, and non-Jewish anti-Zionists explain how justice required the admission of the DPs into Palestine, how justice required that they not be admitted, how a Jewish state would right historic wrongs done to the Jews, and how a Jewish state would wrong the historic rights of the Arabs. The most prominent figure to address the committee at its Washington hearings was Albert Einstein, who denounced British imperialism, the 1939 British White Paper, and—surprisingly—the notion of a Jewish state. Recalling the moment afterward, British committeeman Richard Crossman wrote, "The audience nearly jumped out of their seats."[11]

Departing America, the committee members sailed to Europe. They held additional hearings in London before visiting the refugee camps in Germany, Austria, and Poland that sheltered the DPs. They continued on to Cairo and Jerusalem, where for the first time they learned the full depth of Arab animosity to the Zionist program.

After an exhausting three months, the committee members retired to Switzerland to produce their report. Two recommendations summarized their findings: first, that the 100,000 DPs be admitted to Palestine at once, and second, that Palestine become a binational state under international supervision, in which Jews and Arabs would receive equal representation.

Both recommendations could be expected to outrage the Arabs, and did—the first for amounting to repeal of the 1939 White Paper, the second for denying the majoritarian principle implicit in the idea of self-determination. In Palestine, Arabs rioted in opposition to the committee's report; in other Arab countries, the response exhibited less violence but hardly less hostility.

The Zionists liked the part of the report relating to the DPs, but they decried the report's failure to specify an independent Jewish state. David Ben-Gurion, destined to be Israel's first prime minister, castigated the report as a shameful document designed to thwart Jews' aspirations for a state of their own. Hoping to salvage what they could from the committee's work, the Zionists pressed for acceptance

[11]Richard Crossman, *Palestine Mission* (London, 1947), p. 49.

of the DP provision while rejecting the recommendation for a binational state.

The Truman administration found itself torn on this issue as on others touching Palestine. The State Department heeded warnings from Arab diplomats that American backing for the committee report would undermine, potentially fatally, American relations with the Arab world, and perhaps with the larger Muslim world as well. The White House discounted these warnings as typical Arab rhetoric and argued that humanitarianism demanded accepting the recommendation on the DPs, independent of the matter of the future governance of Palestine. The White House received support in its thinking from a survey done by United States army officers responsible for conditions in the refugee camps in Europe, who predicted violence in the camps if the DPs didn't gain permission to leave.

The British perceived in the White House response more of what they were coming to expect from the Americans: credit-seeking for aspects of policy that played well with the Zionists, and responsibility-dodging for the hard work and opprobrium associated with the aspects of policy the Zionists disliked. Despite pressure from the Truman administration, London refused to allow the two halves of the Anglo-American committee's report to be separated. The Attlee government didn't want to have to deal with the anger the admission of the DPs would produce among the Arabs unless that admission pushed Palestine closer to a solution of its problems and Britain closer to getting out of the country. When it became evident that the British wouldn't reconsider, the report died.

The report's demise prompted the Americans and British to try another tack. Each government appointed delegates to a commission charged with hammering out a settlement for Palestine that both Washington and London, if not necessarily the Jews and Arabs, could live with. Henry Grady, a former assistant secretary of state, headed the American delegation, while Herbert Morrison, Britain's lord president of the council, chaired the British side. Morrison suggested a plan for a single state in Palestine in which Jews and Arabs would occupy separate and largely autonomous provinces. Grady grew convinced that only American backing for such a scheme would persuade the British to give visas to the DPs, despite the fact that the Anglo-American committee had rejected a similar plan as unworkable. Consequently, Grady threw his support to Morrison's plan.

But notwithstanding efforts by the principals to keep the Morrison-Grady plan secret until all the details had been arranged, dissenters on Grady's staff leaked the plan to the press. The Zionists would have nothing to do with anything that gave them less than a sovereign state, and they immediately launched a campaign to kill the plan. The campaign succeeded famously, with critics charging that Jews who had escaped the ghettos of Europe now would find themselves trapped in ghettos in Palestine. Truman, though still sympathetic to Zionist objectives, found the Zionists' obstructionist tactics exasperating. "Jesus Christ couldn't please them when he was here on earth," the president complained, "so how could anyone expect that I would have any luck?"[12]

Truman survived his exasperation, and a few weeks later he made a statement that pleased the Zionists no end. On the day before Yom Kippur—and one month prior to the 1946 congressional elections, as the career diplomats in the State Department noted with disgust—Truman reiterated his backing for the admission of the 100,000 DPs into Palestine and advocated efforts to reconcile the Morrison-Grady provincial autonomy plan with a fresh proposal by the Jewish Agency for a Zionist state. Truman declared, "I cannot believe that the gap between the proposals which have been put forward is too great to be bridged by men of reason and good will." Truman added a prediction that a Jewish state in Palestine "would command the support of public opinion in the United States."[13]

The part of Truman's message about a Jewish state was the most important. Whether or not public opinion in America supported creation of a Jewish state—as it did, although without particular enthusiasm and without much understanding of what the consequences might be—Truman's comment indicated that *he* supported creation of a Jewish state. This fact made his assertion of the possibility of bridging the gap between the Morrison-Grady proposal and the Jewish Agency plan basically a throwaway line. Whatever else it was, the Morrison-Grady scheme was *not* a design for Jewish sovereignty; whatever the Jewish Agency plan wasn't, it *was* a design for Jewish sovereignty. Truman's statement of support for a Jewish state, together with his reassertion of the need to allow the DPs into Palestine, in effect told the Zionists not to compromise. Sit tight, and with American help you'll get your state.

[12]Louis, op. cit., p. 436.
[13]*Public Papers*, 1946, pp. 442–444.

The Zionists did sit tight. In January 1947, the British sponsored yet another effort to find a solution to the Palestine problem. This time they brought representatives of the Arabs and Jews to London to thrash out a settlement. The London meeting of bodies produced nothing closer to a meeting of minds than previous efforts, and the British decided they had had enough. Not long after the London conference adjourned, the Attlee government announced that it would refer the Palestine question to the United Nations.

By 1947, the United Nations was already becoming the dumping ground of choice for insoluble conflicts. As the world was witnessing, the postwar falling out between the United States and the Soviet Union decreed the stillbirth of the international organization as an instrument of collective security. It was a rare issue on which the chief antagonists in the Cold War could agree, and because each wielded a veto in the United Nations Security Council, their disagreement typically produced paralysis of the organization as a whole. The Security Council was the arm of the United Nations for substantive action; the other arm, the General Assembly, served as an arena for the expression of opinion but possessed no enforcement powers.

All the same, referral of the Palestine question to the United Nations afforded a respite for the Truman administration, if not for the Jews and Arabs of Palestine or for the British rulers of the country, all of whom found themselves in an increasingly bloody cycle of violence. Through the summer of 1947, the Truman administration let a United Nations committee hold hearings on Palestine while the administration tended to other matters, such as the recently approved package of aid for Turkey and Greece and a second aid program, just proposed by Secretary of State George Marshall, for the reconstruction of Europe. The Zionists continued to lobby the administration for support of their dream, which looked closer than ever to fulfillment; the Arabs continued to threaten dire consequences if the United States helped the Zionists steal Palestine from the Palestinians. Everyone awaited the outcome of the deliberations of the United Nations committee.

That committee showed no more skill at finding a solution than the committees that had tackled the problem before—as was to be expected, since at this late date, no one anticipated any brilliant new schemes that would satisfy all parties. In fact, the United Nations committee showed less skill than its predecessors, being unable even to reach a unified recommendation. The committee delivered a divided report, with the majority favoring partition of Palestine into three sections: an Arab state, a Jewish state, and the city of Jerusalem, the last under a United Nations trusteeship. The minority proposed a single federal state with Jerusalem as capital.

Over the vehement opposition of the State Department, which predicted immediate war and continuing turmoil if the majority plan took effect, the Truman administration opted for partition. In October 1947, the American representative at the United Nations, Herschel Johnson, announced that the United States would support the majority plan, subject to minor modifications.

The split in the American government didn't end with Johnson's announcement. The State Department, hoping to minimize the damage caused by what it perceived to be the president's unwise decision, refused to campaign within the United Nations for approval of the majority plan. Loy Henderson asserted that the United States had no obligation to carry the flag for partition, and good reason not to. "If we carry the flag," Henderson said, "we shall inescapably be saddled with the major if not sole responsibility for administration and enforcement." Henderson predicted that peaceful partition could be imposed only by means of the threat of external force, probably American. Unenforced partition would lead to "outside intervention from the Arab States, the Soviet Union and, eventually, ourselves, in one form or another."[14]

While the career diplomats sat on their hands, the White House waged a vigorous battle to gain United Nations approval of the majority plan. Persons close to the administration made contact with friends and acquaintances in wavering countries. David Niles enlisted financier Bernard Baruch to talk with Baruch's French banker friends; Baruch warned that a French vote against partition would mean the end of American aid to France. Baruch was bluffing, as the French might have guessed, but at a moment when Congress had yet to approve money for the Marshall Plan, Paris preferred not to take any chances. The French delegate voted for partition.

The Philippines, a country in which the vast Catholic majority worried about Jewish control of Christian holy places, and which contained a restive Muslim minority, had already announced against partition when the American arm-twisting began. The Philippines had

---

[14]*Foreign Relations,* 1947, 5:1195; Henderson memo, Nov. 4, 1947, State Department file 867N.01.

only just gained political independence from the United States, and, facing enormous war-reconstruction costs, it remained economically dependent on the United States. At this very moment, Congress was considering a large package of aid for the Philippines. To convey the message that Manila might wish to rethink its position on Palestine, the White House got Felix Frankfurter and another Supreme Court justice, former Philippine high commissioner Frank Murphy, to buttonhole the Philippine ambassador. Simultaneously, a group of pro-Zionist senators sent a cable to Manuel Roxas, the Philippine president, reminding Roxas of the importance of a correct vote on the Palestine issue. Roxas ordered a change of mind, and the Philippines supported partition.

Liberia, another economic colony of the United States, received the attention of industrialist and former secretary of state Edward Stettinius. Steel-man Stettinius happened to be a close friend of rubber-man Harvey Firestone, whose company dominated the Liberian economy. Stettinius called the Liberian president, William Tubman, to indicate his concern over reports that Liberia would vote against the majority plan. He hoped these reports weren't true. Tubman made sure they weren't.

Haiti, even poorer than Liberia, had also announced against partition. Niles lined up a collection of American businessmen with operations in Haiti to suggest that an unfavorable decision on Palestine would not improve the business climate. Former assistant secretary of state Adolph Berle personally telegraphed the Haitian president, Dumarsais Estimé, to remind the Haitian leader of the importance of the Palestine question in the eyes of the American government. Estimé wired back that on second thought Haiti would vote for partition.

The pressure paid off. When the United Nations General Assembly voted on the majority plan at the end of November 1947, partition passed by two votes.

The General Assembly's acceptance of the majority plan cleared the path for the creation of Israel. For the Zionists, the vote for partition gave an international seal of approval to their long-held aspirations. For the British, it provided convenient cover for dropping a burden they no longer desired to carry. For the Arabs, the United Nations vote represented another setback to their desire to. restore Palestine to the Palestinians. The British colonialists, who had supplanted the Ottoman colonialists, were leaving, but were giving way to another group of interlopers. Although these latest interlopers had deeper roots in Palestine than either the British or the Ottomans, the deeper roots made them all the more threatening to Palestinian goals. The Ottomans had gone, and the British were going, but the Zionists quite evidently intended to stay. To be sure, the majority plan specified a state for the Palestinians as well as a state for the Jews. In this case, though, half a loaf looked hardly better than none, and no Palestinian leader volunteered to step forward and agree to an arrangement that signed away a large part of the national patrimony. Recognizing Israel, in the Palestinian view, amounted to a sellout.

For the United States, the United Nations approval of partition was a mixed blessing. Most Americans applauded the return of the Jews to the biblical homeland, some from not wanting more Jews in America, but many more from admiration for the Jews' grit and from a desire to make amends for what the Jews had suffered. For the Truman administration, the United Nations vote represented both a moral victory and a political success: Truman and his White House advisers sincerely believed in the Zionist cause; at the same time, they understood that a pro-Zionist policy served the administration on the hustings. New York might easily decide the outcome of the 1948 presidential election, and New York's Jews might decide New York.

The months following the United Nations decision witnessed an escalation of violence in Palestine, as both Jews and Arabs positioned themselves for the day when the last British soldiers left. The bloodspilling caused the Truman administration briefly to reconsider its backing for partition. Diehards at the State Department tried to capitalize on the reconsideration and prevent partition from being implemented, or at least to dissociate the United States from the implementation. They succeeded only in embarrassing, and therefore infuriating, the president. Truman wasn't about to welsh on his support for a Jewish state—and, in any case, the Zionists in Palestine weren't about to be denied their country at this eleventh hour, regardless of what the United Nations or the United States said or did.

As the moment of Israel's birth approached, the Truman administration had to decide when and how to grant diplomatic recognition. The diplomats resisted to the last. At a meeting on May 12, Undersecretary of State Robert Lovett pointed out to the president that the United States didn't know what kind of government the Zionists were setting up, and that to extend recognition prematurely would be "buying a pig in a poke." Secretary of State Marshall likewise urged care. White House counsel Clark Clifford was advocating immediate recognition; Marshall blasted Clifford's proposal as "a transparent dodge to win a few votes." During his long career as a soldier, Marshall had carried the principle of political nonpartisanship to the degree of never voting for president. Now the secretary of state told Truman to his face that if he were a voter and the president followed Clifford's advice, he would vote against him.[15]

But the State Department lost this round, as it had lost the others. Truman decided in favor of immediate recognition, evidently believing that delay would be politically foolish and diplomatically quixotic. He ordered the diplomats to work out the details of recognition, which they did with little grace. On May 14, 1948, fifteen minutes after the official proclamation of Israel's existence, the United States recognized the government of the new country.

✿   ✿   ✿

By the summer of 1948, the future of American relations with the Middle East was taking recognizable shape. World War II had demonstrated the absolute essentialness of petroleum in international affairs. Without secure sources of oil, no country could hope to achieve a major, independent role in the game of nations. The Middle East contained a giant part of the world's oil supply; this guaranteed that the region would draw the attention of American leaders.

By mid-1948, the Cold War had well begun. The United States and the Soviet Union had demonstrated their antagonism toward each other, and each adopted as a primary goal the frustration of the other's ambitions. The Soviets hoped to expand their influence in the Middle East; Washington sought to keep the Soviets out.

The establishment of Israel in May 1948 added a new and unsettling wrinkle to Middle Eastern politics. By itself, the existence of the Zionist state would have complicated the relations of any country with interests in the region; the fact that the United States provided crucial support for Israel's creation vexed American dealings with the Middle East all the more.

---

[15] H. W. Brands, *Inside the Cold War* (New York, 1991), p. 187.

Chapter 2

With Friends Like These: 1948–1956

1. TO THE TRIPARTITE DECLARATION

The first war of the Arab-Israeli conflict, which broke out as the final British soldiers were leaving Palestine, lasted the longest. From May 1948 until January 1949, with intermittent truces, Israeli military units battled the forces of Israel's Arab neighbors—Egypt, Syria, Transjordan (soon to be renamed Jordan), Lebanon, and Iraq—and what fighters the Palestinians could put in the field. Although such a war was precisely what the dismalists in the State Department had been warning of, its outbreak to some degree lifted a burden off the American government. All interested parties concentrated their attention on events in the area of combat; the diplomats in foreign capitals and at the United Nations receded into the background.

Almost regardless of developments in the Middle East, the United States probably would have receded into the background of affairs of the region anyway. The period of the first Arab-Israeli war was a frantic time for Washington. In June 1948, the Soviet Union began blockading Berlin; shortly thereafter, the Truman administration ordered an airlift of necessary supplies to the stranded city. Also in June, Yugoslavia's Tito broke with Moscow, opening a gap in the Eastern front that American policy makers did their best to widen. Elections in France and Italy threatened to bring communists to power there; American Marshall Plan aid, along with some secret assistance to the noncommunist parties, attempted to keep them out of power. In China, the armies of Mao Zedong's Communists landed heavy blows on Chiang Kai-shek's Nationalists, sending American strategists scurrying to discover a fallback position in East Asia. All these press-ing concerns required the Truman administration to focus attention and resources on areas other than the Middle East.

Fortunately for the administration (not to mention Israel), the Zionists managed to hold their own—and then some—against the Arabs. During the first few weeks of fighting, the Israelis beat back the invading armies, in the meantime appealing to the United Nations to condemn the aggression. After a month, the Arabs agreed to a ceasefire. This proved to be a miscalculation, since the Israelis used the respite from fighting to resupply themselves with weapons, no-tably from Czechoslovakia. In the second stage of the war, which began as the ceasefire progressively unraveled, the Israelis shifted to the attack, pushing beyond the frontiers assigned them in the Novem-ber 1947 United Nations resolution.

The Truman administration initially adopted a low profile in the diplomacy that accompanied the fighting. Washington's representative at the United Nations, Warren Austin, contributed chiefly the senti-ment that the Muslims and Jews fighting over the holy places ought to settle their differences in a "true Christian spirit." The American role increased following the September assassination of the United Na-tions mediator, Sweden's Count Folke Bernadotte, by Jewish terror-ists. American diplomat Ralph Bunche replaced Bernadotte, guaran-teeing greater visibility for the United States in the talks that ultimately ended the first Arab-Israeli war in January 1949.[1]

That the war ended in an armistice rather than a peace treaty re-sulted from the fact that although the Israelis could defend them-selves and prevent an Arab victory, they couldn't accomplish an Arab defeat. For now, anyway, the Arabs could simply withdraw back across their borders, waiting to fight another day.

Yet if the Israelis didn't win the war in a strict military sense, they won politically by securing (and extending) their borders and forcing the Arabs to deal with Israel as a state-in-being, albeit one the Arabs didn't recognize diplomatically. After 1949, the Arabs might fulminate and threaten, but they couldn't credibly deny that Israel existed. While the armistice agreement explicitly declared that the truce lines should not be construed as territorial frontiers, in practice they be-came just that—until modified by later fighting.

---

[1]George T. Mazuzan, *Warren R. Austin at the U.N.* (Kent, Ohio, 1977), p. 99.

The second consequence of the Palestine War was the creation of the Palestinian problem. Before and during the fighting, several hundred thousand Palestinians fled the territory assigned to Israel by the United Nations and the territories occupied by Israeli troops. The majority of the refugees entered camps in the Gaza Strip, situated along the Mediterranean between Israel and Egypt, and on the West Bank of the Jordan River, both of which had been assigned to the Palestinians by the United Nations partition plan. Following the Palestinians' rejection of the plan, the West Bank soon fell under the rule of Jordan, while the Gaza Strip drifted in a political no man's land, grudgingly administered by Egypt. Egypt's grudge reflected the hard conditions in Gaza, where a quarter-million persons now tried to live on land that had previously strained to support 60,000.

American leaders appreciated that if peace should ever arrive in the Middle East, a solution to the Palestinian problem would precede it. Washington sporadically expostulated with Israel to allow the return of some significant number of the refugees. But Israel resisted, citing security considerations. An additional cause of Israeli reluctance was the fact that now that Israel existed, the 100,000 (and more—the number had grown) DPs in Europe had a place to go—so long as Israel wasn't full of Palestinians. Indeed, under Israel's Law of Return, every Jew in the world enjoyed the automatic right to immigrate to Israel. A population of several million would require lots of land—which led some Arabs, recognizing the demographics of the situation, to speak of the Zionists as latter-day Nazis, seeking "living space" for their own kind at the Arabs' expense. Israel eventually consented to be persuaded by the United States to allow a minor portion of the Palestinian refugees to return to their homes, but far fewer than the Palestine War had displaced.

The 1949 armistice pushed the Arab-Israeli struggle onto the back burner of American foreign relations. This location didn't sit well with those in the United States who thought Israel deserved better from Washington, and such persons regularly agitated for more attention to Israeli concerns. The pressure succeeded in moving the Truman administration to approve a $100 million loan to Israel, an action that commenced a continuing and crucial (to Israel) financial connection between the United States government and Israel. To this flow of public dollars was added a substantial stream of private donations from American Jewish groups—a stream that also would grow over the coming years.

The pressure from Israel's friends in the United States likewise succeeded, although more slowly, in allowing the flow of American arms to Israel. In the spring of 1948, the Truman administration had embargoed weapons shipments from the United States to the vicinity of Israel. Since then, Israel had received much of its arms supply from the Soviet bloc. But the communist-made weapons weren't everything Israel's generals desired, and Israel's politicians disliked the idea of depending on a single source of supply. Both the generals and the politicians looked to the United States for a remedy for their problems. At the same time, they desired to counter British arms sales to the Arabs. When the Israelis presented their case to Washington, officials in the Truman White House sympathized, not wanting Israel to become addicted to Soviet weapons and not wanting to upset Israel's backers in the United States. The State Department took the opposite view: the diplomats feared further antagonizing the Arabs and warned of an arms race in the Middle East.

Attempting to strike a balance between these two opinions, Truman lifted the arms embargo, but simultaneously arranged an agreement among the United States, Britain, and France—France being the third major potential source of Western arms for the Middle East—to exercise restraint in selling weapons to the parties to the Arab-Israeli dispute. What became known as the Tripartite Declaration of May 1950 affirmed the three governments' understanding that the countries of the Middle East required weapons "for the purposes of assuring their internal security and their legitimate self-defense." Yet the declaration also served notice of the opposition of Washington, London, and Paris to the development of a weapons race between the Arab states and Israel. It explained that the three governments would require purchasers of weapons to provide guarantees that the weapons would not be used aggressively, and it reiterated the three governments' opposition to the use of force to alter the status quo in the region.[2]

For the United States, the Tripartite Declaration represented an effort at evenhandedness between Israel and the Arabs. To the Arabs, it asserted the United States' intention to oppose further Israeli expansion; to the Israelis, it promised access to American arms and indicated American acceptance of the 1949 borders. The declaration obviously didn't solve the Arab-Israeli problem, but at the time it

[2]*The New York Times*, May 26, 1950.

seemed to many to be the first step toward a solution. At the least, it promised to calm things in the Middle East down a bit.

2. QUICK FIX: THE CIA IN IRAN

At the beginning of the 1950s, American leaders desperately wanted the Middle East to calm down, since so much of the rest of the world was continuing to do just the opposite. In the spring of 1949, the Senate had approved American membership in the North Atlantic alliance, the United States' first peacetime entanglement since its ill-starred experience with France at the end of the eighteenth century. The Atlantic treaty provoked enormous discussion and sizable opposition; that the Senate ratified the treaty testified to the great alarm Americans felt regarding the future of democracy. Later that year, the Chinese Communists ran the Nationalists off the Chinese mainland, effectively completing the triumph of Marxism-Leninism (soon amended to Marxism-Leninism-Maoism) in the most populous country on the planet. In June 1950, communist North Korea attacked anticommunist South Korea, an attack widely thought to be instigated by Moscow. The Truman administration again declared the American way of life endangered, and ordered American forces to the defense of South Korea.

In three months of desperate fighting, the South Koreans and the Americans, with help from several other countries, managed to stem the North Korean advance; in September, they launched a stunning counteroffensive that carried them far into North Korea, all the way to the border of China. The Chinese, after warning the Americans not to get too close, entered the fray in massive numbers. The Chinese assault threw the Americans into confusion and pushed the world to the brink of another general conflict. American leaders didn't anticipate that the Soviet Union would enter the ongoing fight in East Asia; instead, they feared that the Soviets would take advantage of the United States' preoccupation with Korea and China to put the squeeze on Berlin again, or perhaps attempt once more to destabilize pro-Western regimes in the Middle East.

If Moscow did intend destabilizing the Middle East, Iran seemed as good a place to start as any. The boost to Iranian confidence provided by American diplomatic support in 1946 had largely worn off; the country's monarch, Muhammad Reza Shah Pahlavi, had made himself neither loved nor feared by the country's chief political factions. On the political right, members of the old aristocratic families resented the shah as the son of the usurper Reza Shah Pahlavi, who had illegally seized the Peacock Throne. The large estate holders distrusted him for holding perniciously progressive views on such matters as land reform. On the left, the powerful, well-organized, and pro-Moscow Tudeh party reviled the shah as the representative of a corrupt and archaic form of government, and a lackey of the Western capitalists to boot. Somewhere between left and right, or perhaps on a different political spectrum, Islamic fundamentalists denounced him as illegitimate and anathematized him for leading Iran away from the true teachings of the prophet Muhammad.

The most influential of the shah's opponents, however, was Muhammad Mossadeq. Americans never quite knew what to make of Mossadeq, with his flair for oratory and histrionics, his sometimes bizarre—to American and other Western eyes—yet always entertaining political tactics, and his capacity for concentrating the attention of his country and of much of the world on his own person. Born into one of Iran's most prominent families in the 1880s, Mossadeq claimed as cousins two individuals who between them had served as Iran's prime minister twenty times. (The family didn't talk about the stability of the governments the cousins headed.) Other relatives had held several scores of ministerships. Mossadeq himself had been a provincial governor, finance minister, and justice minister. Years earlier, he had learned to hate Reza Shah, and his antipathy carried over to Reza's son. Most of all, Mossadeq despised the British, whom he charged with subverting Iranian politics in the pursuit of oil profits.

He had a point. The Anglo-Iranian Oil Company, with the British government as majority stockholder, had from the first decade of the century held an exclusive concession to find and pump oil in a half-million-square-mile area of Iran. Almost from the start, the Iranian government expressed dissatisfaction with the terms of the concession and agitated for change. London resisted, on grounds both financial (profits from oil operations swelled the British treasury's coffers) and strategic (Iranian oil fueled the British navy). On numerous occasions, the British couldn't resist meddling in Iranian politics, and when the British troops arrived in 1942, they appeared to many Iranians to be mercenaries in the service of the rapacious Anglo-Iranian company.

It was during the war that Mossadeq began attacking the company and the foreign domination of Iran's economy he claimed it symbolized. He didn't get very far at the time, but he gained a reputation as a spokesman of Iranian nationalism. In 1949, he employed this reputation in helping to establish the National Front, an umbrella organization uniting various groups advocating liberal reforms and an end to foreign control of Iranian economic and political life.

In 1951, as a member of the Iranian parliament's lower house, or Majlis, Mossadeq chaired a committee that drafted a legislative measure aimed at nationalizing the Anglo-Iranian company's Iranian holdings. The measure provoked the opposition of the prime minister, Ali Razmara, who held that likely British retaliation would seriously injure the Iranian economy. But religious extremists assassinated Razmara in March 1951, and in the polarized atmosphere that followed the assassination, the nationalization bill gained parliamentary approval. Mossadeq, the hero of the hour, landed in the prime minister's chair.

The nationalization of the Anglo-Iranian company touched off a struggle to the political death between Mossadeq and the British government. (In fact, *both* Mossadeq and his British counterpart, Clement Attlee, fell from power before the struggle ended.) The British condemned the nationalization as theft and contemplated military action against Iran. Financial and military considerations aside, the British shuddered at the precedent the nationalization might establish for British holdings elsewhere in the Middle East. If the Iranians could get away with taking over the Anglo-Iranian company's assets, which included the world's largest petroleum refinery at Abadan, what would prevent the Egyptians from seizing the Suez Canal? The very thought boggled British minds. To unboggle them, London readied its warships and troops.

But once Washington got wind of British plans, Attlee and his cabinet had to reconsider. Officials of the Truman administration worried that a British move to grab Abadan and the oil fields back from Tehran would trigger another Soviet move against Iranian Azerbaijan, and they relayed their worries, strongly expressed, across the Atlantic. Attlee cancelled the military plans.

The British opted instead for economic pressure. The Anglo-Iranian company shut down operations, throwing thousands of Iranians out of work and depriving the Iranian government of a major source of income. Simultaneously, the company threatened legal action against any other firm dealing in Iranian oil—a threat that in the (especially then) cozy world of international oil amounted to a blockade of petroleum exports from Iran.

In addition, the British applied political and legal pressure. London appealed to the International Court of Justice to enforce what the British claimed to be a no-nationalization clause of the company's contract with the Iranian government. When Mossadeq denied that the court had jurisdiction, and the court agreed, the dispute went to the United Nations.

The Truman administration feared that this latest setback would cause the British to reconsider their reconsideration of military force, and it threw a series of troubleshooters into the breach. First it tried George McGhee, the assistant secretary of state; then W. Averell Harriman, formerly ambassador to the Soviet Union and the Democrats' all-purpose fixer; then McGhee again; then Loy Henderson, whose opposition to the administration's line on Israel had cost him his job as director of the State Department's Middle East division and earned him exile in India and subsequently Iran. Through the end of 1951 and into 1952, none of the troubleshooters had any luck.

The basic problem was that neither the British nor the Iranians had much desire to compromise. For the British, the dispute with Iran held the key to Britain's future in the Middle East. The replacement of the socialist Attlee by the arch-imperialist Churchill at the end of 1951 only reinforced this no-compromise attitude. For the Iranians, the fight with Britain represented nothing less than a fight for Iranian independence. Though Iran, unlike much of the rest of the Middle East, had successfully resisted subjugation by the Western powers, Iranians often felt no less oppressed by Western influences than their subjugated neighbors. To yield on the oil issue would be to admit the legitimacy of these influences. All nations need foreign devils, and for Iran the British filled the bill. (For the United States at this time, the Soviet Union and other communists served.) Mossadeq especially believed the British to be at the root of what ailed Iran. The prime minister told Averell Harriman, regarding the British, "You do not know how crafty they are. You do not know how evil they are. You do not know how they sully everything they touch." To Harriman's reply that the British couldn't be *that* bad, Mossadeq answered, "You do not know them. You do not know them."[3]

Eventually the United States would supplant Britain as Iran's Great Satan, but for now Mossadeq tried to cultivate the Americans, in order to use them against the British. He spoke with Henderson

[3]James A. Bill, *The Eagle and the Lion* (New Haven, Conn., 1988), p. 65.

often and at length. The American ambassador found the prime minister captivating. "Mossadeq was an attractive man although he was neither handsome nor elegant," Henderson later recalled. "He was tall and lanky; his long horselike face topped with rather disheveled gray hair was expressive like that of an actor. He had a large mouth, and when he smiled his whole face lit up and one felt drawn toward him. He liked jokes and liked to laugh at them."[4]

And Mossadeq was sharp. Henderson described him as very shrewd, with an intuitive grasp of Iranian emotions and character. Henderson thought Mossadeq had Britain on the brain, but the ambassador didn't worry that the prime minister would overreact by giving the game to the Soviets. Mossadeq, Henderson said, knew that the Soviets were up to no good in Iran. Putting his finger on what seemed Mossadeq's primary motivation, Henderson concluded that the prime minister was possessed by an "almost megalomaniacal desire to act as the champion of the people in the struggle for 'independence'."[5]

For all his talents and ambitions, Mossadeq walked a tightrope in Iranian politics. The leftist Tudeh wished him ill, staging demonstrations of as many as 100,000 people and demanding that the prime minister take stronger action against the British imperialists and their American accomplices—the latter of whom they identified particularly in the persons of American advisers to the Iranian military. Although nominally illegal, the Tudeh had amassed sufficient strength that neither Mossadeq nor anyone else felt free to move against it; the prime minister instead sought to appease the party. Not surprisingly, this policy of accommodation raised red flags in the minds of American officials watching Mossadeq.

Equally threatening to Mossadeq, if not of such great concern at that time to Washington, were the Islamic fundamentalists. The leader of the fundamentalists was Ayatollah Abd al-Qasem Kashani. Henderson never warmed to Kashani the way the ambassador warmed to Mossadeq, not least since Kashani exuded all the warmth of the average religious zealot. Henderson found him "retrogressive and anti-foreign," disposed to think as poorly of the British as Mossadeq did, although for different reasons, and considerably more hostile to the

[4]Henderson oral history, Truman Library, Independence, Mo.

[5]Henderson to Acheson, Oct. 22, 1951, State Department file 350 Iran, National Records Center, Suitland, Md.

United States. On a visit to the American embassy, Kashani boasted that he pulled the strings that controlled Mossadeq's actions; he added, without explicitly accepting responsibility, that individuals allied to himself had assassinated Ali Razmara. He went so far as to declare that Muslims from India to North Africa were under his control and would obey his every command. Kashani asserted that he and his fellow believers opposed communism most bitterly; accordingly, he did not entirely rule out cooperation with the United States, since he knew that the Americans opposed communism too. Of course, Washington would have to change its ways and recognize the legitimacy of the claims of Shia Islam—Kashani's sect—to rule Iran.

Henderson listened to Kashani with interest. Though much of what Kashani said struck the ambassador as outrageous, he granted that Kashani might serve a valuable purpose for Iran's future—and the United States'—if only temporarily. In Henderson's view, the Islamic fundamentalists knew how to block what they didn't like, but had no positive program. "Religious fanaticism can be used to combat communism, but it cannot be employed as a constructive force for the country's progress," he asserted.

The fourth major element in the Iranian political equation—after Mossadeq, the Tudeh, and the fundamentalists—was Shah Pahlavi. In time, the shah would become a powerful ruler—a veritable tyrant, to his enemies—but at the beginning of the 1950s he was more of a milquetoast. The shah turned 32 in 1951, and although he had occupied his throne for a decade, he ruled less than he reigned. He distrusted Mossadeq, yet while he nominally possessed the authority to dismiss the prime minister and replace him with someone more to the royal taste, he declined to exercise this authority. He feared that he lacked power to match his authority: Mossadeq might well refuse to be fired, and the refusal would humiliate the crown. Henderson, a bull-by-the-horns type himself, found the shah's diffidence exasperating. The ambassador judged the shah indecisive and weak, and regularly despaired that Iran's salvation would ever come if it had to come through the monarch.

Increasingly, during the last part of 1952 and the first half of 1953, Henderson despaired that Iran's salvation would come at all. He never believed that Mossadeq was a communist, nor did he doubt that Mossadeq had anything but the best interests of Iran at heart. In this belief, Henderson generally reflected the opinion of other American officials. Had Iran been a stable democracy, on the model of

France or even Italy, American officials probably wouldn't have considered Mossadeq particularly threatening. Washington has never much liked nationalization as an instrument of other countries' foreign policy, but the American government had long since made its peace with the idea that nationalization was an attribute of the sovereignty of the nationalizing country and not something subject to international debate. (The test case occurred when Mexico nationalized American oil properties during the 1930s and the Roosevelt administration refrained from military or other forcible retaliation.) Besides, the British under Attlee's Labour government had been nationalizing some of Britain's major industries since the end of the war, and still Washington put Britain at the top of the list for Marshall Plan aid. (The British government looked less favorably on *other* countries' nationalizing of British holdings, as the Iran situation, and later the Suez affair, demonstrated.)

The trouble with Mossadeq was not Mossadeq per se, but what Mossadeq might lead to. As the oil blockade took effect, the Iranian economy slid into depression, creating stress and restiveness throughout the country. Most severely hit were the neighborhoods of the oil fields and refineries, which also happened to be the stronghold of Iran's most radical labor unions. The Tudeh battened on the unrest.

At the same time, the anti-Western sentiments both Mossadeq and the Tudeh exploited for their own purposes played into the hands of Kashani and the religious fundamentalists. In the early 1950s, American officials didn't particularly fear the emergence of an Islamic regime in Tehran, at least not for what such a regime would represent on its own terms. They worried that the likes of Kashani would seize the government, but would be unable to solve Iran's problems and would succumb to a leftist power play. Once the Tudeh gained control, Iran would quickly fall into the Soviet sphere.

With neither the Tudeh nor the fundamentalists affording what Washington perceived as relief from Mossadeq, American officials looked to the shah. They had to look hard. Despite repeated urgings from Henderson to stand up to Mossadeq, to assert himself and take charge of the country, the monarch continued to hem and haw. He and his ministers asserted that the time had not yet come for strong moves, that they should give Mossadeq more rope to hang himself. Henderson accounted this argument simply a rationale for inaction and a facade over a lack of nerve. Henderson increasingly felt that the safety of Iran required a coup—a constitutional coup, according to the American reading of the Iranian constitution, but a coup still—by the shah against Mossadeq. Such a coup would require the cooperation of the Iranian military, yet mostly it depended on the determination of the shah. Unfortunately, Henderson predicted, the shah would "take fright at the very idea of a coup."[6]

Until the summer of 1953, the United States government did little to buck up the shah's nerve. Henderson offered verbal encouragement, but not the logistical and financial support required really to make a coup.

In June 1953, however, the situation began to change. The change resulted in part from the continued confusion in Iran. Mossadeq's National Front was crumbling, forcing the prime minister to offer further concessions to the Tudeh and the Islamic fundamentalists. The economy spiraled downward, adding to pressure for change of a radical nature, in favor of either the political radicals or the religious radicals.

Yet an equally important cause of the change occurred in Washington. With the January 1953 accession of Dwight Eisenhower to the presidency, American policy regarding the Soviet Union and its allies shifted from the overt military approach of the Truman administration—represented by NATO and the continuing struggle against China and North Korea—to a covert political approach. Eisenhower had learned to appreciate the possibilities of covert operations and political warfare as commander of Allied forces in Europe during World War II, when resistance fighters and Allied secret agents successfully softened up German defenses before the Normandy invasion and other offensives. Eisenhower assumed the presidency at a moment when the Soviet Union was crossing the threshold into the hydrogen-bomb era, just months behind the United States; he understood how military force was losing its effectiveness in superpower relations. In 1946, during the earlier troubles over Iran, Truman had been able to take confidence from the fact that if things got really sticky, the United States possessed atomic weapons and the Soviet Union didn't. In 1953, Eisenhower had no such advantage.

Covert operations would characterize Eisenhower's foreign policy around the world, involving the United States' clandestine agents in the affairs of Europe, Central America, Asia, and Africa. American spooks were active in much of the Middle East, especially in Iran, where during the late summer of 1953 they achieved what they— dubiously—deemed one of their signal successes.

---

[6]Henderson to Acheson, Aug. 3, 1992, ibid.

Two months earlier, Henderson had traveled to Washington to apprise the Eisenhower administration of the latest developments in Iran. He met with most of the administration's major foreign-policy players. The Dulles brothers—Secretary of State John Foster Dulles and CIA chief Allen Dulles—headed the list, which also included the secretary of defense, Charles Wilson, and a variety of assistant secretaries and other middleweights. The CIA brought in Kermit Roosevelt, the intelligence agency's top hand for the Middle East, to explain a plan—originally devised by the British and still requiring London's cooperation—for the overthrow of Mossadeq and the consolidation of Pahlavi's power. The plan called for a preemptive move by the shah to fire Mossadeq and replace him as prime minister with Fazlollah Zahedi, a prominent army general who until recently had been a Mossadeq ally. Roosevelt couldn't give very many details of the plan, since much would depend on circumstances in Iran at the moment of execution. But, as befit the grandson of Rough Rider Teddy, he was confident of making the scheme work.

John Foster Dulles polled the assembled group to determine their reactions to the scheme. None opposed it, although some expressed greater enthusiasm than others. Most took the view that while the United States shouldn't gratuitously intervene in the affairs of other countries, in this case American security might depend on such intervention. Mossadeq, through inadvertence and incompetence, was leading Iran down a road that ran dangerously close to Moscow. Many Iranians already blamed the United States for intervening; many of the rest blamed the United States for not intervening, for failing to support whichever faction in Iran the blamers belonged to. From the perspective of the United States government, it was a damned-if-we-do, damned-if-we-don't business. Washington ought at least to get some good out of all the blaming—such as a more stable government than Mossadeq's.

The anti-Mossadeq plan, denoted Operation Ajax, succeeded, though not without a few hitches. Mossadeq refused to be fired, arresting the messenger who delivered his dismissal notice and rallying his supporters in the streets. The shah got scared and fled the country, despite some spine-stiffening words from American General Norman Schwarzkopf, formerly adviser to the Iranian gendarmerie (and father of the hero of the Persian Gulf War of 1991). Roosevelt organized counter-riots to Mossadeq's riots by freely dispensing money among rowdies from the slums of south Tehran. Officers loyal to General Zahedi sent tanks into the streets, and after several tense hours, the tide shifted in favor of the shah. The royalists captured Mossadeq, and the shah returned in triumph.

To the Eisenhower administration, the outcome of the operation seemed a victory for the administration's foreign policy, and for American interests in the Middle East. By timely action, the United States had prevented the takeover of Iran by elements unfriendly to the Free World—elements, moreover, that probably couldn't have resisted Moscow's expansionist pressures. The administration didn't acknowledge the American role in the anti-Mossadeq coup; Washington conspicuously congratulated the shah and the Iranian people for saving themselves and their country from a grim fate.

Some Iranians shared this interpretation of events, at least in outline. By the time of the coup of August 1953, Mossadeq's popularity had eroded drastically. Had it not, the CIA's scheme would have failed—as Roosevelt himself admitted afterward. A sizable portion of the Iranian people greeted the prime minister's removal with relief, as betokening an end to the economic distress and political turmoil of the previous few years.

To a significant group within Iran, though, the American role in the coup—which was no secret to Iranians, however little most Americans knew about it—seemed simply an extension of foreign domination of Iranian affairs. When Washington brokered a settlement of the oil dispute between Britain and Iran, in the process forcing the Anglo-Iranian company to grant American firms a share in Iran's oil business, and began sending large amounts of American aid to the shah, whose government grew increasingly repressive with passing time, the United States replaced Britain as the object of Iranian nationalists' hatred and xenophobia. Together, the shah and several American presidential administrations kept a lid on Iranian dissatisfaction for a quarter century. But the tighter they kept the lid, the more the pressure underneath it built.

3. FROM MEDO TO THE BAGHDAD PACT

Strategically speaking, the Middle East matters to the West for two principal reasons. One reason, obviously, is oil. The second, of longer standing, is location. From at least Roman days, the Middle East controlled the trade routes to the Indies; although Vasco da Gama's circumnavigation of Africa in the late fifteenth century opened an alternative route, the building of the Suez Canal three hundred years later restored the Middle East to transportation preeminence. The canal had been operating barely a decade before the British decided they needed to occupy Egypt to assure their easy access to India. The occupation began, as occupations almost always do, as a temporary solution to an immediate problem (in this case, unrest in Alexandria and its vicinity); it continued, as occupations often do, long after the original problem had disappeared. British troops remained in Egypt in the early 1950s. If and how long they would stay, and under what terms, were subjects of acrimonious negotiations between London and the Egyptian government, and the cause of violent skirmishes between Egyptian demonstrators and the British soldiers.

The United States entered the picture from two directions. First, Washington saw Egypt as a key to a settlement of the Arab-Israeli conflict, without which peace and stability would never come to the Middle East. If the Egyptians, perhaps with enticements from Washington, could learn to live with the Israelis, the inhabitants of the smaller Arab states might manage the trick as well. Second, Egypt seemed a likely candidate for membership in a regional alliance against Soviet expansion. Again, as the most prominent of the Arab states, Egypt could set an example for other countries to follow. Here Egypt's location mattered particularly, for whichever side in the Cold War gained Egypt's cooperation would gain control of the Suez Canal. In recognition of Egypt's geostrategic significance, the British had constructed a large military base in the Egyptian desert near the canal; the future of this Suez base constituted the chief haggling point in the ongoing Anglo-Egyptian negotiations.

American leaders saw these two aspects of policy toward Egypt as the front and back of a single coin. An Egypt that received satisfaction from Washington on questions touching Israel would be more likely to cooperate with the United States against the Soviet Union; an Egypt that cooperated against the Soviets would be more likely to receive a favorable hearing in Washington on questions touching Israel.

Through the summer of 1952, the Egyptians didn't get much satisfaction from the United States on the Arab-Israeli question. Although the Truman administration took few active steps on Israel's behalf after extending diplomatic recognition, the Democratic president wasn't about to force the Israelis to convert the 1949 armistice into a peace treaty. A peace treaty may have been impossible at this early date: in Egypt and other Arab states the wounds of the war were probably too fresh. But, in any event, the sympathetic and Democratic Truman was hardly the person to impose concessions upon the Israelis, and without Israeli concessions—for instance, the surrender of the Negev region, captured in the war, or a decision allowing the Palestinians to return—no Arab government could afford to make peace.

Events in Cairo during the summer of 1952 promised a change. The nature of the change, however, was impossible to determine for some time. In July, a group of Egyptian military officers overthrew King Farouk. The officers, led by General Muhammad Neguib, but inspired by Colonel Gamal Abdul Nasser, objected to the monarchy's corruption and backwardness, which had contributed substantially to Egypt's humiliation in the Palestine War. ("Overfed, lazy, and selfish," was how Nasser described his seniors in Farouk's army, adding that they filled their time with "eating, drinking, gambling, carousing, smoking hashish, and engaging in many different forms of corruption and tyranny.") The coup makers also complained at the tardiness of the Egyptian government in ejecting the British from Egypt, and they pledged to accomplish the ejection or go down trying.[7]

Neguib, Nasser, and their colleagues initially looked to the United States for assistance. They knew little about America, but they recalled from their history lessons that the United States had gained its own independence by throwing the British out, and they appealed to this anti-imperialist American heritage. They impressed the American ambassador in Cairo, Lincoln Caffery, with their bona fides, if not their sophistication. "I believe they are well-intentioned, patriotic, and filled with desire to do something for Egypt," Caffery declared. "On the other hand, they are woefully ignorant of matters economic, financial, political, and international." Caffery went on to say that the officers seemed "anxious to learn."[8]

What they were most anxious to learn was whether the United States would help them against the British. London certainly hoped not. In sharp contrast to the situation in Turkey and Greece, where the British had invited the United States to take over from them, and to the situation in Iran, where the British had been happy for Ameri-

[7]Raymond William Baker, *Egypt's Uncertain Revolution under Nasser and Sadat* (Cambridge, Mass., 1978), p. 29.

[8]Cairo to State Department, Aug. 20, 1952, State Department file 774.00, National Archives, Washington.

can efforts to overthrow Mossadeq (although they weren't so happy with the way the oil settlement turned out), the British sought to keep Egypt as their own bailiwick. In certain respects, British policy was anachronistic and illogical. Egypt's importance to Britain had originated in its geographic relation to colonial India, but India had become independent in 1947. Britain's continuing protectorate over the emirates of the Persian Gulf required, or at least strongly indicated, free passage of British vessels to the territories east of Suez, but free passage didn't demand a British sphere of influence over Egypt. As much as anything, Britain's attempt to hang on in Egypt represented a last gasp of British imperialism. And the gasping only grew more pronounced with the return of Churchill and the Tories to power at the end of 1951.

More than any other British prime minister, Churchill—the son of an English father and an American mother—promoted the Anglo-American "special relationship." What Churchill meant by this term varied from circumstance to circumstance; in the Egyptian case, he intended that Washington stay on the sidelines. The Egyptians would try to play the United States off against Britain, Churchill held. They must not be allowed to succeed. If Washington felt utterly obliged to promise the Egyptians something, such a promise ought to be conditioned on prior Egyptian acceptance of a deal granting Britain generous rights to the Suez military base.

Washington saw things differently. While not wishing to make life difficult for the British, and recognizing Britain's importance to American policy in Europe, the American government preferred not to act as a cat's paw for London in the Middle East. Two considerations underlay this preference. First, by associating too closely with Britain, the United States ran the risk of alienating the people of the Middle East, millions of whom despised the British and their brand of imperialism and were already suspicious of the United States for supporting Israel. Second, and related to the first, the British appeared to be living in an imaginary world, thinking they could hold what they had held for so long. In fact, the world had changed beyond the recognition of hidebound types like Churchill and British Foreign Secretary Anthony Eden. To link the United States to Britain in the Middle East, in the face of the rising tide of Arab nationalism and Islamic fundamentalism, would be like boarding the *Titanic* after it hit the iceberg. Ambassador Caffery responded with exasperation to a message from Eden to the Truman administration, urging that the United

States adopt a parallel policy of distancing from the Neguib-Nasser group. "London's Foreign Office tactics have been wrong, and over and over I have predicted the consequences," Caffery said (and he had). "They are wrong again."[9]

American officials in Washington didn't disagree with Caffery, but they hesitated to dissociate themselves as far from London as the ambassador would have wished. General Neguib repeatedly approached Caffery with requests for American aid, especially American weapons. The general and his associates didn't suggest that they ought to get something for nothing; they intimated that in exchange for U.S. arms, they would take part in a regional alliance against the Soviet Union. "If you could find a way to let us have 100 tanks," Neguib said, "various doors would be opened, including one leading to Middle Eastern defense."[10]

Caffery argued vigorously for approval of this request. He convinced the State Department, which in turn swung the Defense Department into line. But the White House balked. As always, Truman paid greater attention to the concerns of his Jewish constituents and to supporters of Israel generally than the professional diplomats did. The Zionist lobby strongly opposed shipping arms to Egypt, which was formally at war with Israel, and which now was headed by a group of soldiers determined to avenge their disgrace at Israeli hands. The State Department countered with the traditional response of backers of questionable characters: These guys may not be perfect, but they're better than what might follow. Of Neguib, the State Department memoed, "He represents our best chance to establish a relationship of confidence between his country and the West. We must support him if he is to overcome opposition which undoubtedly will increase unless he has something to show for his present reasonable and courageous attitude."[11]

Truman wouldn't bite. With only a few weeks left in office, the Democratic president chose to leave this contentious issue to his Republican successor. He refused to grant Egypt American weapons, as the State Department and Pentagon recommended, although he did

[9]Cairo to State Department, Sept. 10, 1952, ibid.

[10]Cairo to State Department, Nov. 25, 1952, State Department file 780.5, National Archives.

[11]Jernegan to Acheson, Dec. 30, 1952, State Department file 774.5 MSP, National Archives.

permit Egypt to *buy* weapons in the United States. Since Cairo lacked cash, this permission counted for little.

With Eisenhower's assumption of office, the Egyptians had reason to believe they would fare better. Jewish groups meant less to the Republicans than they did to the Democrats, and less to Eisenhower personally than to Truman. Therefore the Republican administration presumably would be less susceptible to pressure from the pro-Israel lobby. In addition, if the Republicans' campaign rhetoric, which promised not merely the "containment" of communism but its "roll-back," could be credited, the Republicans would probably tend to agree with the State Department's argument that anti-Soviet considerations required warming to the Arabs.

Eisenhower refused to leap into anything, though. Before deciding what to do about Egypt, he sent John Foster Dulles to Cairo for talks with Neguib and Nasser. The first thing Dulles learned was that Neguib was losing the internal struggle for control of Egyptian affairs; if the United States wanted to do business with Egypt, it needed to deal with Nasser.

Whether Nasser would deal with the United States was another matter. Nasser found the American claim that Soviet communism posed the primary threat to Egypt's well-being ludicrous. "I can't see myself waking up one morning to find that the Soviet Union is our enemy," he snorted. "They are thousands of miles away from us. We have never had any quarrel with them." Imperialist England, not communist Russia, had long been Egypt's enemy, and still was. "I would become the laughing-stock of my people if I told them they now had an entirely new enemy, many thousands of miles away, and that they must forget about the British enemy occupying their territory. Nobody would take me seriously if I forgot about the British."[12]

Dulles tried to change Nasser's mind, without success. As Dulles related to Eisenhower, the Egyptians had fixated on the British so single-mindedly that they neglected nearly all other threats to their country. "Their emotions are so great that they would rather go down as martyrs than concede," Dulles said. "It is almost impossible to over-emphasize the intensity of this feeling. It may be pathological, but it is a fact."[13]

---

[12] Mohammed H. Heikal, *Cutting the Lion's Tail* (New York, 1987), p. 39.

[13] *Foreign Relations of the United States*, 1952–1954, 9:25–26.

This fact had important implications for American policy toward the Middle East. The implication of most immediate consequence was a decision by the Eisenhower administration to scrap plans for a regional defensive alliance centered on Egypt. The alliance in question had been called by various names, most recently the Middle East Defense Organization. The idea had originated with the British a few years before, when London suggested a grouping of Britain, Turkey, and Egypt, connected in some fashion to NATO. American officials at first reacted skeptically, wondering whether the Soviet threat to the Middle East warranted the attention and resources required by an organization of this sort. The outbreak of the Korean War had caused Washington to upgrade its threat assessments, but it also increased the reluctance of the Pentagon to stretch American military forces further than they already were. American officials preferred to leave the Middle East as much as possible to the British. In December 1951, the American joint chiefs of staff declared, "The United States considers that the defense of the over-all area of the Middle East is a British strategic responsibility."[14]

Developments of the next several months—Britain's inability to achieve a settlement of its oil dispute with Iran, sharper fighting in Egypt between British troops and Egyptian nationalists, Korean War–induced British retrenchment in the Middle East and elsewhere—called this conclusion into question. Paul Nitze, the director of the State Department's policy planning staff, asserted in May 1952 that British resources were "wholly inadequate" to defend the Middle East. And the danger to the region was growing. Nitze noted that the United States and its allies had succeeded in strengthening Turkey and Greece against communism during the late 1940s, that United Nations forces currently were barring communist expansion in Korea, and that Franco-American efforts (French troops, American money) were frustrating the communists in Indochina. "In the Middle East, however," Nitze declared, "the general picture appears to be one of such continuing weakness as to constitute an invitation to a shift in the theater of primary pressure if further Communist progress were to be successfully blocked in other areas."[15]

The Middle East Defense Organization, or MEDO, had the aim of remedying this weakness. From the British perspective, it had the ad-

[14]Joint Chiefs of Staff paper 1887/33, Dec. 28, 1951, Joint Chiefs of Staff records, National Archives.

[15]Nitze to Cabell et al., May 26, 1952, ibid.

ditional aim of bringing the United States into the Middle East on Britain's terms. The British, with their long experience in the region and their (self-)presumed sensitivity to the subtleties of regional politics, would guide a joint Anglo-American policy, for which the British would furnish the brains, the Americans the muscle. Shortly after returning to office, Churchill visited the United States and requested American help. Speaking to a combined session of Congress, the prime minister described British troops defending the Suez Canal as "servants and guardians of the commerce of the world," and asked the legislators to approve an American force to join in this noble endeavor.

Congress would have nothing to do with Churchill's design. William Langer, one of the last of the Senate's isolationists, had anticipated just such a request, and had requested that the pastor of Boston's Old North Church, the signal post for Paul Revere's mythic ride, hang two lanterns in the belltower. Congressman Walter Judd dismissed Churchill's request with the comment, "Of course he wants to get his country tied as closely as possible to the United States. What other hope has it?" Seventeen lawmakers issued a demand for full disclosure of meetings between Churchill and officials of the Truman administration, claiming a fear of a secret sellout of American interests. (All seventeen were Republicans, suggesting less high-minded motives as well.)[16]

Congressional concerns hammered the first set of nails into the coffin of MEDO; more pounding accompanied a change of heart among American strategists. As the Pentagon and the State Department observed Britain's continuing troubles with the Egyptians, the defense officials and diplomats began to wonder whether Egypt would ever make a secure centerpiece for a regional alliance. In addition, though Egypt occupied the crucial position in the Middle East in terms of maritime transportation, it lay behind the likely lines of defense of the oil fields of the Persian Gulf against Soviet encroachment. American leaders, not having grown up immersed in the need to guard the route to India, consistently showed more interest in Persian Gulf oil than in the Suez Canal. The deepening crisis in Iran intensified this interest.

In the summer of 1952, J. Lawton Collins, the army chief of staff, outlined current thinking on the diminishing importance of Egypt in American strategic planning. Collins described the defense of the

[16]*New York Times,* Jan. 1, 1952 and Jan. 10, 1952; *Congressional Record,* 1952, pp. 276–279, 288, 317.

Middle East in terms of two "rings": an inner southern ring comprising Egypt and the countries immediately adjacent, and an outer ring arching from the Turkish Straits across the highlands of Asia Minor through the mountains of Iran and into Pakistan. An Egypt-centered MEDO, Collins said, supposing Egyptian cooperation, might hold the inner ring, but it would encounter great difficulty securing the region beyond. "The real hope," Collins continued, "lies in the defense of the outer ring, which would make use of the mountains." The outer-ring—or "northern-tier"—strategy would make optimal use of the Turks, the toughest and most reliable anticommunist fighters in the region. Most important, it would facilitate a defense of the oil fields of the Persian Gulf. "If we are going to hold Middle Eastern oil," Collins declared, "we will have to hold a line in Iran."

Collins went on to say that the active collaboration of Iran was imperative to the success of the entire endeavor. No matter how tough the Turks were, the Soviets could simply bypass Turkey if Iran fell under their sway. At present—while Mossadeq still held the Iranian premiership—forces antipathetic to the West called the tune in Tehran; but Collins suggested that such might not always be the case. "If we could get a stable government in Iran," the general mused, "one which would talk turkey with the Turks, we might be able to do something."[17]

The last nail in MEDO's coffin was driven by Nasser. The Egyptian leader's preoccupation with Britain, and his relative equanimity regarding the Soviet Union, finished off the projected alliance. Dulles returned from his May 1953 visit to Cairo convinced that Washington ought to forget about MEDO; at the same time, he grew increasingly enchanted with the possibilities of an alliance among the northern-tier countries. The secretary of state told Eisenhower that the Turks were champing at the bit, that Syria and Iraq realized the danger communism posed to them and could "probably be induced to join with us," and that Pakistan might easily become "a strong loyal point."

The obvious gap in this lineup was Iran, but the gap needn't always exist. At this moment, the Eisenhower administration's thinking regarding overall security arrangements for the Middle East meshed with its concerns about the internal situation in Iran. By rejecting MEDO, Nasser, in effect, doomed Mossadeq, for Washington now decided that the time had come to give the Iranian prime minister the push he needed to be toppled from power. Dulles told Eisenhow-

[17]*Foreign Relations*, 1952, 9:237–247.

er that the northern-tier strategy would probably work—"if we could save Iran." Therefore the "immediate need" of the United States was "to concentrate on changing the situation there."[18]

Shortly after this meeting, Dulles and Eisenhower approved the CIA's plan for Mossadeq's ouster; within weeks more, Iran had been "saved." Saving Iran from Mossadeq and the Tudeh turned out to be the easy part; subsequent steps to the northern-tier alliance, which acquired the name Baghdad Pact, were more difficult. The basic trouble was that the prospective members of the pact had little in common besides a desire for Western—especially American—economic and military assistance. Furthermore, American assistance to any country of the area upset at least some of the neighbors. Early in 1954, the United States signed a weapons agreement with Pakistan, which outraged India; the Indians thought—correctly, as events proved—that these weapons would be used not against the Soviet Union or China but against India. Israel and Israel's friends in the United States made a fuss whenever the Eisenhower administration hinted at aid to Arab governments, especially to Iraq, the most outspokenly anti-Zionist of the bunch. Saudi Arabia complained that an American alliance with Iraq would demonstrate Washington's favoritism toward Baghdad's Hashemite clan in the Arab world's dynastic wars. Egypt, not surprisingly, and Syria condemned the Baghdad Pact as a continuation of Western imperialism. Britain, liking the idea of being the big fish in a small pond, didn't press for direct American participation.

As a result of all these factors, the United States never joined the Baghdad alliance. Even so, Washington encouraged the group diplomatically and financially. An American representative—the ubiquitous Loy Henderson—sat on important committees connected to the pact, and Henderson's anticommunist pep talks and his fence mending among the diverse membership became a standard feature of alliance meetings during the mid-1950s.

4. DESCENT TO SUEZ

The Eisenhower administration's writing off of an Egypt-centered MEDO didn't imply writing off Egypt, at least not immediately. For nearly three years after Dulles's meeting with Nasser, the administra-

---

[18]*Foreign Relations*, 1953, 9:379–386.

tion continued to woo the Egyptian leader, seeking the same twin objectives the Truman administration had with Neguib: a peace between the Arabs and Israel, and a strengthening of the Middle East against Soviet expansionism. If Eisenhower's policy differed from Truman's, the difference chiefly involved emphasis. For Truman, Arab acceptance of Israel was a goal worth pursuing for its own sake. For Eisenhower, an Arab-Israeli settlement mattered primarily in the context of the struggle against the Soviet Union.

In most instances, the difference was hardly noticeable, since each president believed that peace in the Middle East would promote stability, which in turn would promote resistance to Soviet adventurism. Occasionally, though, the difference in emphasis produced different policy decisions. Truman almost certainly would have handled the Suez crisis of 1956, when Eisenhower slapped down the Israelis (and the British and the French), differently than his Republican successor did.

The Suez crisis arose out of Washington's (and London's and Paris's and Tel Aviv's) frustration with Nasser. Although Nasser nixed Egypt's participation in MEDO, he didn't rule out the possibility of other forms of cooperation with the United States. As matters happened—and as skeptical Arab-watchers predicted at the time—Nasser's professed interest in cooperation reflected no abiding coincidence of American and Egyptian aims, but rather his desire for American weapons and economic aid. While officials of the Eisenhower administration weren't blind to the possibility of mercenary motives in Cairo, they judged the risks of the situation to be worth taking.

The *diplomatic* risks, that is, were worth taking; the political risks were another issue. As in the runup to the establishment of Israel, the pro-Zionist forces in the United States had their ears to the ground, and every time the State Department and the Pentagon thought about sending aid to Egypt, the Israel lobby found out. At the beginning of 1954, congressional friends of Israel asked about reports that the administration was planning to provide assistance to Cairo. Could such shocking news actually be true? they demanded. Congressman Thomas Pelly, a Republican from Washington, declared that military aid to Egypt would be a "terrible mistake." Mixing metaphors, Pelly told his colleagues in the House of Representatives, "Let us have it clearly in mind that we are dealing with a two-edged sword. A loaded gun is not the thing to hand to someone who you are not sure will use it the way you intend." Democrat Emanuel Celler objected to aid to

Egypt on grounds that the Egyptians refused to let Israeli ships transit the Suez Canal. "Today Egypt arbitrarily excludes Israel from access to the canal," the New York congressman said. "Who knows but that the time may come when Egypt would arbitrarily proscribe any other nation, including the United States, from access?"[19]

Eisenhower wasn't about to let the Israel lobby dictate his Middle Eastern policy, but neither did he desire to provoke any unnecessary fights on Capitol Hill. To avoid fisticuffs, the administration devised a program of secret aid to Egypt. The idea of secrecy appealed to Nasser as well: he wanted the American aid, but not the stigma among Arab nationalists of publicly accepting it. In addition, he hoped to avoid the restrictions on use of American aid Congress customarily attached—and would be certain to attach to any aid that conceivably could threaten Israel. Finally, Nasser, who, after all, had come to power as the result of a conspiracy, liked working with the CIA, as opposed to the American embassy in Cairo and the State Department. Nasser hit it off almost at once with the CIA's Kermit Roosevelt. Roosevelt shared many traits of temperament and style with Nasser, and he dealt in cash—some $3 million of which had already been delivered to Nasser's people.

The mutual desire for discretion between Washington and Cairo prompted the Eisenhower administration to offer Nasser a covert package of aid. At a September 1954 meeting of Eisenhower's top-secret Operations Coordinating Board—the administration's clearinghouse for clandestine activities—representatives of the State and Defense departments and the CIA advocated an end run around Congress. The board members recommended telling Nasser that unless he accepted congressional conditions on aid, the administration could not initiate a full-scale military assistance program; however, he should also be told that "in view of our special friendship and our desire to assist his regime to maintain and consolidate itself, we are willing to make available a modest additional amount of economic aid in such a way that it will release dollars for the purchase by Egypt of American military equipment." The board members added, "This would be kept strictly secret."

John Jernegan, the deputy secretary of state for the Middle East, passed this recommendation along to Dulles, with the comment that Nasser could be "very useful to us" if "properly supported and culti-

---

[19]*Congressional Record,* 1954, pp. 410–411, 1674–1675.

vated." Jernegan concluded, "I think a special gesture of this kind is worth trying."[20]

Dulles thought so too, and the project went forward. Unfortunately for its success, although perhaps fortunately for Eisenhower's good name, the two American officers dispatched to Cairo to make the offer quickly learned that the $10 million the administration had in mind wouldn't begin to buy what the Egyptians deemed necessary. Nasser's chief of staff handed the two Americans, Colonel H. Alan Gerhardt and Captain Wilbur Eveland, a list of weapons that included bombers, tanks, and heavy artillery, and ran to well over $100 million. Nasser shortly thereafter made the whole issue moot, however, by indicating that he had changed his mind. He couldn't accept American military aid at this time, secret or otherwise. His government kept secrets badly, and his political enemies would discover any covert program and use it to discredit him for selling out to the Americans. Perhaps later something could be worked out, but not now.

Within a few months, Nasser changed his mind again. Just before the end of 1954, the now-prime minister decided he had things well enough in hand in Cairo to risk accepting American weapons. He still declined to put his signature to the normal agreement covering American military aid, but he said he wouldn't object to writing a personal letter to Eisenhower promising that Egypt would use the aid only for the purposes the United States intended.

By this time, though, the back door for weapons had closed. After the State Department, the Pentagon, and the CIA considered Nasser's counteroffer, Dulles sent a reply explaining that regrettably the administration had already spent the money previously earmarked for Egypt. If the prime minister wished to pursue the question of military aid, he would have to get in line with the leaders of other countries.

The administration's shift on the aid issue was the result of two factors. First, administration officials were feeling increasing heat from the Israel lobby, and they didn't want to be caught trying to help Israel's biggest enemy. On sober reevaluation, even an administration as enamored of covert activities as Eisenhower's had to concede that secret aid to Egypt wouldn't remain secret for long, especially not from the Israelis, who would have every reason to spill the story. The repercussions for the president of being discovered circumventing

---

[20]*Foreign Relations,* 1952–1954, 9:2305–2306.

Congress on behalf of an unpopular government could well be imagined. (Another Republican president, Ronald Reagan, would learn all about such embarrassment thirty years later, when he was found to be dealing arms to Iran on the sly.)

The second reason for withdrawing the offer of secret aid to Egypt was that the Eisenhower administration sensed weakness on Nasser's part. Administration officials asked themselves why Nasser was now requesting something he had refused earlier, and concluded that he needed the United States' help more than the United States needed his. This being the case, the administration ought to drive a harder bargain than previously contemplated. Among other things, the harder bargain should include concessions by Egypt to Israel, as part of a comprehensive settlement between those two antagonists.

During the first half of 1955, a settlement appeared more essential than ever—but also more difficult. In February, Israeli troops responded to guerrilla activities by attacking an Egyptian base at Gaza, killing thirty Egyptian soldiers. Like the mild shakings that often precede major shocks in earthquake zones, the attack signaled a reintensification of the war that had never formally ended since 1949.

Two other events additionally complicated the picture, by straining relations between the United States and Egypt. In April 1955, Nasser attended the Bandung (in Indonesia) conference of nonaligned nations. By itself, Nasser's identification of Egypt with the neutralist movement wasn't grounds for American condemnation. India's Jawaharlal Nehru and Yugoslavia's Tito were two founders of the neutralist movement, and though Washington occasionally had difficulty with the prima-donnaish Nehru, American policy consistently supported both. But if Nasser's association with the nonaligned gang didn't convict him of a hanging offense, it lost him a few more votes on Capitol Hill, where legislators asked why he wouldn't stand up and be counted in the great struggle against communism. (Many, but not quite so many, asked the same question regarding Nehru and Tito.)

The other crucial event of the period answered the congressional critics' question. In September 1955, Nasser announced a barter agreement between Egypt and Czechoslovakia: Nile cotton for East-bloc arms. Nasser had made no effort to hide the impending deal from Washington. Rumors of an agreement had been surfacing for months, and as early as the previous May, Nasser had told the American ambassador in Cairo that Egypt had a firm commitment from

Moscow for the weapons. The Eisenhower administration reacted slowly, suspecting a bluff. When it became apparent that the deal would soon be consummated, the administration sought to forestall it. Dulles first sent Kermit Roosevelt, then George Allen, an assistant secretary of state, to Cairo to try to talk Nasser out of going behind the Iron Curtain for weapons.

The thrust of the administration's argument to Nasser was that Egyptian acceptance of Soviet-bloc weapons—on top of Egypt's animosity toward Israel and its embrace of nonalignment in the Cold War—would make it impossible for the administration to ask Congress for aid to Egypt. Dulles had plenty of evidence to support this position. Although Congress had been adjourned at the time of the announcement of the Czech arms deal, the press had taken up the hue and cry against Nasser. *Newsweek* characterized Nasser's activities as "nonsense on the Nile." The *New Republic* asserted that Cairo's "single preoccupation" was "empire," and likened Nasser to Hitler, asking, "Can Egypt be appeased?" *Time* declared that Nasser's decision for Soviet weapons afforded Moscow "a firm and influential hold on an area hitherto dominated by the West."[21]

For all the animosity Nasser was generating, the Eisenhower administration was not quite ready to give up on him. He might be obnoxious and unreliable, but for better or worse he held one of the keys to peace and stability in the Middle East. His acquisition of Czech weapons could easily lead to a regional arms race, which would probably provoke someone—likely Israel—to a preemptive attack. Should that occur, the Western position in the Middle East might collapse in an instant. Other Arabs would appeal to Moscow for help, and the Russians would be only too happy to oblige. All of the United States' efforts since 1945 to keep the Kremlin out of the Middle East would have gone for nothing.

To avert such an outcome, the administration launched a highly confidential diplomatic initiative. In January 1956, Eisenhower sent Robert Anderson, formerly secretary of the navy and more recently deputy secretary of defense, to Cairo to try to persuade Nasser to make peace with Israel. Anderson already had been to the Middle East once: the previous December he had met separately with Nasser and Israeli Prime Minister David Ben-Gurion to test the possibilities of a settlement. Anderson's efforts had yielded nothing concrete, but

[21]*Newsweek*, June 6, 1955; *New Republic*, April 16, 1956; *Time*, Oct. 10, 1955.

aside from Nasser's refusal to allow him to fly directly between Egypt and Israel, neither had Anderson discovered special cause for pessimism.

Before returning to the Middle East in January, Anderson spoke with Eisenhower and Dulles. The secretary of state proposed a comprehensive package for peace, including American diplomatic support for Egypt against such Arab rivals as Iraq (Dulles conceded that this part of the package would require particular delicacy, on account of the United States' indirect links to the Iraqis via the Baghdad Pact), massive amounts of American aid to develop the Egyptian economy, and American assistance in resettling the Palestinian refugees in countries other than Israel. On the last point, regarding the Palestinians, Dulles admitted that a solution wouldn't come easily. But, like Franklin Roosevelt before him, Dulles had great confidence in the power of American dollars. "Money," Dulles said, would "deal basically with the problem of the refugees."[22]

Robert Anderson departed shortly for the Middle East. For much of the next two months, he shuttled back and forth between Cairo and Jerusalem, stopping at Athens or Rome in between to cleanse his shoes of enemy dust. He offered a variety of sweeteners to the package outlined by Dulles, including an American-built bridge over the Gulf of Aqaba between Egypt and Saudi Arabia, to remedy Israel's geographical splitting of the Arab world. As an alternative to a bridge, he suggested that Israel grant the Arabs transit rights across the Negev, with an overpass-underpass arrangement that would allow Arabs and Israelis to move without blocking each other. Nasser simply laughed at this last idea. "If an Arab on the upper level had to relieve himself and accidentally hit an Israeli," he mocked, "it would mean war!"

At one point in the discussions, Anderson thought he had secured Nasser's assent to start face-to-face meetings with the Israelis. Anderson hurried from the room to cable the good news to Washington. As matters turned out, though, Nasser had found Anderson's Texas accent and idiom incomprehensible, and in nodding what Anderson interpreted as agreement, the prime minister was merely trying to be polite. When Anderson left the room, Nasser asked Kermit Roosevelt, also present, what in the world Anderson had been talking

---

[22]Memo of conversation, Jan. 11, 1956, records of the Office of the Special Assistant for National Security Affairs, Eisenhower Library, Abilene, Kan.

about. Roosevelt replied that Anderson thought Nasser had promised to meet with Ben-Gurion personally. Nasser was flabbergasted. "I could never do that," Nasser said. "I'd be assassinated!" (The fate Nasser described later befell his successor, Anwar Sadat, and for the same reason.)[23]

The Anderson mission failed, and after it did the Eisenhower administration essentially gave up on Nasser. Eisenhower complained that Nasser had proved to be "a complete stumbling block" to peace in the Middle East. "He wants to be the most popular man in the Arab world," the president said, ascribing to Nasser's thirst for popularity his "extremist" views regarding Israel and what Eisenhower deemed Nasser's refusal to take any step that would open him to criticism on any question touching Arab nationalism.[24]

Previously the Eisenhower administration had sought to cultivate Nasser; now it opposed him. The motivation behind the policy shift was partly political, to counter the criticism that was building in Congress and across the United States regarding the administration's easy treatment of Nasser, and partly based on Cold War considerations, to demonstrate to other would-be neutralists that Washington wouldn't let itself be played off against Moscow. Dulles summarized administration opinion on the second point by saying that the United States must "let Colonel Nasser realize that he cannot cooperate as he is doing with the Soviet Union and at the same time enjoy most-favored-nation treatment from the United States."[25]

The principal device for registering American disapproval of Nasser's policy was the suspension of American aid. More precisely, since the United States at this time was supplying Egypt with little aid, disapproval entailed withdrawing offers of future assistance. The biggest package on offer, and therefore the two-by-four most likely to gain Nasser's attention, involved an Egyptian project for a new dam at Aswan on the Nile River. For several years, Washington, working through the World Bank, had been preparing feasibility studies for the Aswan project, which, if all went as planned, would provide irrigation water for hundreds of thousands of acres of otherwise arid Egyptian land, and millions of watts of electricity for Egyptian facto-

---

[23]H. W. Brands, *The Specter of Neutralism* (New York, 1989), pp. 261–262.

[24]Entry for March 13, 1956, Robert H. Ferrell, ed., *The Eisenhower Diaries* (New York, 1981), p. 319.

[25]Dulles to Eisenhower, March 28, 1956, Eisenhower papers, Eisenhower Library.

ries, shops, and homes. Nasser's political rise had occurred just as the engineers were drawing up blueprints, and the project became the centerpiece of his program to bring the Egyptian masses into the twentieth century.

For the Eisenhower administration, the Aswan Dam had initially seemed a good bet. It would show American support for Nasser and for Egypt in a manner that even the most suspicious supporters of Israel would have trouble objecting to—a dam was hardly an offensive weapon. It would demonstrate American interest in humanitarian projects, thereby deflecting criticism that the United States was interested only in military alliances. And it would mix American money with money from other countries, chiefly Britain, in such a way that opponents of foreign aid couldn't say that the rest of the Free World was letting Uncle Sam carry the burden alone again.

In fact, so good did the Aswan bet seem that for a time the administration went to great lengths defending it. In January 1956, while Robert Anderson was in Cairo, the administration sent Herbert Hoover, Jr., to Capitol Hill to speak on behalf of the dam project. In several hours of testimony, the undersecretary of state explained how the dam would more than pay back, in terms of regional stability and good will, the $56 million the administration proposed to give the Egyptians and the several hundred millions it proposed to lend them. Hoover's interlocutors expressed doubt, wondering what political conditions the administration intended to attach to the money. They suggested requiring a promise by Nasser not to get in any deeper with Moscow. Hoover answered that conditions would probably backfire, in that the Egyptians were very touchy about anything that seemed to infringe on their sovereignty. On the whole, the reception Hoover received indicated that the administration might get the money it wanted for Egypt, but not without a fight.

After Nasser's refusal of Robert Anderson's offers, the administration decided it didn't want to make the fight. Backing away from the Aswan package it had already put on the table might have been embarrassing had Nasser not persisted in the kind of behavior that made him a handy villain for American legislators. In May 1956, Nasser announced that Egypt would extend diplomatic recognition to the People's Republic of China, which the United States was trying to isolate. In June, he celebrated the final evacuation of British troops from Egypt—London and Cairo had finally come to terms, basically Egypt's, regarding the Suez base—with a visit from the Soviet foreign minister.

By the summer of 1956, Nasser had become a target for all manner of critics: Israel's partisans, for the usual reasons; anti-Soviet conservatives, for his cozying up to the Kremlin; American budget balancers, for his wanting to spend lots of American money; and, not insignificantly, American cotton growers, for the possibility that the Aswan Dam would help Egypt's farmers undercut American producers.

Things reached such a pass that the administration might have felt compelled to pull back from the Aswan project even if it had still wanted to be friendly to Nasser. The fact that it no longer did simply made reneging easier. On July 19, Dulles summoned the Egyptian ambassador and informed him that the United States government had decided to withdraw its offer of financial assistance for the Aswan Dam.

5. HELL BREAKS LOOSE, IN STAGES

The American decision struck Egypt hard. "This is not a withdrawal; it is an attack on the regime," Nasser declared. In his most bitter criticism of the United States yet, the Egyptian president (his new office following recent election) told American leaders, "Drop dead of your fury, for you will never be able to dictate to Egypt!" He added, "We will not allow the domination of force and the dollar."[26]

Two days later, Nasser announced the nationalization of the Suez Canal Company. This move killed two birds at once: it enhanced Egyptian self-esteem (and Nasser's own political position), since Egypt would now control the operation of this vital waterway; and it would provide the now-needed funding for the Aswan Dam, since the canal annually brought in around $100 million in tolls.

Nasser's move upset the Eisenhower administration, but it absolutely infuriated the British. Anthony Eden, prime minister following Churchill's belated retirement, immediately began speaking of the necessity for strong measures to undo Nasser's reprehensible deed. Eden ordered a freeze on Egyptian assets in British banks and a ban on shipments of British weapons to Egypt, and he conspicuously increased the British military presence in the eastern Mediterranean. In addition, he wrote a letter to Eisenhower, informing the president that London was contemplating still stronger measures. "My colleagues and I are convinced that we must be ready, in the last resort,

[26]Brands, *Specter*, p. 273.

to use force to bring Nasser to his senses," Eden said. "For our part, we are prepared to do so. I have this morning instructed our Chiefs of Staff to prepare a military plan accordingly."[27]

Some American officials thought Eden had the right idea. Nathan Twining, Eisenhower's air force chief of staff, described the Egyptian seizure of the canal as "militarily unacceptable" and asserted that the United States should adopt measures to get the canal back under friendly and responsible control. Two days later, the American joint chiefs of staff advocated contingency planning for an American military response. "Timeliness in effecting this action," the chiefs said, "is essential."[28]

Eisenhower didn't at this stage rule out the use of force, but neither did he desire to encourage the British to do anything rash. After receiving Eden's bellicose note, the president sent Robert Murphy, his most experienced diplomatic troubleshooter, to London to calm the British down. When Murphy discovered the extent of British military preparations and the depth of Eden's animosity toward Nasser, he called for reinforcements. John Foster Dulles caught the next plane across the Atlantic, and together the two diplomats managed to persuade the British to count at least to ten before striking. They repeated their performance for the French, who had their own reasons for detesting Nasser. The French especially objected to Nasser's encouragement of an insurgency against the French government of Algeria. Paris seemed nearly as eager as London to slap the Egyptian president; but, for the present, the French government also agreed to stay its hand.

As events subsequently proved, Dulles and Eisenhower didn't give as clear signals to the Europeans as they might have. Part of the problem arose from the fact that the secretary of state and the president looked on Nasser as being almost as threatening as the British and French did. In a briefing of congressional leaders after Dulles's return from Europe, the secretary asserted that fulfillment of Nasser's bloated ambitions, which evidently included control of Middle Eastern oil, would reduce Western Europe to "a state of dependency." Dulles went on say that Nasser had a "Hitlerite" personality. Eisen-

---

[27]Anthony Eden, *Full Circle* (Boston, 1960), pp. 476–477.

[28]Twining to Joint Chiefs of Staff, July 29, 1956, *Declassified Documents Reference System* (microfiche), 1978, 369b; Wentworth to Joint Chiefs, July 31, 1956, Joint Chiefs of Staff records.

hower agreed, likening Nasser's public pronouncements to Hitler's *Mein Kampf.* The president plainly indicated the administration's resolve. "We can't accept an inconclusive outcome leaving Nasser in control," Eisenhower declared. "We do not intend to stand by helplessly and let this one man get away with what he is trying to do."[29]

Yet the administration determined to exhaust all diplomatic channels before possibly escalating the crisis to the military level. Dulles helped organize an international conference of canal users that met in London in August. Egypt boycotted the conference, which meant that the delegates were mostly wasting their breath. But, as Washington figured things, breath wasted talking was breath not used fighting. After the conference put together a proposal for international operation of the canal, the attending countries appointed a commission to try to sell the proposal to Nasser. The Egyptian president refused to buy, and at the end of September the crisis remained as far from resolution as ever.

Nasser's rejection of the international proposal convinced the British that they had given diplomacy more time than it deserved. They chose to untie the Gordian knot the way Alexander did, with the sword. The French were happy to join, as were the Israelis, who worried about Egypt's access to East-bloc arms and considered this moment of European annoyance an opportunity to smite Nasser before he got too strong. The three governments devised a plan whereby the Israelis would attack Egypt, signaling the British and French to call for a ceasefire. When the Israelis and presumably the invaded Egyptians ignored the ceasefire call, London and Paris would send in planes and troops, ostensibly to protect the Suez Canal. Nasser's fate, and the ultimate disposition of the canal, would be decided on the battlefield, where by then the odds would heavily favor Nasser's foes.

The three conspiring governments went to great lengths to shield their plans from American eyes. Their deception worked, partly because the mobilization the plot required might have been, for all the Americans were able to detect, merely a bluff to scare Nasser. But it was no bluff, and on October 29 Israeli forces invaded the Egyptian Sinai peninsula and headed for the Suez Canal. The following day, on schedule, London and Paris delivered the agreed-upon ultimatum, demanding that shooting stop and the combatants get clear of the canal. The Israelis, after reaching the canal, pulled back ten miles.

[29]Minutes of meeting, Aug. 12, 1956, Eisenhower papers.

The Egyptians, adopting the view that this was their country and their canal, didn't. On October 31, British and French airplanes began bombing Egyptian targets; a few days later, British and French ground forces landed in Egypt.

The attack on Egypt represented a fundamental miscalculation by the British, who were the prime movers in the operation. Eden evidently believed that although the Eisenhower administration might publicly shake a finger at the use of force to dislodge Nasser, Washington would tolerate a quick and successful strike. To some degree, Eden's miscalculation reflected the prime minister's obsession with Nasser, whom Eden considered to be even more dangerously malign than Eisenhower and Dulles did. To some degree, Eden's error was caused by the confusing signals the American administration had given during the previous weeks. Eisenhower had stated that no one could legally challenge Egypt's right to nationalize the canal company and that a solution to the quarrel must be peaceful; but the British could be forgiven for taking such statements in the context of the president's campaign for reelection, which would culminate in balloting that was just days away. Dulles had adopted a firmer anti-Nasser line. While in London, the secretary of state had told British officials that some means must be found to make Nasser "disgorge" what he was trying to swallow. Eden had noted Dulles's remarks carefully. "These were forthright words," Eden later recalled. "They rang in my ears for months."[30]

If the Eisenhower administration was sending mixed signals before the attack on Egypt, once the invasion began it left no doubt where it stood. Eisenhower went on television to deplore the use of force. He said that the United States could not insist on one code of conduct for its enemies and another for its friends.

The president might have used such language had the Suez War been the only event commanding international attention at the time, but his words held particular meaning on account of a simultaneous Soviet invasion of Hungary, where a revolution against Soviet control had just broken out. This coincidence of bullying was one reason why the Anglo-French-Israeli assault infuriated Eisenhower: at just the moment when the Kremlin was showing its true imperialist colors, the United States' two closest allies were doing the same thing. American leaders always denied the argument put forward by nonaligned

[30]Eden, op. cit., p. 487.

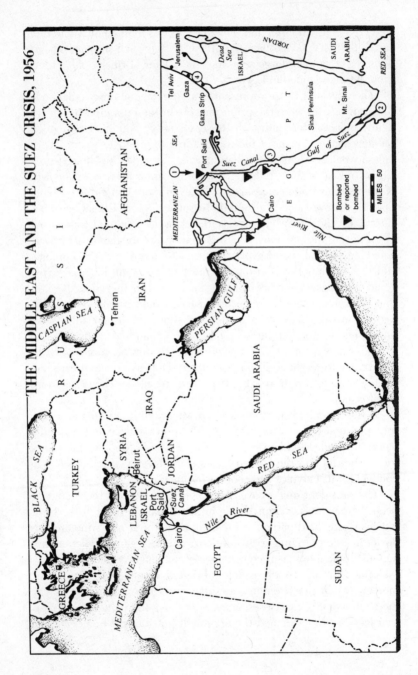

THE MIDDLE EAST AND THE SUEZ CRISIS, 1956

countries that there existed a moral equivalence between East and West in the Cold War; but the juxtaposition of the Suez and Hungarian crises provided powerful evidence of just such an equivalence.

Beyond thundering rhetorically against the invasion of Egypt, the Eisenhower administration took diplomatic and economic measures to halt the fighting. At the United Nations, American representatives worked for passage of resolutions designed to restore peace to the Middle East. More coercively, the administration clamped down on Britain's supplies of those two mainstays of modern warfare: money and oil. When the Middle Eastern war triggered a run on the British pound, Eisenhower ordered American treasury officials to sit on their hands; and when London sought to shore up the British currency by a loan from the International Monetary Fund, he directed his treasury secretary to block it. Similarly, when the crisis disrupted Britain's network of oil supplies, the administration sabotaged Britain's efforts to cover the gap with deliveries from western-hemisphere sources.

The combined effect of these actions, which threatened to leave Britain broke and on empty, compelled Eden to back down. On November 6, London suspended the anti-Nasser operation. The French, grumbling, went along, as did the Israelis, who grumbled even louder.

Untangling the combatants required more time. The British and French withdrew from Egypt within several weeks, but the Israelis stayed in Sinai until March of the following year. They retreated only in the face of escalating U.S. diplomatic pressure, and did so with a minimum of grace and a maximum of irritation toward the American government.

✿   ✿   ✿

The Suez War was a turning point in American relations with the Middle East. The war discredited Britain and exploded most of what had remained of British prestige and power in the region. Until 1956, the United States had relied on Britain to help keep the Soviet Union out of the area; with Britain now largely removed from the picture, Washington would have to shoulder the bulk of the burden itself.

From the American perspective, circumstances in the Middle East were growing more complicated by the year. Interconnections were developing among the three factors that counted most in American assessments of the region, and these interconnections made dealing with each of the factors more difficult than dealing with them in isolation would have been. The question of oil had gotten thoroughly mixed up with the question of the Soviet Union; this was what had caused the Eisenhower administration such concern about Mossadeq and Iran, and prompted the administration to turn the CIA loose against the prime minister. The outcome of the Iranian affair—the shah safe on the Peacock Throne, Persian Gulf oil flowing freely to the West (and American companies sharing in the profits)—seemed to be all Washington could hope for in the short term. But the situation required constant watching.

The Suez War symbolized another interconnection: between the issues of Israel and of the Soviet Union. By accepting Soviet-bloc weapons, Nasser had, in effect, invited the Soviets into the Middle East. The Eisenhower administration, after failing to get Nasser to alter his policies toward Israel and toward the Soviet Union, adopted a policy of opposition to Egypt. Washington withdrew its Aswan aid offer; one thing led to another; war resulted. Although the administration took Nasser's side against Britain, France, and Israel, it did so out of no love for Nasser. American officials distrusted Nasser more than ever now that he was cultivating the Kremlin. American policy, always anti-Soviet in the Middle East, soon became effectively anti-Nasser.

Chapter 3

Deeper and Deeper: 1957–1965

1. PICKING UP THE PIECES: THE EISENHOWER DOCTRINE

Nature, said to abhor a vacuum, had nothing on American policy makers during the Cold War. It was a cardinal tenet of American strategic thinking that wherever Western forces suffered a setback, the Soviet Union would seek to gain an advantage. Although Eisenhower's refusal to countenance the British-French-Israeli aggression against Egypt briefly enhanced the United States' reputation in the Middle East, the net result of the Suez War was to diminish Western influence in the region. After Suez, the British lion scared no one. Because, in the opinion of the Eisenhower administration, certain people in the Middle East needed scaring, Washington decided it had to do the job itself.

Dulles explained the situation to the Senate Foreign Relations Committee at the beginning of 1957. "There is today a vacuum of power as a result of the recent British-French action," Dulles said. Unless the United States found some way to bolster the security of the region, "that critical area will almost certainly be taken over by Soviet communism, with disastrous effects upon our own security position in the world." The secretary of state went on to say that for more than a century, Britain had served as a bulwark against czarist and Soviet ambitions in the Middle East. "That bulwark has been swept away." Dulles concluded, "Only the United States can, I think, save that area and, indeed, save itself from very great peril."[1]

---

[1] *Executive Sessions of the Senate Foreign Relations Committee* (Historical Series), 9:3, 21.

Getting specific, Dulles proposed a particular vacuum filler. Congress should explicitly authorize the president to employ American military force to defend friendly regimes in the Middle East against communist aggression.

This proposal, which upon congressional approval would become known as the Eisenhower Doctrine, signified both a narrowing and a reinforcing of the Truman Doctrine. It narrowed the Truman Doctrine, which had potentially global applicability, by targeting a single geographic region: the Middle East. It reinforced the Truman Doctrine, which had produced only a flow of American money, equipment, and advice, by declaring the United States' readiness to go to war.

After Eisenhower's smashing victory at the polls in November 1956, not many legislators cared to challenge the president politically; yet neither did the Democrats intend to hand him his doctrine on a tray. The function of an opposition party is to oppose, and, besides, the Democrats felt a special obligation to register their concern at the president's brusque treatment of Israel during the Suez War. While that short conflict might have been chiefly an exercise in anachronistic imperialism for Britain and France, for Israel it was a matter of national life and death. The Israelis could look only with trepidation on an Egypt allied to the Soviet Union, and the fact that Moscow had growled threats at Egypt's enemies during the war worried the Israelis still more. (Although the threats weren't very convincing, what with the Red Army busy beating up on Hungary, Eisenhower had responded by placing American military units on alert. The British and French had called it quits before the matter went further.) The Democrats in the Senate, headed by Majority Leader Lyndon Johnson of Texas, wanted reassurance regarding Israel before they would approve the Eisenhower administration's proposal on the use of military force in the Middle East.

Questioning Dulles, the Democrats on the Foreign Relations Committee wondered what the administration's proposal would mean for the United States. Chairman Richard Russell, remarking the region's penchant for violence, said he feared that the United States was "going to get chewed up over there over a period of time with a lot of little wars." Mike Mansfield, the majority whip, pointed out that American resources were stretched thin already. "There are other vacuums in the world," Mansfield said, "and we cannot be expected to cover the world with our armed forces." Hubert Humphrey didn't like what the president's resolution would do to congressional authority in a vital matter of foreign policy. The administration's proposal, the Minnesota Democrat said, amounted to "a predated declaration of war."[2]

But these were only quibbles. The real issue for the Democrats, and a few Republicans, was the administration's attitude toward Israel. Though the British and French had pulled their troops out of Egypt, the Israelis refused to withdraw from the Gaza Strip and a slice of the Sinai near the port of Eilat. Nor did they appear about to withdraw before receiving guarantees that Palestinian guerrillas not use Gaza again for attacks against Israelis and that Egypt not interfere with ship traffic to Eilat. The pro-Israel faction in the Senate judged the Israeli position understandable; Johnson and his associates among the leadership of the upper house dragged their feet on the administration's resolution in an effort to get the White House to agree.

Eisenhower and Dulles wouldn't. Dulles told a group of influential senators and representatives called to the White House in February 1957 that if the Israelis remained obstinate they might precipitate no end of turmoil. Guerrilla war would break out, oil would cease flowing to Europe, and Soviet influence in the Middle East would grow. "In short," the secretary said, "there would be all those disasters that the United States has been trying to avoid since the creation of the state of Israel." Henry Cabot Lodge, Eisenhower's representative to the United Nations, asserted that the United States would have no alternative to accepting an Arab resolution calling for sanctions against Israel if the Israelis continued to refuse to withdraw. Citing the surprised satisfaction among the Arabs that had greeted the administration's actions during the Suez crisis, Lodge declared, "The Arabs will feel we have abandoned our position if we do not support some effective measures to accomplish Israeli withdrawal."

The Democrats at this meeting soon recognized that they weren't going to change Eisenhower's mind, but they refused to yield to the administration without making their point. They declined the president's invitation to join in a statement urging the Israeli government to pull back. Some of the Democrats, like Johnson, opposed pressure on Israel on principle. Others—and Johnson, too, for that matter—desired that the president bear the onus for any policy decision construable as anti-Israel. Russell urged the president to argue his case to the American people. Johnson's Texas colleague, House Speaker Sam Rayburn, concurred, saying, "America has either one voice or none,

[2]Ibid., 9:5–28.

and the one voice is the voice of the president, even though not everyone agrees with him."³

Eisenhower accepted the advice. In the last week of February, he delivered a televised address emphasizing the need for Israel to withdraw from the territory it had taken by force. At the same time, Eisenhower wrote a letter to Israeli Prime Minister Ben-Gurion, in which he counseled the Israelis to pull back before they found themselves with fewer friends than they had already.

The Israelis chose to be persuaded. On March 1, the Israeli foreign minister, Golda Meir, told the United Nations that Israel would withdraw.

Eisenhower also got what he wanted from Congress. The House already had approved his Middle East resolution; now the Senate leadership, with no further pretext for delay, brought the Eisenhower Doctrine to a vote. The administration won by a wide margin.

2. TO BEIRUT AND BEYOND: LEBANON, 1958

One of the administration's selling points regarding the Eisenhower Doctrine was that if Congress granted the president the authority he requested, to use American military force in the Middle East, this force would probably never have to be used. Merely knowing that American warships, planes, and troops were just over the horizon would deter potential aggressors. Had American legislators seen that their approval would lead to the actual landing of American troops in the Middle East within eighteen months of their vote, they might have weighed their ballots more carefully. On the other hand, had they known how the 1958 intervention in Lebanon would turn out, they might not have.

Events of 1957 prepared the administration for action in Lebanon. In the spring of that year, pro-Nasser army officers in Jordan launched a revolt against King Hussein, on the model of the revolt against Farouk that Nasser himself had spearheaded in Egypt. But Hussein soon began earning his reputation as the great survivor of the Middle East; he called on Washington for help and received

---

³Minutes of meeting, Feb. 20, 1957, Eisenhower papers, Eisenhower Library, Abilene, Kan.

$10 million in emergency aid, as well as a conspicuous visit from the U.S. Sixth Fleet. The outcome pleased both Hussein and Washington: he held his throne, while the United States improved its standing in Jordan.

In August 1957, the Sixth Fleet again steamed toward the eastern end of the Mediterranean. Trouble in Syria was the occasion this time. The Syrians were following Nasser's lead in looking to Moscow for arms, and when Damascus announced a hefty increase in shipments from the Soviet Union, Syria's conservative neighbors got nervous. To calm them, the Eisenhower administration stepped up deliveries of weapons to Jordan, Lebanon, and Iraq. (The Suez crisis, coming after the commencement of Soviet arms sales to Egypt, had effectively abrogated the 1950 Tripartite Declaration.) Eisenhower also repositioned American fighter planes to Turkey, while the Turks massed troops on the Syrian border. Lastly, the president instructed American naval vessels to cruise the Syrian coast.

Nothing came of all the huffing and puffing, except that American officials grew increasingly sensitive to the groundswell of support for Nasser that was developing throughout much of the Middle East. Most of the region's governments remained conservative, but how long the conservative rulers could keep radical army officers, radical students, and radical popular leaders under control was an open question. Farouk's regime had seemed as stable as several others before it collapsed; a similar fate might easily befall some of those others.

In the first half of 1958, Lebanon appeared a likely candidate for such a scenario. At the beginning of the year, Egypt and Syria merged to form the United Arab Republic, an unequal and ill-fated union that combined Nasser's charisma and Arab-world prestige with the revolutionary socialism of the Syrian Baath party. Nasser tried to act as though he were taking part in a shotgun wedding; he told the U.S. ambassador in Cairo that the union would prove "a great headache." Nasser had reason to worry, since Syria's president, Shukri al-Quwatli, himself had warned Nasser of the difficulties Egypt was getting into. "You don't know what you have taken on," Quwatli said. "You have taken on people of whom every one believes he is a politician. Fifty percent consider themselves national leaders; twenty-five percent of them think they are prophets; and at least ten percent believe they are gods. You have taken on people of which there are those who worship God, and there are those who adore fire, and there are those who idolize the devil." Nasser had to accept the Syrian leader's word on the subject, never having been to Syria. But the riotous welcome he received in Damascus after the announcement of the union stilled at least some of his worries.[4]

It only made Washington worry the more. Nasser hadn't tried to conceal his desire to unify the Arab world, and he had hidden barely better his intention to head the powerful new nation that would result. The merger with Syria seemed a first step on the pan-Arabist path. Washington hadn't liked Nasser when he confined his ambitions to Egypt; it liked him even less when he took his show on the road.

A paper written for Eisenhower's National Security Council assessed the prospects for success in Nasser's endeavors and, indirectly, the prospects for American interests in the Middle East. The paper asserted that the struggle between the United States and the Soviet Union for predominance in the region was not a contest of arms but a "battle for men's minds." The United States wasn't winning this battle, although it wasn't losing either. The predominant mood among the Arabs was neutralist rather than pro-American or pro-Soviet, for two reasons. First, the Arabs hoped to play East against West to their own benefit. Second, they feared the consequences of another world war.

A slightly revised version of this NSC paper went on to describe the phenomenon of Arab nationalism, which was, to a large degree, the positive form of Arab neutralism. Arab nationalists, with Nasser in the lead, dreamed of "an Arab empire reaching from Casablanca to the Persian Gulf." This dream was almost completely unrealistic, given the deep fissures that ran through the Arab world, but it motivated much of Arab politics just the same. It also explained a large part of the Arabs' resentment against the West, since they blamed the West, somewhat ahistorically, for carving up the Arab world into more than a dozen separate political entities. By contrast, the Soviet Union, not having taken part in the carving, could and did cast itself as the friend of Arab nationalism. Communism held scant attraction for most Arabs, but neither did it seem especially threatening. As far as the Arabs were concerned, Zionism posed a far greater danger to Arab interests. The NSC paper offered little concrete in the way of guidance for American policy makers. Arab nationalism was a force essentially beyond the capacity of the United States to influence. The

[4]Anthony Nutting, *Nasser* (New York, 1972), p. 218; Tawfig Y. Hasou, *The Struggle for the Arab World* (London, 1985), p. 113.

best American officials could hope for was to mitigate its more radical influences. To this end, the United States might "discreetly encourage" conservative governments in the Middle East, particularly in Jordan, Saudi Arabia and Iraq, by means appropriate to circumstances.[5]

American leaders didn't know it at the time, but Iraq's government faced the greatest danger. At just this moment, officers in the Iraqi army were plotting against the Hashemite monarchy in Baghdad. In July 1958, the plotters staged a coup that resulted in the murder of the royal family and the prime minister, Nuri al-Said. Because Nasser had been railing against Nuri, and because the rebel officers demonstrated certain affinities with Nasser's brand of Arab nationalism, observers both within the region and outside initially perceived Nasser's hand in the revolt.

The Iraqi affair sent chills down spines throughout the Middle East, not least on account of the brutality with which Nuri and the royal family were killed. The government in Lebanon shivered especially, since the administration of President Camille Chamoun had been facing the danger of civil war for several months. Chamoun had embraced the Eisenhower Doctrine with enthusiasm, antagonizing Arab nationalists; he compounded his difficulties by indicating that he would seek an amendment to the Lebanese constitution—a charter designed to ensure a delicate balance among the country's different religious groups—that would allow him to be reelected. Nasser contributed to Chamoun's troubles with propaganda, money, and weapons. In May 1958, fighting broke out, prompting Chamoun to ask Washington to put teeth—troops, rather—into the Eisenhower Doctrine.

Eisenhower considered Chamoun's request seriously, but before he reached a decision, the fighting died down. A stalemate ensued, with the country divided between regions controlled by rebels and those held by forces loyal to the government. Through June, the violence remained sporadic—and sometimes senseless. The American ambassador in Beirut, Robert McClintock, described the shooting of an unarmed worker near his car by a Christian militiaman. The soldier explained that the worker might have been carrying a bomb. McClintock commented to Washington, "Result: No bomb, one dead laborer." But the violence had yet to achieve the levels that would

[5]NSC 5801, Jan. 16, 1958, and NSC 5801/1, Jan. 24, 1958, National Security Council records, National Archives, Washington.

typify Lebanese politics thirty years later, and when Chamoun changed his mind and declared publicly that he would step down at the conclusion of his current term, an end to the crisis seemed in sight.[6]

The July coup in Baghdad, however, revived the crisis. Chamoun immediately summoned McClintock. "You see what's happening?" he said. "Lebanon is in real danger." Chamoun demanded that the United States send troops at once. "I want your assistance," he said. "I want an answer within twenty-four hours. Not by words, but by action."[7]

Eisenhower responded swiftly. He called his top foreign-policy advisers to the White House, where all agreed that the administration had to move swiftly to stabilize the situation in the Middle East. If not, they believed, Nasser would take over much of the region. Having placed its credibility on the line with the Eisenhower Doctrine, the administration couldn't afford to fall short. After hearing assessments of the situation from the State and Defense departments and the CIA, Eisenhower turned to his chairman of the Joint Chiefs of Staff, General Twining. "How soon can you start, Nate?" the president asked. Twining said the plans were already in place. Eisenhower shot back, "What are we waiting for?"[8]

Despite his alacrity in deciding for the use of force, Eisenhower understood the hazards of putting U.S. troops on the ground in the Middle East. The president, as was his custom whenever he made important decisions, brought the leaders of Congress to the White House so he could explain what he was up to. Dulles began the briefing with a prediction: "If we go in, our action is likely to accentuate the anti-Western feeling of the Arab masses." This would be true despite the fact that the conservative governments of the region would welcome American intervention; they were largely unrepresentative of their peoples. Dulles cautioned against expecting a fast, easy solution. "While we will probably be able through the presence of our forces to hold Lebanon's independence, we would be drawn into the area and it is not clear how we could withdraw."

But if intervention posed problems, so did nonintervention. "The first consequence of not going in," Dulles said, "would certainly be

[6]*Declassified Documents Reference System* (microfiche), 1976, 100c.

[7]Camille Chamoun oral history, Princeton University, Princeton, N.J.

[8]Robert Cutler, *No Time for Rest* (Boston, 1965), pp. 363–364.

that the non-Nasser governments in the Middle East and adjoining areas would be quickly overthrown." Lebanon doubtless would cave in to the radicals. Even more harmful would be the effect on American allies around the world. "The impact of our not going in, from Morocco to Indochina, would be very harmful to us. Turkey, Iran and Pakistan would feel, if we do not act, that our action is because we are afraid of the Soviet Union. They will therefore lose confidence and tend toward neutralism."[9]

Eisenhower decided that the costs of staying out surpassed those of going in, and shortly after this meeting, he gave the order for the marines to land. Within hours, the first troops hit the beaches of Beirut; within days nearly 15,000 American soldiers occupied the Lebanese capital and its neighborhood.

From a military perspective, the Lebanese intervention turned out to be remarkably uneventful. The American forces fired on no one, and no one fired on them. Although the Lebanese opposition suspected that the purpose of the intervention was to keep Chamoun in office, American diplomat Robert Murphy visited the rebels and persuaded them otherwise. Lest Chamoun have second thoughts about stepping down, Murphy did some preemptive persuading with the Lebanese president as well.

In fact, the intervention was essentially a matter of symbolism: to demonstrate to conservative regimes in the Middle East that the United States cared for their survival and to demonstrate to Nasser that Washington wouldn't retreat in the face of his anti-Western agitation. Ironically, though, the outcome that emerged after the U.S. troops had been in Lebanon for a few weeks was one that Nasser himself had suggested in June: General Fuad Chehab, the Maronite Christian commander of the Lebanese army, as president; Rashid Karami, the Sunni Muslim insurgent leader, as prime minister.

Doubly ironically, the assumption that had set the American intervention in motion—that Nasserists were taking over Iraq—proved false. The assumption, while broadly accepted at the top of the Eisenhower administration, was not shared throughout the Foreign Service. From Baghdad, the American ambassador asserted that Abd al-Karim Kassem, the new head of the Iraqi government, might be a radical but wouldn't subordinate his own and his country's interests to Nasser's and Egypt's. Some State Department officials recalled the millennia-

[9]Memo of conference, July 14, 1958, Eisenhower papers.

old rivalry between the valley of the Tigris-Euphrates and the valley of the Nile, and suggested that the rivalry would continue.

Eisenhower sent Robert Murphy from Beirut to Baghdad to evaluate the situation in Iraq personally. Murphy found Kassem committed to charting his own course, not Nasser's. Murphy later described the "quiet ferocity" with which Kassem spoke of Nasser and of the activities of Nasser's agents in Iraq. Kassem conceded that in some areas Iraq's foreign policies might agree with Egypt's, but he seemed, in Murphy's words, "grimly determined" to maintain Iraq's freedom of action.[10]

Kassem proved as good as his word, and before long the airwaves of the Middle East sizzled with the denunciations Baghdad and Cairo were hurling at each other. Thoughtful Middle East watchers in the United States and elsewhere couldn't help asking what benefit the American show of force in Lebanon had accomplished. The staff of Eisenhower's National Security Council answered frankly: Not much. A policy paper of November 1958 explained that despite the intervention in Lebanon, the two basic trends in the Middle East—the emergence of the radical pan-Arab nationalist movement and the intrusion of the Soviet Union into the area—continued unabated. If anything, the radicals' momentum was increasing, and the nationalists and the West were more at odds than ever. The threat to the United States had increased proportionately. The paper stated, "The virtual collapse during 1958 of conservative resistance, leaving the radical nationalist regimes almost without opposition in the area, has brought a grave challenge to Western interests." Until this point, the United States had sought to block Soviet penetration of the Middle East by opposing the nationalists. But this opposition had rested on the conservative base that had largely vanished; consequently, the United States was left without a policy.

Given these developments, the NSC paper said, the U.S. government must change its strategy. The overall objectives remained as before: most notably, to keep the Soviet Union out of the Middle East, and to preserve Western access to oil. But where the United States previously had pursued these objectives by resisting the tide of Arab nationalism, now it should try to accommodate the nationalists. For better or worse, they controlled the only game in town. "The prevention of further Soviet penetration of the Near East [essentially, the

[10]Robert Murphy, *Diplomat among Warriors* (Garden City, N.Y., 1964) pp. 412–414.

Middle East] and progress in solving Near Eastern problems depend on the degree to which the United States is able to work more closely with Arab nationalism and associate itself more closely with such aims and aspirations of the American people as are not contrary to the basic interests of the United States." The touchstone of this new approach would be Washington's attitude toward Nasser. "In the eyes of the great mass of Arabs, considerable significance will be attached to the position which the United States adopts toward the current foremost spokesman of radical pan-Arab nationalism, Gamal Abdel Nasser."[11]

Considering that the Eisenhower administration had just sent 15,000 troops to Lebanon to prevent pro-Nasserist expansion, this statement was a striking admission of failure—or, rather, of the irrelevance of the policy on which the intervention was based. When the administration requested congressional approval for the Eisenhower Doctrine, it had defended the request in terms of combatting communism. At the time, critics had suggested that the administration was missing the point: if anything threatened American interests in the Middle East, it was not communism, whose atheism offended the region's Muslims even more than it did Americans, but Arab nationalism. This latest statement of policy represented an admission that the critics were right. It also signaled that the Eisenhower Doctrine was a dead letter, scarcely a year and a half after its enunciation.

Fortunately for the rethinkers in Washington, Nasser found cause to reconsider his own position. During the couple of years after Kassem's seizure of power in Baghdad, the new Iraqi regime politically outflanked Nasser on the left. Kassem turned to the Iraqi Communist party and to the Soviet Union for help in Iraq's rivalry with Egypt. Nasser counterattacked; when communists in Syria, still part of the United Arab Republic, began fighting with Nasserists, Nasser ordered a crackdown. Hundreds of communists landed in jail. Nasser replied to Soviet Premier Nikita Khrushchev's complaints about this rough treatment of the Kremlin's co-ideologists by saying that Moscow should mind its own business. In order to strengthen his position further, Nasser reinforced political ties to the West. He went so far by the end of 1959 as to resume diplomatic relations with erstwhile arch-enemy Britain.

Nasser took his campaign of rapprochement toward the West into the American popular press during the summer of 1959. He cooper-

[11]NSC 5820/1, Nov. 4, 1958, National Security Council records.

ated with *Life* magazine in producing a feature article outlining his philosophy of foreign affairs. In marked contrast to his discussion with Dulles in 1953, when he had claimed that Western imperialism posed a far greater danger to Egypt than communism did, now he indicated that he feared imperialism of the East more than imperialism of the West. His struggle with the communists was to the bitter end. "We know they can never relent in their opposition to Arab nationalism and the U.A.R.," he said. "Their ultimate objective is that of Communist parties everywhere: to take power." He noted for his audience that Egypt had outlawed its Communist party—a prudent precaution, he couldn't resist adding, that the Israelis had not seen fit to implement. Egypt would continue to be vigilant and strong.[12]

Between the Eisenhower administration's recognition of the need to accommodate Arab nationalism, and Nasser's judgment that the time had come to edge back toward the West, the last years of Eisenhower's tenure as president witnessed the beginning of a mutual effort at improving Egyptian-American relations. Nasser turned his propaganda guns away from the West and toward the communists; Eisenhower approved the first new economic aid for Egypt since the seizure of the Suez Canal.

In the autumn of 1960, Nasser and Eisenhower met in New York, where the United Nations was celebrating its fifteenth anniversary. The two presidents spoke in friendly fashion. Eisenhower said he welcomed recent statements by Nasser that Egypt didn't seek to destroy Israel. Nasser, without accepting Israel's legitimacy, remarked that it would be foolish to try to liquidate the Zionist state. "Nowadays anyone can begin a war," Nasser declared, "but it will not stay limited, and no one can win." Eisenhower had been saying such things for years.[13]

3. HARD CASES MAKE BAD POLICY: THE YEMEN WAR

During Eisenhower's second term, struggles among the Arabs filled Washington's Middle East viewfinder. The battle between radicals and conservatives, between Nasserists and anti-Nasserists, and between Egypt and Iraq kept U.S. foreign-policy planners working over-

[12]*Life*, July 20, 1959.

[13]Memos of conversation, Sept. 26, 1960 and Sept. 28, 1960, Eisenhower papers.

time devising appropriate ways to safeguard American interests amid the turmoil. The Eisenhower administration got involved in a major way in the intra-Arab quarrels when it sent troops into Lebanon; it joined the fray less dramatically in other areas. American aid continued to prop up friendly regimes in Lebanon, Jordan, and Saudi Arabia; American covert operatives quietly electioneered for favored candidates in Syria. After the fall of Nuri and the Hashemites in Iraq, the Baghdad Pact reconstituted itself as the Central Treaty Organization, or CENTO, this time with full American membership—although, following Iraq's withdrawal, without any Arab participation.

While the Arabs were squabbling among themselves, their common struggle against the Zionists got short shrift. This was all to the good, in Washington's opinion, since the Arab-Israeli problem constituted a no-win situation for the United States. The basic division in American thinking regarding the Arab-Israeli conflict remained as previously. Strategically, the Arabs counted for more, since they produced most of the Middle East's oil, held or shared control of vital communications choke points (the Suez Canal, the Strait of Hormuz at the entrance to the Persian Gulf), and owned military facilities (Dhahran in Saudi Arabia, Wheelus in Libya) used by U.S. troops and planes. Politically, Israel held the advantage, since the Israelis had more friends in high places in Washington, their form of government possessed greater appeal for democratic-minded Americans, and their religion and culture constituted the first half of the "Judeo-Christian heritage" beloved of American orators. As a rough approximation, when things were calm between Arabs and Israelis, strategic issues took precedence in U.S. policy making, and American relations with the Arabs improved. When troubles escalated in the neighborhood of Israel, political considerations predominated, and relations with the Arabs suffered.

The Suez War of 1956 contradicted this rule briefly, but primarily because of the inept actions of the British and French. The several years after the war generally confirmed the rule. The Arabs continued to learn to live with Israel, if not happily; and as they did, American-Arab relations improved. The rapprochement between Washington and Cairo at the end of Eisenhower's second term and the broader acceptance by American officials of the need to accommodate Arab nationalism were the most conspicuous instances of the trend.

The trend continued into the Kennedy administration. John Kennedy had cast himself as a friend of the Third World while a senator. He took a particular shine to India, pushing legislation that increased American aid to that exemplar of nonalignment, but his solicitude extended as well to issues dear to Arab hearts. In 1957, he made a long speech attacking the Eisenhower administration for siding with Paris in France's struggle to hold on to Algeria. As with most such performances, it was difficult to know what portion of Kennedy's concern owed to genuine care for the Algerians and what portion to his desire to make trouble for the Republicans and a name for himself. But regardless of the mix of motives, the Massachusetts legislator gained a reputation as one who might be less obligated to the Israel lobby than some other Democrats.

However much the gaining of this reputation might have cheered the Arabs, though, it was no way to get elected president, which was what Kennedy wanted. Accordingly, as his 1960 campaign shifted to fast-forward, he conferred with the most prominent leaders of the American Jewish community. He assured them that he had not inherited the pro-German sympathies of his father, who had been ambassador to Britain as Hitler plunged Europe into war. He explained that his solicitude for the Algerian rebels did not signify an inclination to appease Arab radicals. He declared that he understood Israel's need to remain economically and militarily strong.

Kennedy continued to cultivate the Jewish community after his election—which victory resulted in no small part from the overwhelming support of American Jews, who found Republican nominee and vice president Richard Nixon too domestically conservative for their predominantly liberal tastes and too tied to Eisenhower's strategic policies for their pro-Israel sensibilities. Kennedy had promised White House access to the friends of Israel, and after his election he followed through. He appointed Abraham Ribicoff and Arthur Goldberg, both energetic proponents of a strong American-Israeli relationship, to cabinet posts. He made Myer Feldman his own version of Truman's David Niles. He encouraged Lyndon Johnson, his vice president, to maintain the close ties to the Jewish community Johnson had formed on Capitol Hill.

Between his senatorial rhetoric and his White House staffing, Kennedy positioned himself to pursue an even-handed policy between Arabs and Israelis. Yet events elsewhere in the world—crises in Cuba and Berlin and the Congo in 1961, in Laos and again Cuba in 1962, the deepening American involvement in Vietnam throughout the Kennedy years—conspired to distract the Democratic administration from the Middle East. Much as had occurred during Truman's second term, the Middle East was overshadowed by currently hotter spots in the Cold War.

To the degree Kennedy paid attention to the Middle East, he concentrated on Egypt. This fact alone indicated that Nasser had achieved one of his aims: to be considered the chief spokesman of the Arab world. Eisenhower had resisted conceding any such recognition to Nasser, preferring King Saud; but after the revolution in Iraq and the anticlimactic outcome of the intervention in Lebanon, Eisenhower had been forced to admit that if anyone spoke for the Arabs, Nasser did. Kennedy inherited this conclusion and had no inordinate difficulty with it, perhaps partly because he was much closer in age to Nasser (they were one year apart) than Eisenhower was.

From the first, Kennedy indicated a desire for good relations with Egypt. He declined to be provoked by Nasser's criticism of American intervention in the Congo and of the failed Bay of Pigs operation, accounting it the sort of thing any self-respecting Third World leader had to say under the circumstances. Privately, he conveyed his views regarding world affairs to Nasser in correspondence demonstrating a spirit, as he said in a May 1961 letter to the Egyptian president, "of mutual respect and confidence."[14]

Nasser reciprocated. He assured Kennedy that reaching an Arab-American understanding was an important aim of Egypt's. "We should keep trying, and never despair in our attempts to reach it," he said. He sent his ambassador in Washington, Mustapha Kamel, to the State Department and the White House, with a message that differences between the two countries over Israel need not block improvements in other areas. Nasser himself told the American ambassador in Cairo, John Badeau, that there was nothing to be gained by starting every conversation between representatives of the two countries with an argument about Israel. He suggested putting the Arab-Israeli question "in the icebox" and devoting the energies of the two countries to more constructive matters.[15]

[14]Kennedy to Nasser, May 3, 1961, Kennedy papers, Kennedy Library, Boston.

[15]Nasser to Kennedy, Aug. 22, 1961, Kennedy papers; Douglas Little, "From Even-Handed to Empty-Handed: Seeking Order in the Middle East," in Thomas G. Paterson, ed., *Kennedy's Quest for Victory* (New York, 1989), p. 161.

Substantively, Kennedy expressed his desire for good relations with Egypt through increased amounts of American aid. Under Public Law 480 (PL-480), the U.S. government purchased wheat and other commodities from American farmers and shipped the produce to deserving foreign countries. The program developed a strong constituency, since it served to boost the income of farmers and truckers and longshoremen, to name three of the more obviously benefiting domestic groups, in addition to alleviating hunger and poverty abroad. Egypt had received small quantities of PL-480 grain for a few years, allotted on an annual basis. Kennedy proposed to increase the amount of aid, and to apportion it out in multiyear packages, so that Egyptian economic planners might know what to expect for the future. During the final months of 1961, the director of the State Department's policy planning staff, Walt Rostow, worked out a three-year, $500 million package with Ambassador Kamel. The package took time to wend its way through the bureaucratic process, with proponents having to rebut the usual charges that subsidizing neutralists like Nasser would sap the will of America's allies; but in June 1962 Kennedy put his signature to the agreement.

Nasser valued the aid and the vote of confidence it represented. Kamel remembered later: "Nasser appreciated Kennedy's efforts to treat him as an equal and as an important world leader."[16]

Unfortunately, Middle Eastern affairs were too complicated for some wheat to remedy the underlying problems in the Egyptian-American relationship. Tension persisted throughout Kennedy's three years in office, sometimes remaining submerged, occasionally surfacing. One occasion on which the tension surfaced took nearly everyone by surprise.

In September 1962, a group of dissidents in Yemen staged an attack on the Yemeni government. The country's aged monarch died of natural causes amid the excitement, and the crown prince fled into the hinterlands of Yemen's north. There he rallied loyal tribesmen and, with the support of royalist Saudi Arabia, launched a campaign to oust the radical republicans from the capital.

Egypt got involved because Nasser felt he ought to have a role in most disputes among Arabs, especially one taking place just across the Red Sea. Nasser hadn't much liked the Yemeni monarchy, and he took the opportunity to back the rebels currently in control in Sana, eventually sending 50,000 troops. This threw him into opposition to Saudi Arabia. What had begun as a coup and blossomed into a civil war now threatened to blow up into a regional conflict.

Only the most miniscule portion of the American public had the foggiest notion of who the opposing Yemeni factions were and what they were fighting for. Even among professional Arab-watchers, the significance of the struggle for Yemen wasn't always clear. The United States had almost no interests in Yemen itself, which was why so few Americans knew anything about the country. But the backers of the opposing sides, Saudi Arabia and Egypt, *did* matter in American policy, and the Kennedy administration had to figure out how to deal with them. In Egypt's favor was the administration's desire to extend the recent improvement in relations with Cairo. In Saudi Arabia's favor was the oil that had made and would continue to make the Saudis wealthy and powerful far beyond their numbers.

Kennedy sought to straddle the fence. After considerable pulling and hauling among the involved elements of the bureaucracy, the president chose to grant diplomatic recognition to the republican regime in Sana. This decision pleased Nasser and other Arab radicals. At the same time, though, Kennedy attempted to reassure the Saudis that he had nothing against royalism. He went so far in the latter direction as to dispatch special envoy Ellsworth Bunker to Saudi Arabia to present the Saudi regime with eight U.S. air force planes for use in the defense of Saudi towns near the border with Yemen.

Two-timers occasionally get away with their double games, but rarely if the games last very long. Despite predictions by American intelligence agencies of an imminent victory by the Yemeni republicans, the royalists fought doggedly on, leaving the Kennedy administration in an embarrassing predicament. The administration provided the Saudis with enough assistance to provoke Nasser but not enough for the royalists to win the war, in turn dismaying the Saudis.

The Saudis' disappointment was in some respects the less serious consequence: because the West constituted the only significant market for their oil, the Saudis had nowhere else to turn. Egypt, on the other hand, enjoyed the option of turning—further—toward the Soviet Union. Nasser wouldn't give the Kremlin the keys to his country; he was far too much of a nationalist for that. But he might grant military basing rights to Moscow in exchange for East-bloc weapons and economic aid. The mere thought of Soviet ships and planes stationed next to the Suez Canal gave American planners fits.

In an attempt to avert such an outcome, Kennedy directed the State Department and the White House staff to work on a ceasefire between the two Yemeni factions and their outside seconds. Various American diplomats sought a formula that would end the fighting in Yemen and allow Egypt and Saudi Arabia to disengage. Ellsworth Bunker shuttled back and forth between Nasser and Saudi Prince Faisal, aiming for a mutual withdrawal of forces. Bunker's efforts hung up on the usual you-go-first objections, but eventually he succeeded in getting agreement to a disengagement plan—which broke down shortly after the signing.

The contest dragged on, with no end in sight. Only the onset of the Arab-Israeli war of June 1967 convinced Cairo that the time had come to cut losses and leave Yemen to the Yemenis.

In the shorter term, the Yemen War let the air out of Kennedy's policy of seeking rapprochement with Nasser. American critics of Egypt had generally not appreciated Kennedy's policy of accommodation of Nasser, and the Egyptian president's meddling in Yemen simply confirmed Nasser's reputation as the big troublemaker of the Middle East. Nasser took the U.S. support of Saudi Arabia, belated and half-hearted though it was, as evidence that in any crisis the Americans could be counted on to act like other Western imperialists. They might speak fine words about democracy, but as soon as anyone threatened their oil supply, the words went out the window.

Nor did the Yemen War do much for the United States' relations with Saudi Arabia. Dealings between the two countries had been strained before the war started; the Saudis didn't like Kennedy's cultivating of Nasser. Faisal responded by refusing to extend the lease on the U.S. air base at Dhahran, which in turn prompted Washington to trim plans for American aid to Saudi Arabia. Saudi rumor merchants spoke darkly of retaliation against Aramco, the oil consortium. Faisal interpreted Kennedy's recognition of the Yemeni republicans as an insult, a challenge to the principle of legitimacy, and a further indication of Washington's Nasser-appeasing tendencies. Kennedy's reassurances—he wrote to Faisal that "Saudi Arabia can depend on the friendship and cooperation of the United States" and that the United States had "a deep and abiding interest in Saudi Arabia"—and the subsequent delivery of the American planes and accompanying advis-

ers eased Saudi complaints somewhat. But as long as the war continued, so did Saudi suspicions of American constancy.[17]

4. ARMS FOR ISRAEL

If American policy in the Yemen War irritated both the Egyptians and
the Saudis, it didn't earn much applause in Israel either. The Israelis
had never accepted the American reasoning behind a policy of placat-
ing Nasser; to them he remained a bitter enemy who challenged Israel directly and who fomented unrest among the already restless
Palestinians. For Israel, the consequences of Nasser's policies were
the economic and psychological strains of perpetual readiness for war
and the toll in human life and suffering of terrorist attacks. Saudi Arabia seemed hardly better. Although the Saudi regime was too nervous
about its own future to meddle with Israel straightaway, it followed
the indirect route of funding anti-Israel Palestinian guerrillas. The
Kennedy administration's decision to send the Saudis airplanes and
military advisers simply gave the American seal of approval to another
country dedicated to Israel's destruction.

Repeatedly, when the Israelis have noticed their Arab neighbors
getting militarily stronger, they have taken steps to go the neighbors
one or two better. Often they have turned to the United States for
help in such steps. During the Kennedy years, the Israelis particularly
sought permission to purchase American Hawk antiaircraft missiles.
The request wasn't new; the Israeli government had asked the Eisenhower administration for Hawks, but been turned down. The State
Department, as Arab-inclined as ever, explained that Washington
didn't want to contribute to a Middle East arms race. The Eisenhower White House, still annoyed with the Israelis for their role in the
Suez conspiracy, refused to overrule the State Department.

Israeli officials tried again after Kennedy entered office. They argued that an American policy of abstention from a Middle East
weapons race might make sense in the abstract, but in the real world
the Soviets had been arming Egypt and Iraq, creating the sort of dise-
quilibrium that could easily lead to war. The United States had sup-

[17]George Lenczowski, *American Presidents and the Middle East* (Durham, N.C.,
1990), p. 81.

ported the establishment of Israel; did the Americans now wish to see Israel succumb to its communist-backed enemies?

The argument persuaded Myer Feldman and the other pro-Israelists in the Kennedy administration, but made less headway with the State Department and a small pro-Arab contingent in the White House. The two sides thrashed the matter over until Kennedy, with the 1962 elections approaching, decided in favor of selling Israel the missiles.

This decision marked a significant shift in relations between the United States and Israel. Until the early 1960s, Washington had treated Israel as a country much like most others: one with whom it might agree or disagree, with whose interests or from whose interests America's might converge or diverge. Harry Truman had provided crucial assistance at the birth of Israel, but once it was born he had left it largely on its own. Dwight Eisenhower had kept his distance from the Israelis, to the extent of publicly chastising them during the Suez War and coercing them afterward into accepting a settlement they didn't like.

Although Kennedy had initially sought an evenhanded policy between Israel and the Arabs, his policy gravitated irresistibly toward Israel, particularly after the Yemen War spoiled the honeymoon with Nasser. At the end of December 1962, the president met with Golda Meir in Florida. Kennedy told the Israeli foreign minister that the United States had "a special relationship" with Israel comparable only to the relationship it had with Britain. Kennedy went on to say that this special relationship shouldn't prevent the United States from seeking closer ties with Arab countries; indeed, he asserted, it was to Israel's interest as well as to America's for the United States to communicate freely and amicably with the Arabs. "To be effective in our own interest, and to help Israel, we have to maintain our position in the Middle East generally." Kennedy continued, "If we pulled out of the Arab Middle East, and maintained our ties only with Israel, this would not be in Israel's interest." Yet the United States would look after Israel. "This country is really interested in Israel," the president affirmed. "We are interested that Israel should keep up its sensitive, tremendous, historic task."[18]

Kennedy's decision on the Hawks reflected this interest in terms directly understandable to Israel's enemies. A follow-up decision to fi-

---

[18]Memo of conversation, Dec. 27, 1962, Kennedy papers.

nance the Hawks on generous terms reinforced the point. From Kennedy onward, American presidents treated Israel in accordance with the "special relationship" Kennedy described; before long, Israel was a de facto ally of the United States, with most of the rights and privileges allies usually received—including lots more weapons and dollars. Whatever this development did for Israel's self-confidence and security, it further complicated American relations with the Arab states.

Recognizing that it would, the Kennedy administration undertook another effort to solve the Arab-Israeli dispute. The administration developed and promoted a plan, unofficially named for Joseph Johnson, the president of the Carnegie Endowment, for dealing with the problem of the Palestinian refugees. During its eighteen months of life, the plan generated enough support among both Israelis and Arabs to let optimists feel hopeful, but enough opposition to let pessimists feel dismal. The Kennedy administration worked to keep it alive, as other administrations have done with other initiatives, partly out of a desire to appear to be making some progress toward a solution to the Middle East's most intractable problem. Ultimately, the plan foundered on Israel's belief that it would allow too many Palestinians back into Israel, and the Arabs' belief that it would allow too few.

Though Israel could reasonably have little to complain of regarding Kennedy's time in office, Israel's partisans couldn't help but think that the cloud of tragedy that brought Kennedy's death had a silver lining: Lyndon Johnson. While majority leader in the Senate during the 1950s, Johnson had distinguished himself as a loyal and powerful friend of Israel; that he did so coming from a state without a conspicuous Jewish constituency distinguished him further. Of course, Johnson recognized that supporting Israel made good Democratic politics, and even had he not recognized this fact—an impossible premise, given Johnson's acute political sensibilities—he would still have found himself rubbing elbows with the many Jews who shared his liberal philosophy.

East-coasters and others intrigued by Johnson's Texas background liked to explain his solicitude for Israel as a manifestation of a kind of remember-the-Alamo syndrome. There may have been something to this analogy, but a more prosaic explanation probably revealed as much. Johnson admired the stubborn determination of the Israelis to pull themselves up by their national bootstraps, as he himself had done in his own career. At least one close observer saw a strong psychological affinity in Johnson for Jews. White House aide Harry McPherson suggested that "some place in Lyndon Johnson's blood" there resided "a great many Jewish corpuscles." McPherson continued, "I think he is part Jewish, seriously. Not merely because of his affection for a great many Jews but because of the way he behaves. He really reminds me of a six-foot-three-inch Texas slightly corny version of a rabbi or a diamond merchant on 44th Street."[19]

Johnson had demonstrated a concern for the welfare of the Jewish people as early as the 1930s. A friendship with Jim Novy, an Austin businessman of Russian-Jewish background, sensitized the Texas congressman to the special problems facing Jews in Europe at that time. During the last years of the peace and the first years of the war, Johnson helped procure visas and other documents that allowed hundreds of Jewish refugees from countries controlled by the Nazis to escape to the United States. Afterward, Novy said of Johnson, "We can't ever thank him enough for all those Jews he got out of Germany during the days of Hitler."[20]

As president, Johnson proved himself to be one of the best friends Israel ever had. Two months after he succeeded Kennedy, Johnson received a proposal to sell Israel several hundred American tanks. As in the case of the Hawk missiles, the Israelis contended that they needed the tanks to keep pace with the radical Arabs, whom Moscow continued to arm. The Israelis added that American military aid to Saudi Arabia, while designed to secure that oil kingdom against the radicals, might one day find its way into battle against Israel.

The State Department argued against the tanks, for the usual reasons; the CIA also opposed the deal. The intelligence agency asserted that the Arabs were watching the new president carefully to determine whether he would be a captive of the Israel lobby, especially in an election year. The CIA noted the important military distinction between Hawks, which were strictly defensive weapons, and tanks, which could be used offensively as well. Citing this distinction, the agency said that approval of the tank deal would signify "a fundamental break with the fifteen-year-old U.S. policy of not being a major supplier of arms, especially offensive ones, to either Israel or the Arab states." Such a break likely would result in the further intrusion of the

---

[19]Harry McPherson oral history interview, Johnson Library, Austin, Tex.

[20]Robert Dallek, *Lone Star Rising: Lyndon Johnson and His Times, 1908–1960* (New York, 1991), pp. 169–170.

superpower conflict into the Middle East—a development the Israelis would exploit. "The dominant policy makers in Tel Aviv would welcome the opportunity to use the Cold War as a device to assure themselves of closer U.S.-Israeli ties, particularly in the military."[21]

At the White House, Myer Feldman rebutted these objections. Feldman described the logic behind a decision to provide the tanks as "inexorable." Johnson's predecessors and Johnson himself had committed themselves to defend Israel, if Israel were attacked. The idea behind approving the tanks was to avert an explicit test of this commitment. "Our basic policy must be directed toward the prevention of any aggression," Feldman declared. "Our policy must be such that American intervention will not be necessary."[22]

Johnson chose to delay a decision on the tanks. Israeli Prime Minister Levi Eshkol had scheduled a visit to Washington, and the president hoped to do some horse trading. In particular, Johnson desired guarantees from Eshkol that the Israelis wouldn't develop nuclear weapons. Israel had every right to defend itself, Johnson believed, but to introduce nuclear weapons into the Middle East would eventually render Israel *less* secure rather than more so, since such escalation would force the Arabs to try to get nuclear weapons of their own. To encourage the Israeli government to see things similarly, Johnson decided to withhold the tanks Eshkol wanted until the prime minister gave satisfaction on the nuclear issue.

Eshkol did, agreeing to allow American scientists to inspect Israel's nuclear facilities to assure Washington that only peaceful activities were taking place there; but even then, Johnson hesitated regarding the tanks. Although he thought the Israelis ought to get them, he was reluctant to incur the Arab wrath that would descend on whatever government provided the tanks. The president suggested that Eshkol go shopping elsewhere—in Germany, perhaps. The Germans owed the United States some favors, and Washington would recommend that they be helpful in this regard. But the president said that if all else failed, the United States would supply the tanks.

All else did fail. Though Johnson got West German Chancellor Ludwig Erhard to consent to sell Israel the tanks, word leaked out of the impending sale, threatening serious disruption of German-Arab relations. Several of the Arab governments moved toward breaking

---

[21]CIA memo, Feb. 25, 1964, Johnson papers, Johnson Library.

[22]Feldman to Johnson, Mar. 14, 1964, Johnson papers.

diplomatic ties with Bonn and recognizing East Germany. Erhard judged that what he owed Johnson stopped short of such a sacrifice, and at the beginning of 1965, Bonn suspended weapons sales to Israel. At this point, Eshkol cashed Johnson's promissory note: he demanded the American tanks. Shipments of the tanks began shortly. Through the end of 1965, more than 200 had arrived in Israel.

The tank deal, after the sale of the Hawks, accelerated the trend toward the United States' becoming the armorer of the Israelis. So, ironically, did a decision by the Johnson administration to send weapons to one of Israel's declared enemies, Jordan. King Hussein, remarking the largess the United States had been bestowing on fellow conservative and monarch Faisal of Saudi Arabia, thought he deserved more from Washington than he was getting. Not entirely convincingly, but with sufficient verve to worry the Johnson administration, the Jordanian king threatened to appeal to the Soviets for help. To keep him happy, Johnson decreed an increase in U.S. military aid to Amman.

The hard part of the bargain was getting the Israelis to go along. Obviously, Israel didn't possess a veto over American policy decisions, but political realities were such that if the Israelis stirred a stink, Congress would catch a whiff and Johnson would catch hell. For Johnson, a principal objective of foreign policy was to keep the legislature undistracted from his agenda of domestic reform; to this end, preventing Israel from raising a row became a priority.

As a means to the end, Johnson sent W. Averell Harriman, the undersecretary of state, and White House staffer Robert Komer to Israel. The two envoys told the Israelis that U.S. assistance to Jordan was intended to preempt the Soviets. "The dangers to Israel would clearly be greater if we did not help Jordan," Harriman said. President Johnson remained committed to Israel's security, and in return for Israel's cooperation, he was willing to increase the Israelis' slice of the American military-aid pie. But Israel must help the president with his political difficulties. Harriman said that Israeli officials should place the administration's aid package to Jordan in the "proper perspective" for the American Jewish community. Such perspective-placing constituted "an essential part of our relationship."[23]

An offer of increased U.S. aid was precisely what the Israelis

---

[23]Steven L. Spiegel, *The Other Arab-Israeli Conflict: Making America's Middle East Policy, from Truman to Reagan* (Chicago, 1985), pp. 132–134.

wanted to hear. Eshkol and Foreign Minister Meir pressed for specifics. They demanded a public statement of Washington's willingness to provide weapons to Israel, and they insisted on receiving more and better arms than Jordan. They also requested American support in a long-running water dispute with Jordan.

Harriman and Komer refused to commit the administration publicly to the kind and extent of arms sales the Israelis desired. To do so, Harriman said, would provoke the Arabs excessively. The two envoys explained that the administration backed Israel's water claims in principle, but they told Eshkol to refer the matter to the United Nations. Lest Israel think about acting unilaterally on the water question, they stated explicitly that Washington would not accept unilateral measures by Israel to prevent water diversion.

Closing the distance between the American and Israeli positions required several days of jaw-numbing bargaining. Harriman gave up and went home, leaving the matter to Komer, who eventually struck a deal with Eshkol. The United States agreed to guarantee that Israel get advanced military aircraft: the Israelis would first seek the planes from third countries, but if they couldn't find what they needed, the United States would furnish the aircraft. In compensation, the Israeli government would counsel its friends in America not to create a fuss over the arms deliveries to Jordan. The water question was left unresolved.

As had happened regarding the tanks, the administration within several months had to make good its pledge to act as Israel's supplier of last resort. After window shopping Western arms marts, the Israelis decided that their security required American A-4 fighter-bombers. Nothing else would do. Johnson, ever cognizant of the trouble unsatisfied Israel-supporters could cause in his campaign for a domestic Great Society, reluctantly approved the transfer of the planes.

Although the administration tried to preserve the pretense that it wasn't contributing to the arms race in the Middle East, the A-4 sale demonstrated that it would soon be doing so if it wasn't already. Looking back from the perspective of mid-1966, Walt Rostow described what Washington had been sending in the way of weapons to Israel. In 1962, America had supplied Israel with five batteries of Hawk missiles, worth $21.5 million. In 1965, the Israelis got 210 tanks, worth $34 million. The A-4 agreement included 48 planes, worth $72 million. In addition, the Israelis had received large quantities of ammunition, spare parts, and communications equipment. All this, Rostow commented, without apparent irony, had been delivered or scheduled for delivery despite America's "standing policy not to become a major arms supplier in the Middle East."[24]

5. THE TROJAN WAR REVISITED: CYPRUS

On its own terms, the Middle East was explosive enough for the most jaded geopolitician, but what made the crises there *really* worrisome was the possibility that they would lead to war between the United States and the Soviet Union. In 1956, in 1967, and in 1973, fights between Israel and its Arab neighbors immediately aroused leaders in Washington and Moscow, who scrambled airplanes, redirected naval task forces, and recalled soldiers to bases. In no instance did the superpowers approach quite so near to direct combat as they did in the 1962 Cuban missile affair, but the risk of nuclear war between the chief antagonists in the Cold War was large enough to sober all but blinkered fools.

In 1964, a crisis developed that varied this theme. Here the risk of war involved not the opposite camps in the Cold War but two members of the same camp. To persons whose grasp of world affairs stretched no further back than about 1945, this might have seemed strange, but not to those who understood the deep roots of rivalries in the Middle East. Since 1952, Turkey and Greece had been members of NATO, admitted as a reward for their cooperation with the United States and its Atlantic partners, and as part of an effort to extend the Western cordon around the Soviet Union into the Middle East (where it connected to the Baghdad Pact). For a bit longer—since the implementation of the Truman Doctrine in 1947—Turkey and Greece had been de facto allies of the United States. But before that, going back to the days Homer sang about, the two countries had more often been enemies than collaborators. In 1964, they came very close to being enemies again, approaching to within hours of war before Johnson read the riot act and enforced peace—or at least nonwar.

The focus of the Turkish-Greek dispute was Cyprus. The roots of the island's troubles were similar to those of the Arab-Israeli conflict: two distinct groups of people trying to live on the same plot of

[24]Rostow memo, May 19, 1966, Johnson papers.

ground. Another similarity existed: both conflicts had assumed their present form upon the relinquishment of British control. In 1960, the British handed sovereignty in Cyprus to a government headed by the religious and political leader of the island's majority Greek community, Archbishop Makarios III. A complicated constitution protected the rights of the minority Turkish community, or tried to; and a more complicated diplomatic-military arrangement among Britain, Turkey, and Greece—the so-called guarantor powers—protected the constitution, or tried to. In actual practice, neither guarantee worked very well, and at the end of 1963, widespread violence between Greek Cypriots and Turkish Cypriots broke out. The former appealed to Greece for help, the latter to Turkey, while the British wrung their hands and appealed to Washington. London proposed a peacekeeping force involving troops from the United States and other NATO countries. Failing this, the British government would turn the matter over to the United Nations.

American officials didn't like the idea of pulling Britain's Cyprus chestnuts out of the fire, but they liked the idea of war between Turkey and Greece—which was what hotheads in both countries were talking about—even less. Turkey by now had become the linchpin of U.S. policy in the Middle East. In case of war with the Soviet Union, NATO could use its control of the Turkish Straits to close the exit from the Black Sea. Bombers stationed in Turkey could strike deep into Soviet territory. During peacetime, American spyplanes based in Turkey overflew the Soviet Union—or had, until Soviet gunners shot down an American U-2 in 1960, causing a diplomatic furor. Electronic listening posts in Turkey kept track of Soviet missile tests and other events of interest to U.S. intelligence agencies.

When it became evident that the British were serious about dumping responsibility for Cyprus on the United Nations—from which American leaders had learned to expect little—the Johnson administration consented to join the other NATO countries in trying to keep the peace in Cyprus. The president ordered Undersecretary of State George Ball to Cyprus to present the issue to Cypriot President Makarios.

Ball expected difficulty with Makarios. The undersecretary's main briefing on the archbishop had come from the American ambassador to the United Nations, Adlai Stevenson. A few years earlier, Stevenson had spent three days with Makarios in Nicosia; he had left Cyprus feeling nothing but contempt for the archbishop. The only method of dealing with Makarios, Stevenson told Ball, was by "giving the old bastard absolute hell." Stevenson added, "I have sat across the table from that pious-looking replica of Jesus Christ, and if you saw him with his beard shaved and a push-cart, you would recall the old saying that there hasn't been an honest thief since Barabbas."

At Ball's first meeting with Makarios, on the porch of the archbishop's residence, Makarios greeted the undersecretary in the luxurious costume of the Orthodox prelate. But once the formal reception ended, the archbishop took Ball to his private study and performed what the undersecretary later described as "an astonishing striptease." Off came the headgear symbolizing his episcopacy. Off came the gold chain and medallion signifying his function as confessor. Off came the robes of the priest. Ball had expected to find a venerable ecclesiastic. "Now I found myself facing a tough, cynical man of fifty-one, far more suited to temporal command than spiritual inspiration." Makarios's actions during the next few days caused Ball to question the numerical part of this description. "He must be cheating about his age," Ball told Johnson. "No one could acquire so much guile in only fifty-one years."

Makarios attempted to assure Ball that the trials afflicting Cyprus were nothing unusual. "Mr. Secretary," the archbishop said, "the Greeks and Turks have lived together for two thousand years on this island, and there have always been occasional incidents." Ball, upset by the mayhem that was taking place at that very moment, responded, "Your Beatitude"—despite his dismay, Ball stuck to protocol—"I've been trying for the last two days to make the simple point that this is not the Middle Ages but the latter part of the twentieth century. The world is not going to stand idly by and let you turn this beautiful little island into your private abattoir." Unruffled, Makarios responded, "You're a hard man, Mr. Secretary, a very hard man."

Later during Ball's visit, the archbishop addressed the undersecretary alone in his study. With disarming frankness, he said, "I like you, Mr. Secretary. You speak candidly, and I respect that. It's too bad we couldn't have met under happier circumstances. Then, I'm sure, we could have been friends." Pausing a moment, he proceeded, "We've talked about many things, and we've been frank with one another. I think it right to say we've developed a considerable rapport. Yet there's one thing I haven't asked, and I don't know whether I should or not. But I shall anyway. Do you think I should be killed by the Turks or the Greeks? Better by the Greeks, wouldn't you think?"

Ball, always the diplomat, refused to commit himself. "Your Beatitude," he answered, "that's your problem."[25]

(Yet Ball thought Makarios's question not entirely inappropriate to the search for a solution to the Cyprus problem. A few years later, in a moment of greater than usual exasperation, Ball commented in confidence, "That son of a bitch will have to be killed before anything happens in Cyprus."[26])

For all his idiosyncrasies, Makarios made one thing clear to Ball: he wouldn't accept the peacekeeping force London and Washington had in mind. Cyprus didn't appreciate being treated as a pawn in NATO politics. If peacekeepers were to come to Cyprus, they would have to represent the broader spectrum of the United Nations.

Makarios eventually got his United Nations force, after Britain made good on its threat to divest itself of responsibility for Cyprus. But the blue-helmeted peacekeepers had little luck stemming the flow of blood on the island. At the beginning of June, Turkey decided it could no longer stand by and watch Turkish Cypriots get massacred. Ankara brought its military to full alert. Major hostilities appeared imminent.

A war in the eastern Mediterranean was the last thing the Johnson administration needed, especially at a time when the war in Vietnam was going badly. Johnson fired off a blistering letter to Turkish Prime Minister Ismet Inonu—a message Ball described as "the diplomatic equivalent of an atomic bomb." After reading Johnson's letter, Ball told Secretary of State Dean Rusk, "That may stop Inonu from invading, but I don't know how we'll ever get him down off the ceiling."[27]

Johnson's letter left nothing to Inonu's imagination. By invading Cyprus, the president said, Turkey would fail utterly in its obligations to the Atlantic alliance. "There can be no question in your mind that a Turkish intervention in Cyprus would lead to a military engagement between Turkish and Greek forces." Such a conflict between two NATO allies was "unthinkable" and would comfort only the enemies of freedom. The Soviet Union, which had already taken advantage of the division in NATO ranks to offer support to Makarios, would be tempted to involve itself in any war that erupted. Should the Kremlin succumb to the temptation, the Turks had better look to their own

---

[25]George Ball, *The Past Has Another Pattern* (New York, 1982), pp. 340–346.

[26]Laurence Stern, *The Wrong Horse* (New York, 1977), p. 84.

[27]Ball, op. cit., p. 350.

defense. "I hope you will understand," Johnson said, "that your NATO allies have not had a chance to consider whether they have an obligation to protect Turkey against the Soviet Union if Turkey takes a step which results in Soviet intervention without the full consent and understanding of its NATO allies." It went without saying—although Johnson did—that the Turks could forget about further U.S. aid if they invaded Cyprus. Johnson concluded, "You have your responsibilities as Chief of the Government of Turkey. I also have mine as President of the United States."[28]

Johnson's ultimatum froze the Turks in their tracks, as the administration expected it would. At the same time, it alienated Inonu, again as expected. Inonu told the American ambassador that his government would consult with the United States before acting, but he complained at the undue severity of Johnson's letter. Allies didn't speak to allies thus, the Turkish prime minister said. Inonu denied that Turkey intended a permanent occupation or partition of Cyprus; it merely intended to protect Turkish Cypriots from the violence they encountered every day. He asked bitterly who would protect the Turkish Cypriots now that Turkish troops were forced to sit in their barracks.

American officials understood that they had won only a momentary reprieve from war, not a solution to the problems that had brought war close. In order to find a solution, the Johnson administration undertook a new diplomatic initiative. Washington arranged talks in Geneva between Turkish and Greek representatives. Former secretary of state Dean Acheson, the principal author of the Truman Doctrine and the grand old man of U.S. relations with Turkey and Greece, would mediate.

The Geneva talks began in July. Acheson negotiated alternately with the Turkish and Greek representatives, who refused to occupy the same room simultaneously; eventually he devised a plan that would eliminate the Cyprus problem by eliminating Cyprus (which was why Makarios hadn't been invited to send a representative). Under this first Acheson plan, Cyprus as an independent country would disappear, partitioned between Greece and Turkey. An elaborate system of guarantees would protect the rights of the relatively few Greek Cypriots and Turkish Cypriots caught on the wrong sides of the partition line.

[28]Johnson to Inonu, June 5, 1964, Johnson papers.

Turkey liked the idea of partition, but Greece didn't. The Greek government called it a denial of the rights of the Cypriot people—by which Athens meant the Greek Cypriot majority. Makarios's violent opposition to the plan contributed to Athens's rejection; the Greek government didn't want to have to implement a Cyprus solution over the head of the spokesman of the Greek Cypriots, the very people it purported to protect.

The failure of the first Acheson plan coincided with another notching up of the bloodshed on Cyprus. Responding to renewed attacks on Turkish Cypriots, Ankara sent jets against Greek Cypriot positions. The Turkish army again mobilized, as did the Greek army. Again Johnson appealed for calm, sending identical letters urging forbearance to Inonu, Makarios, and Greek Prime Minister Andreas Papandreou.

To give Ankara additional reason not to invade, Johnson complemented words with covert measures. Since June, U.S. intelligence operatives in the Cyprus area had been keeping a close eye on General George Grivas, the hero of the Cypriot revolt against British colonialism and the commander of the sometimes-terrorist organization EOKA. Grivas and Makarios had long been rivals for leadership of the Greek Cypriot community, partly for personal reasons, but mostly because Grivas favored *enosis* (union of Cyprus with Greece), while Makarios wanted to be president of an independent country. Though Grivas was no more pro-American than Makarios, to the Johnson administration he appeared more predictable. Via one of Grivas's associates, the administration learned that Grivas was hatching a plot to overthrow Makarios and effect *enosis*, with an important proviso pledging compensation to Turkish Cypriots who chose to leave Greece's new province and legal protection for those desiring to stay. Washington let Grivas know that the United States didn't look unfavorably on his scheme.

Perhaps Makarios got wind of the American backing for Grivas. Perhaps that was the point. Perhaps Johnson's appeal for peace had an effect. Whatever the causes, Makarios chose to accept a United Nations call for a ceasefire. When Turkey joined the truce, the August crisis passed.

Attention once again shifted back to Geneva, where Acheson was at work on a revised plan. The new version specified a fifty-year lease of the northern portion of Cyprus to Turkey, rather than outright cession; otherwise it resembled the first Acheson plan. Turkey rejected the new proposal on the ground that while fifty years might seem a long time to Americans, in Turkey's neighborhood it was the blink of an eye. Greece liked the new plan better than the old one, but in the end, Athens refused to break with Makarios, who denounced the new scheme as violently as he had the old.

On this sour note, the Geneva talks adjourned. American officials, Acheson especially, considered the Greeks primarily responsible for the talks' failure. Acheson described Papandreou privately as "a garrulous, senile windbag without power of decision or resolution." Had Papandreou possessed such power, Acheson believed, the outcome might have been different.[29]

Acheson was disgusted, but he hadn't run out of ideas. On his return to Washington at the beginning of September, he proposed that the administration essentially tell the Turks to go ahead and invade Cyprus. Acheson thought he had good reason for advocating what amounted to a complete reversal of U.S. policy so far, which had aimed precisely to *prevent* the Turks from invading. In the first place, he was convinced that neither Makarios nor the Greek government would agree to anything the Turks could live with. In the absence of a fresh approach, the Cyprus question would plague the United States and the world indefinitely. In the second place, Makarios was flirting with the Soviets and they were flirting back. If a solution at all favorable to the West was to appear, it would have to arrive before a Makarios-Moscow alliance developed. In the third place, the combination of Turkish determination and Greek ineptitude the recent events had revealed suggested strongly that the Turks could invade Cyprus and seize what they would have gotten under the first Acheson plan, before the Greeks got into the fight. Athens would be left with nothing to do but annex the rest of the island, again as per the first Acheson plan.

With the help of George Ball, who also favored this bold solution, Acheson pitched his idea to Johnson. The president was intrigued. What would happen to the Turkish Cypriots in the Greek sector? he asked. Ball said that most would stay on the island; of these, the particularly nervous would move to the Turkish zone. Would Athens really follow the script? the president inquired. Ball thought so. Evidence indicated that Papandreou's government had a contingency plan for "instant

[29]David S. McLellan and David C. Acheson, eds., *Among Friends: Personal Letters of Dean Acheson* (New York, 1980), p. 284.

enosis" in case of a Turkish invasion. How about casualties during the operation? wondered Johnson. Acheson, who apparently had broached the subject with Turkish leaders, said the military in Ankara could be relied on to carry out the operation with relatively little violence. Acheson added that the invasion would entail minimal use of American weapons and such "internationally unpopular" tactics as bombing raids. Ball commented, "With luck, bloodshed would be limited."[30]

After further discussion, Johnson said he'd think the matter over. He did, and ultimately decided against the Acheson-Ball recommendation. The president probably questioned whether the plan would go as smoothly as Acheson and Ball predicted. He must have worried that the U.S. role in the plan would be discovered. And with the war in Vietnam already creating a great deal of controversy, he certainly feared the domestic political fallout of a military conflict between Turkey and Greece—just weeks before the 1964 election, in the campaign for which he was presenting himself as the peace candidate. As he told Acheson and Ball, the present period was "not a good season for another war."[31]

❖   ❖   ❖

During the several years after the Suez War, the United States grew more deeply involved than ever in the affairs of the Middle East. The Eisenhower Doctrine of 1957 turned out to be a false start: following the landing of U.S. troops in Lebanon in 1958, Washington recognized the ineffectiveness—for the time being at least—of directly applying American military force to the region's troubles. Far more portentous was Kennedy's decision to develop a "special relationship" with Israel. This decision undercut the Democratic president's efforts to promote good relations with the Arabs, particularly Egypt, and it led to the United States' becoming Israel's chief weapons supplier. The United States hadn't taken Israel under its wing as an official ally—through the early 1990s, it never would—but it had gone far toward identifying American interests with Israeli interests. This identification would have a most profound effect on American Middle East policy.

[30]Memo for record, Sept. 8, 1964; Komer and Bundy to Johnson, Aug. 18, 1964; Tuesday lunch notes, Sept. 8, 1964; all in Johnson papers.

[31]Memo for record, Sept. 8, 1964, Johnson papers.

Chapter 4

More War: 1966–1973

1. EGYPTIAN BRINKMANSHIP, ISRAELI IMPATIENCE

Whether another season would have been better for war, Johnson didn't say. Presumably, the president could have done without war in the Middle East entirely. But though he refused to give the nod to a war over Cyprus, and earlier had thrown the United States' weight energetically against it, he showed less resolve in seeking to prevent a renewed outbreak of the Arab-Israeli conflict. At least partly as a result of his irresolution, war returned to the Israel-Palestine area, with consequences that changed irrevocably the face of the Middle East and the position of the United States therein.

The deep roots of the June 1967 war lay in the same troubled soil that had sprouted the two previous Arab-Israeli clashes, but the shallow feeders that actually triggered the fighting ran only to the previous year. In February 1966, a coup in Syria led to the ascendancy of an ardently socialist and militantly anti-Israel regime in Damascus. As so often occurs with governments that lack compelling domestic agendas, the Syrian leaders launched into foreign adventures. They proclaimed their desire for warmer relations with the Soviet Union and simultaneously commenced a guerrilla offensive against Israel, from bases in Jordan as well as in Syria. The Soviets and the Israelis both reciprocated the attention: the former with economic and military aid, the latter with armed reprisals.

A major Israeli attack on the Jordanian village of Samu in November 1966 silenced the Syrians for a time, but the following year brought a resumption of violence. By the beginning of April 1967, the regular artillery exchanges across the Israel-Syria frontier in the Golan Heights hardly made the nightly news, even in the countries involved. On April 7, Israel staged air raids against the Syrian gunners, provoking Damascus to loft its own planes and join the air battle. The Israelis shattered the Syrian force and rattled windows in the Syrian capital to emphasize their scorn.

Though Syria had seceded from its ill-starred union with Egypt in 1961, Nasser, still aspiring to leadership among the Arabs, felt heavy pressure to respond to the Israeli attacks. Nasser possessed a more realistic sense of the power balance between the Arab states and Israel than the Syrians did, and he had no overwhelming desire to take on the Israelis. But because opposition to the Zionists was almost the only issue holding the Arab movement together, he couldn't allow anyone to seem more anti-Zionist than he. In November 1966, he signed a mutual defense pact with Syria. Following the April 1967 Israeli air assault, the Syrians demanded that he honor his commitment.

Nasser felt pressure on another front as well. Since the Suez War of 1956, a United Nations Emergency Force had separated the armies of Egypt and Israel in the Sinai desert. Arab irredentists charged Nasser with cowering behind UNEF; hardliners in Syria, Jordan, Iraq, and elsewhere complained that the Egyptian president knew only how to talk. If he were serious about Arab unity and the struggle for Palestine, he would order UNEF out of Egypt and punish the Zionist aggressors.

Nasser bowed to the criticism. On May 16, he told the United Nations to withdraw its troops from Egyptian territory. Two days later, the secretary general, Burma's U Thant, ordered compliance with the Egyptian demand.

On May 22, Nasser cranked the tension tighter. Just as the last UNEF troops left Sharm el Sheikh on the Tiran Strait at the entrance to the Gulf of Aqaba, the Egyptian president announced that Egypt would close the strait and thereby the gulf to Israeli ship traffic. Meanwhile, he increased the number of Egyptian troops near Israel's southwestern border.

To Israel, Nasser's actions represented an intolerable provocation. The ouster of UNEF and the massing of troops appeared to foretell an attack on Israeli territory, while the closing of Tiran and Aqaba deprived Israel of reasonable access to countries to its east and portended a trampling of Israel's rights.

The Johnson administration watched these events with mounting concern and counseled caution. Johnson wrote to Israeli Prime Minister Eshkol on May 17 explaining that while he understood Israel's fears, he expected the Israeli government to exhaust all peaceful avenues for resolving the crisis. "I know that you and your people are having your patience tried to the limit," the president said, before continuing, "I would like to emphasize in strongest terms the need to avoid any action on your side which would add further to the violence and tension in the area." Johnson warned against rash measures, especially ones that took Washington by surprise. "I urge the closest consultation between you and your principal friends," he said, meaning himself and his associates. "I am sure you will understand that I cannot accept responsibilities on behalf of the United States for situations which arise as the result of actions on which we are not consulted." A short while later, Johnson wrote Eshkol again, calling on the prime minister to demonstrate "steady nerves" and pledging the United States to resist aggression in the Middle East.[1]

Johnson wrote to Nasser, too. He asserted the United States' friendly feelings toward Egypt and the Arab people, and he promised Nasser that the United States would listen sympathetically to Cairo's legitimate grievances. He also acknowledged difficulties between the United States and Egypt in the past, but he stressed that these were not the present issue. "Your task and mine," he said, "is not to look back but to rescue the Middle East—and the whole human community—from a war I believe no one wants." Johnson offered American support for new efforts to solve the problems between countries of the Middle East, and he volunteered to send Vice President Humphrey to the region in such an effort—"if we come through these days without hostilities."[2]

For good measure, Johnson contacted Soviet Premier Aleksei Kosygin. The Johnson administration rightly suspected the Soviets of encouraging Syria's tendency toward troublemaking. Beyond causing problems for Israel, and through Israel for the United States, Moscow evidently thought Syrian pressure on Nasser would encourage unity between the primary radical regimes of the region and would relatively weaken the conservative, pro-Western governments. Johnson

---

[1]Johnson to Eshkol, May 17, and May 21, 1967, Johnson papers, Johnson Library, Austin, Tex.

[2]Johnson to Nasser, May 22, 1967, ibid.

warned Kosygin that the stakes of conflict between Arabs and Israelis might be higher than the Kremlin had calculated. "The increasing harassment of Israel by elements based in Syria, with attendant reactions within Israel and within the Arab world, has brought the area close to major violence," Johnson told the Soviet leader. "Your and our ties to nations of the area could bring us into difficulties which I am confident neither of us seeks. It would appear a time for each of us to use our influence to the full in the cause of moderation, including our influence over action by the United Nations."[3]

Johnson complemented these private cautions with a public statement of American intentions. On May 23, the president went on television and radio to reiterate a position adopted by Eisenhower in 1957, to the effect that the Gulf of Aqaba was an international waterway that must be open to free navigation by ships of all countries. He declared the Egyptian blockade illegal and gravely threatening to world peace. He said he was distressed at the withdrawal of UNEF. He regretted the violence in the region. He deplored the buildup of military forces. Significantly, however, he stopped short of declaring explicit support for Israel, and he left responsibility for a resolution of the crisis to the international community.[4]

During the last week of May, Johnson walked a diplomatic tightrope. He aimed to convince each side that strident talk and bellicose posturing might get out of control; at the same time, he tried to avoid unduly frightening the potential belligerents. Once either party became convinced of war's inevitability, that party would feel a nearly irresistible temptation to hit first. This was particularly true of the Israelis, who enjoyed almost no room for retreat if a war started badly. Toward them, Johnson had to offer reassurance that they wouldn't be left to fight alone—but only if they didn't start an avoidable war.

Reassurance, with a warning, was what the Johnson administration gave when Abba Eban, the Israeli foreign minister, visited Washington. Eban first spoke to Dean Rusk, who described the session to Johnson. As the secretary of state explained, the Israelis didn't anticipate constructive action by the United Nations. "They have absolutely no faith in the possibility of anything useful coming out of the U.N.," Rusk said. The secretary asserted that he had pressed Eban hard about the need for Israel to refrain from preemptive moves; he advo-

---

[3]Johnson to Kosygin, May 19, 1967, ibid.

[4]*Weekly Compilation of Presidential Documents,* May 29, 1967.

cated that Johnson do likewise. The president might also underline the fact that if war came, the question of who started it would be vitally important.[5]

Johnson prepared carefully for his meeting with Eban. He convened his top advisers to sound out their assessments of the recent developments. Rusk presented the latest intelligence reports and said he judged the current situation "serious but not yet desperate." To what the president had already heard about Egypt and Israel, Rusk added that the Soviets were still agitating affairs, albeit more vigorously for public display now than in private. "Privately we find the Russians playing a generally moderate game," Rusk said, "but publicly they have taken a harsh view of the facts and have laid responsibility at Israel's door—and by inference at ours." While Egypt and Syria continued to claim they had the Kremlin's backing, this backing seemed rather less than complete.

Johnson asked for a military assessment of matters. Earle Wheeler, the chairman of the Joint Chiefs of Staff, indicated that forcing passage through the Tiran Strait would present problems for the U.S. navy during the next couple of weeks. Egypt had two submarines in the area, and the nearest available American antisubmarine vessels were currently at Singapore, fourteen days away. Wheeler said that the Sixth Fleet, of course, had antisubmarine capabilities, but if Nasser was serious about closing Tiran, he wasn't likely to let U.S. antisubmarine craft through the Suez Canal. Wheeler went on to say that a war Israel started for the purpose of lifting the Egyptian blockade could quickly spread. "If the Israelis move, it might not be possible to localize a strike designed simply to open the straits." Wheeler discussed possible use by Israel of "unconventional"—that is, nuclear—weapons. The notes of this portion of the meeting remained classified a quarter century later. But the excisers spared Wheeler's firm conclusion: "The Israelis can hold their own."

Defense Secretary Robert McNamara expanded on the prospects of a wider war. McNamara predicted that the outset of the conflict would witness a struggle for air superiority. Each side would run through its supply of airplanes, or at least through the rockets and other armaments the planes required. Each would then turn to its prime supplier: Israel to the United States, Egypt and Syria to the Soviet Union. Presumably, the Israelis would shoot down more MiGs than they lost planes of their own. If the MiGs went down with pilots

[5]Rusk to Johnson, May 26, 1967, Johnson papers.

aboard, Moscow might feel obliged to send not only new planes but Soviet pilots. Soviet pilots would complicate matters in one or both of two ways. If they showed greater ability than the Arabs they replaced, they might destroy lots of Israeli planes and kill lots of Israeli pilots, evening the battle and increasing pressure on the United States to respond in kind. If they did no better than the Arabs had, they would get themselves killed, requiring Moscow to escalate or risk humiliation.

Johnson asked for opinions regarding the objectives and motives of the Egyptians and the Soviets. He wondered specifically whether Moscow was aggravating the current situation to distract the United States from the Vietnam War, then hotter than ever. Wheeler and CIA Director Richard Helms guessed not, though the two agreed that the Kremlin would take full advantage of any distraction the Middle East offered. Helms suggested that the Soviets liked the level of tension about where it was. They also seemed to like the idea of forcing a more complete association of the United States with Israel. "The Soviets would like to bring off a propaganda victory," the intelligence director said, "with them as the peacemakers and saviors of the Arabs, while we end up fully blackballed in the Arab world as Israel's supporter." Regarding Egypt, Helms estimated that Nasser had achieved his primary objective for the moment: he had adopted a hard line against Israel, thereby confirming his credentials as defender of the Arabs against the Zionist interlopers.

Lucius Battle, recently ambassador to Egypt and now assistant secretary of state for the Middle East, took issue with Helms. Battle said that until a week before, he would have agreed that Nasser chiefly sought a political triumph. But Nasser's announcement of the Aqaba blockade indicated greater military seriousness than Cairo had shown previously—and greater danger for Israel and the United States. Either Nasser had a more solid and more sweeping Soviet commitment than the administration knew, or he had gone "slightly insane." Battle elaborated: "It is most uncharacteristic for Nasser not to leave a door open behind him, and that is exactly what he appears to have done in this case." The assistant secretary pointed out the variety of problems Nasser faced—food shortages in Egypt, a fundamentally failing economy, challenges to Egypt's leadership of the Arab movement from both political radicals and religious conservatives— and suggested that Nasser might be trying to recover his position with a stunning stroke against Israel.[6]

[6]Minutes of NSC meeting, May 24, 1967, ibid.

On the other hand, it might be the Israelis who would strike first; preventing their doing so was the primary purpose of Johnson's meeting with Foreign Minister Eban. The president promised Eban that the United States would apply its "best efforts and best influence" to keep the Tiran Strait open, but he said he could do nothing until the United Nations secretary general, now investigating the affair, delivered his report. "If we move precipitously," Johnson declared, "it would only result in strengthening Nasser." The president understood that Israel expected little good to come of U Thant's actions. The United States, he said, had no illusions on the subject either. Still, the United Nations process must run its course. Afterward would be the time for other measures. "When it becomes apparent that the U.N. is ineffective, Israel and its friends, including the United States, who are willing to stand up and be counted can give specific indication of what they can do." In particular, the president mentioned an international naval force to challenge Nasser's blockade.

Johnson tried to calm Israel's fears. "Our best judgment is that no military attack on Israel is imminent," he told Eban. Moreover, U.S. intelligence analysts predicted that if Israel was attacked, the Israelis would lick their attackers. Israel could afford to wait until Thant reported to the security council. Although maintaining full mobilization was not without disadvantages, the alternatives were worse. "We know it is costly economically," Johnson said, "but it is less costly than it would be if Israel acted precipitously and if the onus for initiation of hostilities rested on Israel rather than on Nasser."

Eban probed Johnson: "I would not be wrong if I told the Prime Minister that your disposition is to make every possible effort to assure that the strait and the gulf will remain open to free and innocent passage?" Johnson replied that that was correct.

The president reiterated, "We are Israel's friend. The straits must be kept open." Yet an answer to the current problem required time. "We cannot bring about a solution the day before yesterday." He told Eban that it was "inconceivable" that Israel would decide for war while peaceful efforts to end the blockade were still under way. Very deliberately, and repeating himself for emphasis, Johnson declared, "Israel will not be alone unless it decides to go alone."[7]

---

[7]Memo of conversation, May 26, 1967, ibid.; State Department administrative history, v. 1, part 4, section H, p. 57, Johnson Library; Abba Eban, *An Autobiography* (New York, 1977), pp. 354–359.

From the United States, Eban flew back to Israel for a crucial meeting of the Israeli leadership. While awaiting the outcome of the meeting, the Johnson administration continued efforts to calm the international atmosphere. Malcolm Toon of the State Department's Soviet bureau spoke with the chargé d'affaires of Moscow's embassy, Yuri Chernyakov. Toon said the United States was engaged in a "maximum effort" to restrain the governments involved in the current dispute. He made a point of adding: "including Israel." Toon remarked that the United States was encouraged by a recent statement from Moscow calling for peaceful resolution of the Middle Eastern troubles. He said he hoped Moscow's actions mirrored its words.[8]

The meeting of the Israeli government came and went, and nothing happened. "It looks as though they have decided not to go to war at this time," Walt Rostow commented to the president on May 28.[9]

Nasser likewise indicated a desire to avoid immediate hostilities. At a news conference on the same day—a transcript of which American officials examined carefully—the Egyptian leader placed the present crisis in longer perspective. The problem involving Israel, he said, was not a matter of the Tiran Strait; the problem was the "aggression which took place and continues to take place against one of the homelands of the Arab nation in Palestine." Nasser didn't say so explicitly, but because this problem was the same one that had set Arabs and Israelis at odds for nearly twenty years, he gave the impression that its solution didn't have to come in the next few days or weeks.

Even so, Nasser was not about to fold his hand. A reporter asked him if he was taking account of possible American intervention in the Arab-Israeli dispute. "I do not take the United States into account," he replied, "because if I take the United States, the Sixth Fleet, the Seventh Fleet and the U.S. generals into account, I shall never be able to do anything or to move." Regardless of the course the Americans followed, Egypt would not retreat. "If the United States intervenes, we must defend ourselves and defend our rights."[10]

The U.S. embassy in Cairo interpreted these remarks to mean that though Nasser wouldn't back away from a military showdown with Israel, neither would he instigate one. For the time being, a bel-

---

[8]Memo of conversation, May 27, 1967, Johnson papers.

[9]Rostow to Johnson, May 28, 1967, ibid.

[10]Nasser press conference transcript, May 28, 1967, ibid.

ligerent posture appeared to suit his purposes better than actual belligerence. Nasser added to this impression on May 29 by inviting the American government to send a special representative to discuss the situation with him.[11]

Johnson quickly dispatched Robert Anderson, formerly Eisenhower's secret envoy to Nasser, to Cairo. Simultaneously, the president weighed a proposal from the State and Defense departments for opening the Tiran Strait. Rusk and McNamara offered a three-stage plan for ensuring free passage. Stage one entailed more of what the administration was doing already: working through the United Nations. While this failed, as it certainly would, the administration should prepare to move to stage two: a declaration by the major maritime nations of support for the principle of unfettered navigation of the strait and the Gulf of Aqaba. Such a declaration would convey conviction only to the extent that the administration accompanied it with arrangements for stage three: a confrontation against the Egyptians by a multinational fleet. The more nations that contributed vessels to the fleet the better. Rusk and McNamara thought the United States could depend on Britain, with Canada and the Netherlands as maybes. Beyond these three, volunteers would come harder.

The two secretaries cautioned that the military risks of blockade breaking were "not negligible." If shooting started, it might not easily stop. Nor were the political risks negligible, and, consequently, the administration should purchase insurance. "We believe that a joint congressional resolution would be politically necessary before U.S. military forces are used in any way." Despite expressions of strong support for Israel in the legislature, the administration would have to exercise care. Vietnam had lawmakers skittish about attaching American prestige to foreign causes, however worthy. Rusk and McNamara granted that "many congressional doves may be in the process of conversion to hawks"—doves on Vietnam becoming hawks on the Middle East, they meant—but they added, "The problem of 'Tonkin Gulfitis' remains serious." (Though Congress had passed the administration's Tonkin Gulf Resolution by an almost unanimous vote in 1964, many legislators were having second thoughts about this broad delegation of Vietnam War-making authority to the president.)[12]

[11]Yost to State Department, May 30, 1967, ibid.; Rostow to Johnson, May 29, 1967, ibid.

[12]Rusk and McNamara to Johnson, May 30, 1967, ibid.

Johnson agreed with McNamara and Rusk on the politics of intervention in the Middle East. The president intended to ask Congress for authority to use U.S. ships in the Middle East if the situation came to that. Meanwhile, he began checking congressional views. Congressmen Emanuel Celler and Thomas Morgan, after polling their colleagues, told Johnson that a clear majority in support of Israel existed in the House of Representatives. They said that members of this majority felt that Nasser was trying to push Israel around, and that sooner or later the United States would have to take steps to open the Gulf of Aqaba. Celler offered Johnson a strong statement backing the administration. He said he had gotten more than a hundred representatives to sign it, "without even trying." Johnson asked Celler to keep the statement handy, but not to make it public just yet.[13]

One reason for Johnson's desire to delay was that he wanted to hear what Nasser had to tell Robert Anderson. The American envoy met with the Egyptian president on June 2. Nasser said he didn't desire war. He promised that Egypt wouldn't initiate hostilities, although he conceded that Syria or radical elements among the Palestinians might. Egypt would wait until Israel moved. Yet Egypt would not allow itself to be caught unprepared, as it had been in 1956. He said he had ordered troop levels and readiness increased in Sinai in order to prevent surprise. Egypt had developed elaborate plans for "instant retaliation" in the event of Israeli attack. He was confident that Egypt's military forces could hold their own if war came.

Nasser explained Egypt's position regarding the Tiran Strait. For eight years after 1948, the strait had been closed to Israel. The channel was less than three miles wide, and therefore didn't qualify as an international waterway. The strait had only been opened by the "illegal act" of Britain, France, and Israel as part of the 1956 war. In closing the strait, Nasser said, he was simply returning to the status quo ante bellum. Besides, because the armistice agreements of 1949 and 1956 had never given way to a peace treaty, Egypt remained legally at war with Israel. As long as Israel insisted on acting like an enemy, it must expect to be treated like an enemy.

Anderson asked what Egypt required in order to make peace with Israel. Nasser replied at once: a solution to the Palestinian problem. Anderson queried whether permission for a limited number of the refugees to return, with monetary compensation for the rest, would

[13]Rostow to Johnson, June 1, 1967, with Johnson note, ibid.

suffice. Nasser said it wouldn't. Nearly all the Palestinians insisted on going home; they would continue to insist even if offered compensation.

Nasser said he wanted friendly relations with the United States. He reemphasized that he was in no sense a communist, despite Egypt's ties to the Soviet Union. He criticized American policy for being unduly influenced by the large Jewish vote in the United States.

After the meeting, Anderson cabled his impressions to Johnson. On the crucial question of Nasser's willingness to go to war, Anderson wrote: "He kept reassuring me that he was not going to start a war, but that he was not responsible for all groups, and that he would intervene in any actual conflict begun." As to whether Nasser might modify his current position, Anderson commented, "For the time being I think he will remain firm."

Anderson had stopped in Lebanon on the way to Egypt. In Beirut, he had sought out acquaintances from other countries of the region. He had discovered, significantly, that even Saudis, Kuwaitis, Lebanese, and Iraqis who opposed Nasser on most issues were now rallying to his cause. Nasser knew this, of course, and the Johnson administration must bear it in mind in formulating U.S. policy. With the backing of nearly all the Arabs, Nasser would probably resist attempts to force passage into the Gulf of Aqaba. "I believe he would regard any effort to open the Straits of Tiran as hostile," Anderson said.[14]

Anderson's message reinforced the Johnson administration's belief that Egypt wouldn't initiate an armed conflict, but it afforded little hope beyond that. Nasser's words suggested that the Egyptian president was unwilling to try to control the Syrians and the Palestinians, either of whom might happily provoke a war. Egypt would then join the fray, with the same result as if Nasser had started it.

Nonetheless, Johnson worried more about Israel than about the Arabs. On Eban's visit to Washington, the Israeli foreign minister had indicated less confidence in Israel's ability to defeat the Arabs than U.S. officials thought conditions warranted. The Joint Chiefs of Staff predicted an Israeli victory within five to seven days. If Israel struck first, the briefer prediction would hold, and Israel would suffer fewer casualties. If Egypt or Syria got in the initial blow, the war would last a few days longer and would exact from Israel a higher price. But by no means was the essential security of Israel at risk.

[14]Anderson to Johnson, June 2, 1967, ibid.

Yet the Israeli government thought so, or at least the Israelis chose to give the appearance that they did. Perhaps they were simply building a case for teaching the Arabs a lesson. Whatever the reality, Johnson felt obliged to restate his commitment to Israel's safety, in hopes that this would ease the pressure for preemption. On June 3, he wrote Eshkol congratulating the prime minister and his associates for their "resolution and calm in a situation of grave tension." Johnson affirmed two basic principles of U.S. policy pertinent to the current crisis: support for the territorial integrity and political independence of all countries of the Middle East, and support for freedom of the seas. He added explicitly that the United States judged the Aqaba Gulf to be an international waterway.

In the same letter, Johnson once more urged Eshkol to refrain from hasty action. The United States was seeking international cooperation in formulating measures to lift the blockade, the president declared. American representatives at the United Nations and in foreign capitals were working around the clock to gain this cooperation. But their efforts required time to yield results. Israel must provide the time.[15]

2. THE JUNE WAR

But Israel couldn't wait. On the morning of June 5, it attacked Egypt. The Israeli air force struck by surprise, destroying more than 300 Egyptian planes in the first three hours of the war and losing fewer than 20 of its own. Shortly thereafter, the Israelis flew against Jordan, eliminating that country's air force in minutes. Syria received similar treatment early in the afternoon. Israel's victory in the air essentially guaranteed victory on the ground. Israeli armor, supported by Israeli jets, invaded the Sinai, severing Egyptian lines and advancing rapidly toward the Suez Canal. Israeli forces occupied the West Bank and seized the Old City of Jerusalem.

Johnson learned of the outbreak of fighting at 4:30 A.M., Washington time, on June 5. He immediately wanted to know who had started it. Walt Rostow, on the other end of the telephone line, couldn't say for certain. The Israeli defense ministry was claiming that Egypt had moved first; U.S. officials in the area couldn't confirm or deny. Abba

[15]Johnson to Eshkol, June 3, 1967, ibid.

Eban repeated the cover story in a call to the State Department. The administration refused to accept the tale, believing that Nasser wasn't foolish enough to tempt fate so egregiously. Johnson's spokesman George Christian told reporters that the White House was investigating the matter.

Within hours, the Israeli story fell apart. The Israelis failed to produce evidence of an Egyptian incursion, while the wrecks of Egyptian planes caught on the ground testified convincingly against it. When Eshkol sent a message to Johnson on the afternoon of June 5, the prime minister didn't—quite—say that Israel had responded to an Egyptian attack. Yet he did claim that Israel had acted out of self-defense. "After weeks in which our peril has grown day by day, we are now engaged in repelling the aggression which Nasser has been building up against us." Reminding Johnson of the 6 million Jews killed by the Nazis, Eshkol thanked the president for the United States' support of Israel in the past, and said he looked forward to American support in the future. While he indicated that Israeli forces could handle the Arabs, he had a favor to ask the president. "I hope that everything will be done by the United States to prevent the Soviet Union from exploiting and enlarging the conflict."[16]

Such was precisely Johnson's intention. The president appreciated the diplomatic difficulties the Israelis' preemptive attack created for the United States, but he also realized that Israel's swift success at arms had averted a far more difficult scenario, one in which Israel appeared likely to *lose* the war. If the Israelis had stumbled, the administration would have been sorely tempted to go to their rescue. Since the early 1960s, Israel had become almost an ally of the United States; for an American president to acquiesce in Israel's destruction would have been unthinkable.

After the initial hours of fighting, only intervention by the Soviets could have tilted the battlefield odds against Israel. Consequently, Johnson concentrated his attention on Moscow. As soon as he got out of bed on the morning of June 5, the president sent a message to Kosygin expressing the United States' desire to see the conflict end as quickly as possible. He urged the Soviet Union to join in efforts toward this objective.

The Soviet leader replied a short while later. Kosygin concurred with Johnson's judgment that protracted hostilities would raise grave

[16]Eshkol to Johnson, June 5, 1967, ibid.

dangers. The Soviet Union would work for a truce, Kosygin said. He hoped the United States would use its influence with Israel to do likewise.

Johnson liked the idea of a truce, but the truce terms Moscow initially sought differed from those the president deemed appropriate. The Soviet delegate on the United Nations Security Council proposed a measure calling not only for the shooting to cease but for invaders—meaning the Israelis—to withdraw behind the 1956 armistice lines. The Israelis, still smashingly successful in the field, saw no reason to comply. They remembered the Suez War, following which they had succumbed to international pressure to give up territory won in fighting. They determined this time to establish and retain buffer zones around their borders. Johnson refused to override the Israelis, and he instructed Arthur Goldberg, his United Nations representative, to seek a ceasefire-in-place.

In the early phase of the war, some U.S. officials believed that the Israeli successes might open new opportunities for solving the Arab-Israeli problem once and for all. According to this line of thinking, an Israeli victory would demonstrate to the Arabs the futility of pretending that Israel could be destroyed; at the same time, the Israelis would win territory they could barter for peace treaties and recognition of Israel's right to exist.

But a comprehensive settlement proved elusive, not least because the Israelis, despite their brilliance on the battlefield, remained touchy on all matters affecting their security. Their touchiness showed plainly on the first day of the war. A spokesman for the U.S. State Department, asked to describe the Johnson administration's policy toward the conflict, said the United States was "neutral in thought, word, and deed." From the reaction that followed, one might have thought that the administration had announced it was about to start sending weapons to Egypt—except that the Egyptians complained too. The statement triggered an instant uproar among Israel's American backers, who expected far more than neutrality from Washington in what they considered a just war for Israel's existence. Regardless of which side had fired first, they contended, Egypt and Syria had provoked the conflict. In Israel's hour of trial, Washington seemed to be reneging on its oft-given promises of support. Blame for the war and pressure to relinquish territory might follow.[17]

---

[17]*American Foreign Policy: Current Documents,* 1967, p. 506 n. 67.

Johnson immediately acted to silence the howling and allay the fears. Obviously, the president couldn't declare American unneutrality, but through his many contacts with the American Jewish community he spread word that his devotion to Israel hadn't diminished. Israel could count on Lyndon Johnson, as it always had. The president had Dean Rusk announce—from the White House rather than from the State Department—a correction to the neutrality statement. Rusk told a news conference that neutrality, while narrowly accurate as a description of American nonbelligerency, didn't cover the American attitude. "Neutrality does not imply indifference," Rusk explained. Without specifying Israel by name, Rusk said the policy of the United States remained unchanged. The American government and people were as committed as ever to the search for a lasting and stable peace in the Middle East, which implied, as Washington had often declared—so often that Rusk didn't need to at this ticklish hour—Arab recognition of Israel's right to exist. "There is the position at law that we are not a belligerent," he summarized. "There is the position of deep concern, which we have as a nation and as a member of the United Nations, in peace in that area."[18]

The Arabs never accused the United States of neutrality; at first, many didn't even believe American claims of nonbelligerency. Upon the outbreak of the war, the Egyptian government charged that planes from U.S. aircraft carriers had taken part in the raids on Egyptian airfields. Cairo found it impossible to accept—or admit, anyway—that the Israelis by themselves could have delivered such a crushing blow.

But after Johnson requested that Kosygin point out to Nasser what Soviet intelligence knew—that American warplanes had been nowhere in the vicinity at the time of the attacks—the Egyptian government shifted its ground for complaint. It alleged that American support for Israel before and during the fighting rendered the United States, in effect, a belligerent. On June 6, Cairo broke diplomatic relations with Washington. Syria and Iraq soon followed suit.

The anti-American movement among the Arabs might have turned into a stampede if the Soviet Union hadn't also set itself up for Arab criticism. On June 6, Moscow altered its position on the issue of

[18]Eshkol message in Rostow to Johnson, June 6, 1967, Johnson papers; State Department *Bulletin*, June 26, 1967.

a ceasefire. Reasoning that the longer the war lasted, the more territory Egypt would lose, the Kremlin voted in favor of a United Nations resolution recommending a ceasefire-in-place. Restoring the status quo, if such ever became possible, would have to wait.

At a White House meeting the next day, the top officials of the Johnson administration examined where they stood. Dean Rusk recapitulated the events of the first forty-eight hours of the war. Rusk said that Nasser had misjudged both the military situation between the Arabs and Israel and the degree to which the Soviets would back him. As a result, he had suffered a "stunning loss." There now existed widespread disillusionment among the Arabs with the Egyptian president. Soviet prestige in the Middle East had plunged on account of Moscow's failure to follow through on earlier professions of support. Israel was riding high. The Israelis' demands would be "substantial."

Richard Helms focused on the Soviet reaction. The CIA director considered the damage to Soviet prestige almost as great as that to Nasser's. Moscow, Helms said, had badly underestimated what it was letting itself in for with Nasser and the Syrians. Its error was even greater than the error Khrushchev had made during the Cuban missile crisis.

Llewellyn Thompson, the U.S. ambassador to the Soviet Union, then in Washington for consultation, thought the Kremlin would be relatively easy to handle despite its present discomfiture. Unlike Khrushchev, the current Soviet leadership didn't enjoy gambling or confrontational diplomacy. Barring a direct Israeli threat against Cairo, the Soviets would probably cut their losses and avoid deeper involvement.

Johnson wasn't so sure. The Soviets would have a hard time walking away from their investment in Egypt and Syria, the president said. The United States must keep a close eye on the Kremlin.

Rusk thought the Israelis would present a bigger problem than the Soviets. Israeli successes, which had saved the administration from one set of problems, created another. The Arabs identified the United States with the Israeli aggressors, as the recent severing of relations indicated. The only way to salvage the situation was to keep Israel's demands within reason. This would require the greatest care. Overt and official pressure on Israel would probably fail, even if political conditions in the United States had allowed it. Instead, the administration must work from the inside, relying on its many direct and indirect connections to the Israeli government. Administration officials must make themselves "attorneys for Israel," Rusk said. Johnson agreed regarding the delicacy of the task. The administration should try to create "as few heroes and as few heels" as possible, he said. Yet matters could be far worse. "We are in as good a position as we could be, given the complexities of the situation." Significant troubles remained, though. "By the time we get through with all the festering problems, we are going to wish the war had not happened."[19]

A new and flabbergastingly unanticipated problem emerged several hours after this meeting. Out of the—literally—clear blue sky, Israeli fighter-bombers attacked the American intelligence ship *Liberty* off the Egyptian coast. The casualties numbered over two hundred; thirty-four men died. The ship barely escaped sinking. The attack almost certainly wasn't a case of mistaken identity, since the vessel was plainly marked and visibility was excellent. Israeli reconnaissance planes repeatedly flew close overhead prior to the assault.

The most probable explanation for the attack is that the Israelis didn't like the idea of Americans eavesdropping on Israeli communications, a job the *Liberty* was outfitted to do. The war against Jordan had ended on June 7, when Amman accepted the United Nations ceasefire resolution. Egypt was on the ropes and would quit on the day of the *Liberty* attack. Yet the Israelis, predictably full of themselves, had one more goal: the capture of the Golan Heights. The invasion of Syria would commence within hours. If the Americans found out about it ahead of time, they might object and try to prevent the accomplishment of what the Israeli defense ministry considered a vital task. To prevent any such complication, someone in the Israeli chain of command—a subsequent CIA report cited confidential sources naming Defense Minister Moshe Dayan—ordered the *Liberty* destroyed.[20]

The Israeli government shrewdly guessed that Washington wouldn't investigate the incident closely, at least not until too late to do anything about it. The Israelis declared the attack an error. Abba Eban sent Johnson an apology: "I am deeply mortified and grieved by the tragic accident involving the lives and safety of Americans in Middle Eastern waters." Israeli Ambassador Avraham Harman similarly

[19]Notes of NSC meeting, June 7, 1967, Johnson papers.

[20]Donald Neff, *Warriors for Jerusalem* (New York, 1984), p. 265 n.

told the president of his "heartfelt sorrow at the tragic accident to the U.S.S. *Liberty* for which my countrymen were responsible."[21]

American officials believed the "tragic accident" story as little as they had believed Israel's claim that Egypt had started the war. Clark Clifford, formerly Truman's pro-Zionist aide and now an adviser to Johnson, told the president, "It is inconceivable that it was an accident." Clifford called for an investigation that would set forth the facts and demand punishment of those Israelis responsible. Johnson was irate. "I had a firm commitment from Eshkol, and he blew it," the president said. "That old coot isn't going to pay any attention to any imperialist pressures."[22]

Johnson ordered U.S. planes to go to the area of the attack to find out what they could. To avoid alarming the Soviets, he sent Kosygin a message explaining that this deployment had the sole purpose of looking into the *Liberty* incident. The United States had no intention of intervening in the fighting. The president also told Kosygin he would appreciate the Kremlin's cooperation in passing the message to Nasser.

When the U.S. planes added little new knowledge about the *Liberty* affair, Johnson remained angry but decided to take no action against Israel. The middle of a war seemed an imprudent time for an altercation. The president agreed with Rusk's earlier comment that the only hope for restraining the Israelis—short of a politically inconceivable application of major sanctions—was to remain on friendly terms with them. Consequently, he chose to accept the Israeli government's apologies, and he ordered the incident smoothed over.

The June 9 Israeli invasion of Syria initiated the final phase of the war, and produced a final set of problems for the Johnson administration. As the invasion commenced, Arthur Goldberg was explaining to the United Nations the need for bringing the fighting to an end. Israel's attack didn't reflect favorably on the United States: either the United States lacked the will to stop the Israelis, in which case its professions of evenhandedness were a sham, or it lacked the ability, in which case it wasn't much of a superpower.

While the latest Israeli move was embarrassing, the Soviet response to that move was alarming. The Kremlin had been provoked beyond endurance by the humiliation of its allies, and now decided it

[21]Eban to Johnson, June 8, 1967; Harman to Johnson, June 8, 1967; both in Johnson papers.

[22]Notes of NSC meeting, June 9, 1967, ibid.

had to do something about this most recent outrage. On news of the Israeli invasion of Syria, the Soviets broke off diplomatic relations with Israel. Shortly afterward, Kosygin called Johnson to declare that the situation in the Middle East had reached a "very crucial moment." Kosygin warned of a "grave catastrophe" about to happen, and announced that unless the Israelis halted operations immediately, the Soviet Union would take "necessary actions, including military."[23]

Kosygin's message caught the administration by surprise. Just a day earlier, the State Department had sent a circular to all U.S. diplomatic and consular posts summarizing the administration's understanding of the situation in the Middle East. On the matter of Soviet actions and intentions, the circular explained that the Soviets calculated that any effort on their part to retrieve the Arab military situation "would carry unacceptable risk of confrontation with us." On June 8, the CIA declared flatly, "There is no danger of Soviet military intervention in the Middle East."[24]

Following Kosygin's threat, Johnson responded in two ways. He ordered the Sixth Fleet, hovering off the Syrian coast, to move closer to shore. What the fleet would do when it got there, he hadn't decided; he hoped he wouldn't have to. The point was to convince the Soviets that two could play the brinkmanship game. At the same time, Johnson told Kosygin that his administration was working on getting Israel to accept a ceasefire. An end to the fighting, he said as convincingly as he could, was imminent.

Fortunately for the United States, for the Soviet Union, for Israel, and for Syria, Johnson was right. The Israelis decided they had gained all the ground they needed, and on June 10 they signed a truce with Syria. Fighting continued for some hours afterward, but by June 11 all was still.

With the end of the war, Johnson's Middle East problems moved off the critical list to the merely serious. Until very recently, some administration officials had retained hope that the war's jolting might have shaken loose a solution to the Arab-Israeli conflict. Walt Rostow, the administration's house optimist, thought a settlement was possible, although he conceded that it would require the coincidence of a number of favorable factors. These included concessions from Israel on territory taken, an agreement among the great powers to limit

---

[23]Lyndon Baines Johnson, *The Vantage Point* (New York, 1971), p. 302.

[24]State Department to all diplomatic and consular posts, June 9, 1967; CIA to White House, June 8, 1967; Johnson papers.

arms sales to the Middle East, and a shift in the political center of gravity in the Arab world from radical leaders to moderates. It would also require—this most fundamentally—"a broad and imaginative movement by Israel on the question of the refugees."[25]

Events quickly demonstrated that none of Rostow's conditions were likely to obtain, at least not soon. Israel showed little inclination to give up much of the territory it had seized in battle—Sinai, the Gaza Strip, the West Bank, East Jerusalem and the Old City, and the Golan Heights—or to exercise imagination regarding the refugees. The Soviets, having suffered a severe diplomatic defeat, had almost no interest in collaboration with the Americans to limit arms sales to the region. A moderation of Arab politics would have to await healing of the wounds of the war.

Johnson received a firsthand report on Israel's uncompromising mood. Aide Harry McPherson, just back from Israel, explained that the Israelis were flushed with victory. "The spirit of the army, and indeed of all the people, has to be experienced to be believed," McPherson said. "The temper of the country, from high officials to people in the street, is not belligerent, but it is determined, and egos are a bit inflated—understandably. Israel has done a colossal job." The military wanted to keep all of the territory seized. Everyone wanted to keep the Old City. "Regaining the Old City is an event of unimaginable significance to the Israelis. Even the nonreligious intellectuals feel this way." McPherson sensed room for give regarding Sinai and perhaps the West Bank, among politicians if not among the generals. A demilitarized Sinai, even back in Egyptian hands, might not pose an unacceptable danger to Israel, while trying to absorb the West Bank, with its large population of Arabs, would present problems the Israeli government hadn't figured out how to solve.

But the Israeli government and people were united in opposition to a return to the prewar status quo. "There are constant references and comparisons to 1956. The Israelis do not intend to repeat the same scenario—to withdraw within their boundaries with only paper guarantees that fall apart at the touch of Arab hands." The United States might as well forget about persuading the Israelis to relinquish territory they didn't freely choose to give up. "We would have to push them back by military force, in my opinion, to accomplish a repeat of 1956." Merely cutting off U.S. aid wouldn't do it.[26]

[25]Rostow to Johnson, June 7, 1967, ibid.

[26]McPherson to Johnson, June 11, 1967, ibid.

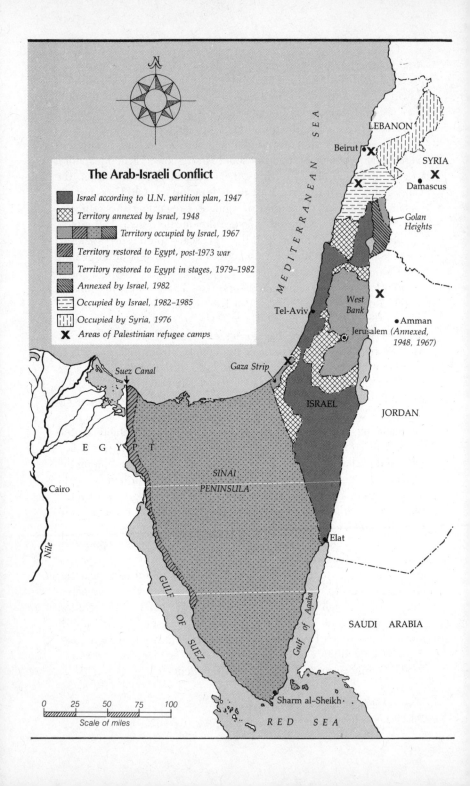

The Arab-Israeli Conflict

- Israel according to U.N. partition plan, 1947
- Territory annexed by Israel, 1948
- Territory occupied by Israel, 1967
- Territory restored to Egypt, post-1973 war
- Territory restored to Egypt in stages, 1979–1982
- Annexed by Israel, 1982
- Occupied by Israel, 1982–1985
- Occupied by Syria, 1976
- X Areas of Palestinian refugee camps

MEDITERRANEAN SEA

LEBANON

Beirut

SYRIA

Damascus

Golan
Heights

West
Bank

Tel-Aviv

Amman

Jerusalem (Annexed,
1948, 1967)

Gaza Strip

ISRAEL

JORDAN

Suez Canal

E G Y P T

SINAI
PENINSULA

Cairo

Nile

GULF OF SUEZ

Gulf of Aqaba

Elat

SAUDI   ARABIA

Sharm al-Sheikh

RED   SEA

0   25   50   75   100
Scale of miles

3. THE SPECIAL RELATIONSHIP BECOMES MORE SPECIAL

The use of U.S. military force against Israel, of course, was unthinkable, and the United States began adjusting itself to the new reality the June War (frequently called the Six-Day War) had created. Two aspects of this reality figured most prominently: the occupation by Israeli forces of territories with large Palestinian populations, namely the West Bank and Gaza; and the still-closer identification of the United States with Israel.

The occupation of the West Bank and Gaza rendered the Arab-Israeli dispute more intractable than ever. The occupation became a major issue in Israeli politics, as liberals and conservatives debated whether the territories should be annexed into a "greater Israel," whether Israelis should be allowed or even encouraged to settle there, whether Israel could long hold the territories and remain a democracy, whether the Palestinians should be expelled, given the rights of Israeli citizens, or left in limbo. Beyond the political questions, matters of finances and livelihoods arose as the West Bank and Gaza developed close connections to the Israeli economy, supplying both cheap labor and markets. Interestingly, the informal economic union that developed between Israel and the occupied territories resembled the formal economic union between Israel and the prospective Palestinian state that had been prescribed by the 1947 United Nations resolution partitioning Palestine.

The United Nations took another shot at the Arab-Israeli dispute in November 1967, when the Security Council, with U.S. approval, adopted Resolution 242. This resolution, one of the most important, if unproductive (through 1992), measures that ever gained the Security Council's assent, called for the withdrawal of Israel's armed forces "from territories occupied in the recent conflict," for "termination of all claims or states of belligerency" among area countries, and for acknowledgment by all countries of each other's "right to live in peace within secure and recognized boundaries free from threats or acts of force." Essentially, Israel should give up territories it had taken, in exchange for peace and Arab recognition of its right to exist. Yet, as in most such documents, there were devils in the details. The unqualified "territories" of the first clause were interpreted by the Arabs to mean *all* territories occupied during the war, but by the Israelis to mean *some* territories. The Israelis intended for the termination of states of belligerency and the acknowledgment of Israel's right to exist to come *before* withdrawal, but the Arabs for them to come *after*. The result was that the two sides could claim adherence to the principles of Resolution 242 while advocating conflicting policies.

If the condition of the territories constituted the chief geographic and demographic result of the June War, the closer alignment of Israel and the United States constituted its chief diplomatic and political result. The breaking of relations with Washington by Egypt and other Arab countries, combined with the Arabs' increased drift toward the Soviet Union, left the United States more reliant than ever on Israel for regional influence. At the same time, the facts that the Israelis had struck first and won so big and that they remained entrenched in the territories after the war eroded support for Israel in the United Nations and elsewhere, leaving Israel more reliant than ever on the United States. The particular solicitude of the Johnson administration for Israel's welfare reinforced the mutual reliance. Perhaps the clearest evidence of this reliance was a 1968 Israeli request to buy fifty American Phantom jets—the most potent weapons Israel had yet sought—and Johnson's approval of the sale.

It was a measure of the special relationship between the United States and Israel by the late 1960s that the presidential nominees of both major parties endorsed the Phantom deal. As a consequence, the election of Richard Nixon in November 1968 suggested that there would be no fundamental changes in U.S. policy toward the Arab-Israeli conflict. Yet, with Nixon, voters could never be sure that what they voted for was what they'd get. Nixon hinted at a "secret plan" to end the Vietnam War, but among his most significant actions as president was the widening of that war into Laos and Cambodia. Four years after his election, American bombing of North Vietnam became more intense than ever. Even more surprising was Nixon's opening to China, a country he had done much to ostracize during the 1950s.

In practice, Nixon's policy was as favorable to Israel as Johnson's, but where Johnson operated from a personal and political commitment to Israel, Nixon viewed Israel chiefly as a pro-American asset in relations with the Soviet Union. Johnson's foreign policy was principally reactive. The Democratic president dealt with crises as they occurred, in such a manner as to preserve a favorable climate for American interests; but, chiefly attuned to domestic matters, he had no grand design for international affairs. Nixon, by contrast, found domestic matters boring; his passions he saved for reshaping the world at large.

The most obvious manifestation of Nixon's penchant for world reshaping was detente, the policy of (relative) relaxation toward the communist powers. As Vietnam was demonstrating, the United States no longer possessed the ability—if it ever had—to contain communism all along the boundary between East and West. Nixon's strategy for dealing with the Soviet Union entailed enlisting other countries to aid in the containment. What made Nixon's policy different from that of his predecessors, who also had enlisted other countries—the members of NATO and the Baghdad Pact, for instance—was that Nixon went considerably farther afield in the search for collaborators against Moscow. He went all the way to Beijing, in fact, deep in the heart of the communist camp, where he embraced China's leaders and pledged a common devotion to world peace and resistance to (Soviet) aggression.

Nixon's use of the Chinese against the Soviets was an extension of what came to be called the Nixon Doctrine: a policy of looking to local proxies to guarantee security for American interests in various regions of the world. The doctrine originated as a means of getting the United States out of Vietnam; as applied to that country, it took the name "Vietnamization" and involved combining South Vietnamese manpower with American firepower and dollar-power against the North Vietnamese.

In the Middle East, the Nixon Doctrine produced a deepened U.S. commitment to Iran and to Israel. The commitment to Iran followed a 1968 announcement by the British government that Britain intended to drop its military commitments "east of Suez"—primarily in the Persian Gulf region. The overextension of U.S. forces in Vietnam precluded an American filling of this latest British-induced vacuum; instead, the Nixon administration decided to build up Iran as a pro-Western bulwark in the area. From the 1953 anti-Mossadeq coup until the end of the 1960s, American arms had flowed to Iran at a steady but not especially rapid rate. Beginning in the early 1970s, though, American weapons deliveries increased dramatically. To emphasize the new strategy, Nixon traveled to Tehran in May 1972 and promised the shah that Iran could purchase whatever American weapons it desired, in whatever amounts it desired. The shah took up the offer, and by the end of the decade Iran boasted one of the most formidable military establishments in the world.

The Nixon administration's strengthened commitment to Israel occurred in an analogous fashion. For most of Israel's existence, U.S. planners had viewed Israel as a drain on the United States' diplomatic, and therefore strategic, resources. The career officers in the State Department had judged Israel an unnecessary drain; thus their recommendations that the United States distance itself from Israel. The Truman White House and its Democratic successors had judged Israel a necessary drain; thus their pro-Israel policies. But both sides recognized that support for Israel would cost the United States some significant price among Arabs and Muslims. The Nixon administration was the first to develop a philosophy of Israel as a strategic *asset*—although skeptics in the State Department still harbored doubts.

In the first years after its founding, Israel had demonstrated no particular anticommunist preferences. Its domestic policies reflected a strong socialistic current, and in seeking weapons and other means of national support, it searched wherever such items might be found. But with the rise of radical regimes in Egypt, Iraq, and Syria, and as those regimes turned to the Soviet Union for arms and political support, Israel's foreign policies developed distinctly antiradical overtones. In looking after its own interests, Israel came to serve as an agent of relative conservatism in the Middle East, and, indirectly, as an agent of American influence.

This conjunction of American and Israeli security interests showed most plainly in September 1970, when radicals threatened the monarchy of King Hussein in Jordan. At this time, a number of groups claimed to represent the cause of Palestinian nationalism. The oldest and largest, Fatah, was composed chiefly of Sunni Muslims, and had been around for a decade. The smaller Popular Front for the Liberation of Palestine (PFLP) had been founded in 1967 by George Habash, a Christian, and others dissatisfied with Fatah. Two years later, some disgruntled members of the PFLP followed Nayif Hawatmah, also a Christian, in a walkout; the breakaway faction formed the Popular Democratic Front for the Liberation of Palestine (PDFLP). An umbrella group that would eventually become a shadow government for the Palestinians, the Palestine Liberation Organization (PLO), dated from 1964. In 1969, Yasir Arafat, a leader of Fatah, was elected to head the PLO.

King Hussein had long eyed the Palestinian radicals with suspicion, the more so as they grew increasingly organized and militant.

Hussein liked the idea of controlling the West Bank, which the Palestinians considered the nucleus of the Palestinian homeland. After the Israelis occupied the West Bank in the June War, the Palestinians moved their bases of operations into Jordan proper, which only increased Hussein's discomfort. For their part, many of the Palestinians despised Hussein as a Western lackey; they agitated for his overthrow. Sporadic violence between Palestinian guerrillas and Jordanian troops punctuated the spring and summer of 1970, until in September, after a spectacular multiple-airplane hijacking by the PFLP, a fed-up Hussein ordered his army to destroy the guerrillas' bases. The confrontation escalated quickly when Syria threw its support to the Palestinians. On September 18, Syrian tanks crossed the border into Jordan.

The Nixon administration interpreted the Syrian action, at least partly, as an exercise in Soviet adventurism. "We could not allow Hussein to be overthrown by a Soviet-inspired insurrection," Nixon wrote in his memoirs. The president contemplated the use of U.S. troops to prevent Hussein's fall, but decided against it. Just months earlier, he had ordered the invasion of Cambodia, which had produced an enormous outcry in the United States and abroad; the moment seemed inauspicious for sending American soldiers into any other foreign countries unless absolutely necessary.[27]

Yet intervention by Israel was hardly out of the question. On the contrary, Israel had every reason to try to thwart the overthrow of the moderate Hussein by radicals committed to the destruction of Israel as soon as humanly possible.

The coincidence of interests—the American interest in blocking the expansion of Soviet influence in the Middle East, the Israeli interest in preventing the rise of a radical regime in Jordan—led to a coordinated policy. Washington sent the Sixth Fleet toward Syria, otherwise upgraded the state of U.S. military readiness in the area, and warned Moscow against fanning flames in a region already on the verge of explosion. The Israelis, following consultation with American officials, mobilized for war.

The combined American-Israeli show of force, together with spirited fighting on the part of Hussein's army, and some differences of opinion in Damascus, persuaded the Syrians to withdraw from Jordan. The exercise convinced the Nixon administration of Israel's value as a strategic partner in preserving a pro-Western status quo in the

[27]Richard M. Nixon, *Memoirs* (New York, 1978), p. 483.

Middle East. As he had done with Iran, Nixon rewarded Israeli cooperation by large increases in American weapons and aid. In the middle of the Jordanian crisis, the president informed Golda Meir, now
prime minister, that a shipment of Phantom jets stuck in the bureaucracy would be released and that Israel would receive $500 million in
new American aid. By the last year of his first term, Nixon had authorized more assistance to Israel than all previous American presidents
combined.

4. THE ARABS' REVENGE: THE OCTOBER WAR

As indicated by the fighting in Jordan, which concluded with the retreat of most of the Palestinian guerrillas to Lebanon (and produced
more than 10,000 casualties), the end of the June War had hardly
ended the hostilities between Israel and the Arabs. In 1969, Egypt
denounced the 1967 ceasefire and commenced what Nasser called a
"war of attrition" against Israel along the Suez Canal and in the Sinai.
The Israelis responded with air strikes against both military and civilian targets along the canal and far into the rest of Egypt. The United
States tried to stem the violence by sponsoring a series of diplomatic
initiatives, informally named for Nixon's first secretary of state,
William Rogers. The Rogers plans produced a halt in the shooting
and bombing, but nothing in the way of a permanent resolution of the
Arab-Israeli dispute.

Other events in the region promised to produce motion on the
Arab-Israeli issue, although which direction the motion would take
remained anybody's guess. In 1969, a military coup toppled the
Libyan government of King Idris, replacing the pro-American
monarch with Colonel Muammar al-Qaddafi. Qaddafi pledged opposition to communism, at least in Libya, but he had no patience with
the American backers of the Zionists. In 1969, Qaddafi kicked the
American Peace Corps out of Libya. In 1970, he ejected U.S. forces
from Wheelus air base. In 1973, he nationalized American oil properties in Libya.

More important, though not immediately, was the death of Nasser
in September 1970, and the accession of Anwar el-Sadat to the
Egyptian presidency. Sadat was something of a dark horse; though he
had conspired with Nasser in the 1952 plot that overthrew Farouk, he

wasn't one of Nasser's current intimates. Cairo's insiders couldn't decide among themselves who should follow the great man of Arab nationalism, so they chose Sadat as an interim place-filler. He proved more clever than they, however, and when they tried to elbow him aside, he clapped them in jail.

But no Egyptian leader who aspired to stay in power long, certainly no successor to Nasser, could forget the struggle against Israel. Three years after the June War, the Israelis still occupied thousands of square miles of Egyptian territory in the Sinai. Initially Sadat tried to secure the return of the Sinai by diplomatic means. He sought improved relations with Washington, in the well-founded belief that if anyone could pressure the Israelis to withdraw, it was the Americans. To this end, and also because the Soviets made rude guests, he evicted some 15,000 Soviet military advisers in July 1972.

Yet after their smashing 1967 victory, the Israelis didn't feel like pulling back without guarantees more ironclad than Sadat thought he could give. And with the 1972 American election campaign in full swing, Nixon didn't have much desire to lean on the Israelis, at the risk of upsetting pro-Israel American voters.

Sadat subsequently decided to argue his case on the ground. During the summer of 1973, Egyptian strategists met with their counterparts in Syria, whose government wanted to regain the Golan Heights. Following an elaborate disinformation campaign that disguised war mobilization as military maneuvers, Egyptian artillery and armor attacked Israeli positions along the Suez Canal, while Syrian tanks and infantry stormed the Golan Heights.

The October War (also called the Yom Kippur War, because it commenced on the Jewish holy day) caught both the Israelis and the Americans looking the wrong way. (The Israelis evidently discovered that an attack was imminent several hours before it occurred, but this was too late to do much about it.) The Israelis, overconfident after the 1967 war, had a hard time believing that the Arabs would start a war they almost surely would lose. On the day before the war began, the Israeli government relayed to Washington its evaluation of the current situation. "Our assessment is that the alert measures being taken by Egypt and Syria are in part connected with maneuvers (as regards Egypt) and in part due to fears of offensive actions by Israel," the Israeli report said. "We consider the opening of military operations against Israel by the two armies as of low probability."

Washington was confident of the efficiency of Israeli intelligence and figured that if the Israelis weren't worried, the United States needn't worry either. A CIA memo to the White House reflected the Israeli view and added some opinions of the agency's own. The memo declared that although Egypt and Syria, on one hand, and Israel, on the other, were getting nervous about each other, their nervousness hadn't reached the point of genuine alarm. "The military preparations that have occurred," the intelligence agency concluded, "do not indicate that any party intends to initiate hostilities."[28]

Beyond the Israelis' complacency, the Nixon administration had an additional reason for looking the wrong way. During the period of the October War, the Watergate posse was closing in on the president. The fighting in the Middle East began while Nixon was hiding out in Florida, fending off efforts by the Watergate special prosecutor to secure the audio tapes that had become the centerpiece of the case against the president. Two weeks into the war, Nixon demanded the special prosecutor's resignation, triggering the quitting-and-firing wave at the Justice Department known as the "Saturday night massacre." Meanwhile, Nixon's vice president, Spiro Agnew, was one step ahead of the law on other charges, and losing ground. Agnew quit four days after the war started, pleading no contest to charges of influence peddling while governor of Maryland.

Just as the war commenced with a surprise, its first days introduced a new element into U.S. decision making for the Middle East. Until this point, the saving grace of Zionist assertiveness—from the original fight for Israel, through the 1967 war—had been the Zionists' ability to look after themselves on the battlefield. As a consequence of this ability, Washington had never had to confront the ultimate question of whether it should stand by and see Israel lose a war or send U.S. troops to shoot Arabs. During the initial phase of the October War, the Israelis suffered unexpected reverses. In the Golan Heights, Syrian armor smashed Israeli defenses, and Syrian paratroops captured key Israeli positions on Mount Hermon. After twenty-four hours of fighting, the Syrians appeared poised to rush down into Israel itself. In the south, Egyptian forces leapfrogged the Suez Canal, burst through Israeli lines, and advanced into the Sinai.

To be sure, the Syrians and Egyptians never got close to threatening the national existence of Israel, and the Israelis regrouped and counterattacked. But the October War shattered the record of Israeli

[28]Henry A. Kissinger, *Years of Upheaval* (Boston, 1982), pp. 465–466.

invincibility. In parrying the initial Arab thrusts, Israel lost more than 100 planes and 500 tanks, and 500 soldiers died. Although such numbers were not large, as battlefield statistics go, for a small country like Israel they hurt tremendously. Before the 1973 war, Washington could tell the Israelis they had nothing militarily to worry about from the Arabs—that they could absorb a first blow without serious damage. After 1973, such assurances carried much less persuasiveness than before.

Notwithstanding the early losses, the old pattern of Israeli dominance reasserted itself. Israeli forces split the Egyptians in the Sinai, driving to the Suez Canal and continuing twenty-five miles onto the western side. Israeli armor and infantry regained their footing on the Golan Heights and threw the Syrians back down the eastern slope of the mountains.

Yet Israeli supplies were running thin, and the government of Prime Minister Meir called desperately for U.S. help. Fortunately for Israel, the fact that Israel this time had *not* fired the opening shot made it easier for Washington to respond favorably than would otherwise have been the case. Actually, it took Washington some time to convince itself that the Israelis really hadn't fired first. The initial reports from the front were confusing, as such reports usually are, and American leaders recalled how the Israelis had lied about the beginning of the 1967 war. Hours after the beginning of the October War, officials of the State and Defense departments, the National Security Council, the CIA, and the Joint Chiefs of Staff met to consider the situation. The consensus was that the Israelis had probably moved first. But the true nature of the situation soon came out, and, politically if not militarily, it worked to Israel's advantage. In this instance, Israel was the aggrieved party, the victim of aggression.

Or at least this was how things seemed to most Americans. To the Arabs and many others, who saw Egypt and Syria as merely trying to recapture Egyptian and Syrian territory seized by force in the previous war, the aggressor-aggressee question was more complicated.

The Nixon administration was willing enough to give the Israelis what they wanted. "We will almost certainly approve tomorrow the military equipment within reason that you may need," Secretary of State Henry Kissinger informed the Israeli embassy on the first day of the fighting. "Especially if the Soviets line up with the Arabs, then we will certainly do it."[29]

[29]Ibid., p. 479.

But the administration preferred to keep the Israelis a little off balance. It didn't want them to defeat the Arabs as decisively as they had in 1967; if they did so, they would probably ruin for a generation any chance for peace. "We want the fighting to end on a basis where we can build a lasting peace," Nixon said. A military draw offered the best hope for such a basis. The president described his strategy later: "I believed that only a battlefield stalemate would provide the foundation in which fruitful negotiations might begin. Any equilibrium, even if only an equilibrium of mutual exhaustion, would make it easier to reach an enforceable settlement."[30]

To foster a stalemate, rather than an Israeli triumph, as well as to avoid alienating the Arabs more than necessary, the Nixon administration doled out arms to Israel at a carefully controlled pace. At first, the administration required the Israelis to pick up the weapons themselves, from U.S. military bases, in Israeli planes that had had their Israeli markings painted over. As the war dragged on, and as the Soviets began mounting a major resupply effort of their own to the Arabs, the administration authorized the U.S. air force to deliver the goods in American planes. By early in the second week of the war, the American airlift was landing 1000 tons of supplies a day in Israel. Included in the reinforcement operation was a new batch of American Skyhawk and Phantom fighter-bombers.

The operation succeeded too well. Confident that they wouldn't run out of bullets, the Israelis drove farther into Syria, until they approached the outskirts of Damascus. In the south, they threatened to encircle the Egyptian Third Army and destroy it entirely.

At this point, the Nixon administration decided to push for a ceasefire. Henry Kissinger flew to Moscow—a less dramatic trip now than in predetente days—where he and the Soviet leadership agreed on the advisability of terminating the current war before either superpower's client got humiliated.

Israel didn't much like the idea of a ceasefire; countries that are suddenly winning wars that began badly usually don't. In particular, the Israelis wanted to teach the Arabs not to pick any future fights.

To convince the Israelis, Kissinger paid them a visit. He found them surprisingly unsure of their situation, given the military victories they were in the process of achieving. "Deep down," Kissinger wrote afterward, "the Israelis knew that while they had won the last

---

[30]William B. Quandt, *Decade of Decisions* (Berkeley, 1977), p. 187 n.; Nixon, op. cit., p. 921.

battle, they had lost the aura of invincibility. The Arab armies were not destroyed. The Arab nations had not won, but no longer need they quail before Israeli might. Israel, after barely escaping disaster, had prevailed militarily; it ended up with more Arab territory captured than lost. But it was entering an uncertain and lonely future, dependent on a shrinking circle of friends." Prime Minister Meir suspected that the Americans and the Soviets had reached an agreement to impose the pre-1967 borders on Israel. Was this so? she demanded. Kissinger denied it. Meir wanted to know whether the superpowers intended to impose any other borders. Kissinger denied this as well. But her questions confirmed his estimate of Israel's unease. "As she explored all possible permutations of American duplicity, she exemplified the enormous insecurity inherent in Israel's geographic and demographic position and its total dependence on the United States."[31]

It was this dependence that caused the Israelis to accede to the Nixon administration's insistence on a ceasefire. When Kissinger allowed that Washington wouldn't complain about a little "slippage" in Israel's adherence to the deadline of the proposed ceasefire, to let the Israeli forces tidy up some loose ends, the Israeli government accepted the proposal. Egypt had done so shortly before.[32]

Almost immediately, the ceasefire started fraying. The Israelis continued their tidying up for more than the few hours Kissinger thought he had granted them; Egyptian artillery bombarded Israeli positions; each side blamed the other for breaking the truce first; and the war was under way once more.

Things got particularly tense when Moscow, acting on a request by Egypt's Sadat, suggested a Soviet-American peacekeeping force. Soviet leader Leonid Brezhnev said he hoped the United States would agree to the suggestion; if it didn't, the Soviet Union would have to move on its own. "I will say it straight," Brezhnev told Nixon, "that if you find it impossible to act with us in this matter, we should be faced with the necessity urgently to consider the question of taking appropriate steps unilaterally. We cannot allow arbitrariness on the part of Israel." To underline Soviet concern, the Kremlin ordered Soviet ships in the Mediterranean to prepare for action, and placed several airborne divisions on alert.[33]

[31]Kissinger, op. cit., pp. 561–564.

[32]Ibid., p. 569.

[33]Ibid., p. 583.

The Nixon administration rejected the idea of Soviet troops in the Middle East. As had been the case since 1945, keeping the Soviets out of the area remained a principal goal of U.S. policy. In the present instance, the consequences of the introduction of Soviet forces, even as peacekeepers, could be imagined. If they interposed themselves between the Israelis and Egyptians, the Israelis might fire on them, accidentally or on purpose. If that happened, the Soviets might retaliate, and perhaps escalate. The United States would be obliged to determine whether to counter-intervene. If it did, it risked a major blowup with the Soviets. If it didn't, it risked letting the Kremlin get away with intimidating its protege Israel. In the aftermath of the U.S. pullout from Vietnam, such intimidation could have especially harmful repercussions on American credibility worldwide.

Nixon's capacity to concentrate on the Middle East suffered at this time from concurrent impeachment hearings in the House of Representatives; but even so, he responded vigorously. The president went Brezhnev one better in the bluff-and-bluster game: he placed conventional and nuclear U.S. forces around the world on alert. He wrote Brezhnev saying that the United States would view unilateral Soviet action as a matter "of the gravest concern, involving incalulable consequences."[34]

Skeptics on the subject of Nixon, their ranks by this time including nearly all non-family-members, thought the president might be overreacting for domestic political effect. He seemed to be making the point that, in a moment of world crisis, impeachment wasn't a good idea. But regardless of its impact on his domestic predicament—none that lasted—the highly visible scurrying around on U.S. military bases across the globe persuaded the Kremlin to drop whatever notions it had of landing troops in the Middle East.

Meanwhile, the administration warned the Israelis to quit while they were ahead. The Israelis resisted briefly, hoping to place Egypt's Third Army entirely at their mercy. But, facing the possibility of a cutoff of U.S. aid, they agreed to stop shooting. On October 27, the 1973 war ended.

       ✿   ✿   ✿

The June War of 1967 literally changed the map of the Middle East, leaving Israel in control of sizable portions of its neighbors' territory. The October War of 1973 indicated that changing the map back to its previous condition would be a long and arduous process, at best. Both wars furthered the identification of the United States with Israel, as did the Nixon administration's decision to treat Israel as a strategic asset in the contest with the Soviet Union. This closer identification appeared—for the short term, at least—to work to the United States' advantage. In the case of the Jordanian crisis of 1970, for example, Israel helped King Hussein defeat the Soviet-backed Syrians and the radical Palestinians, thereby strengthening the status quo in the Middle East.

But the intimate American-Israeli relationship also entailed risks, as demonstrated by the fact that both the June War and the October War brought the United States and the Soviet Union to the point of rocket-rattling at each other. In neither instance did Washington or Moscow really intend to start shooting, but accidents happen, and when they involve the superpowers, they can be very frightening.

The fright factor in the Middle East was increasing with each war. The Palestine War of 1948–49 had been a merely local affair, with largely local dangers and repercussions. The fighting in the Suez War of 1956 included two outside middleweights—Britain and France—whose participation raised the stakes. The June War of 1967 engaged the heavyweights—the United States and the Soviet Union—but only marginally. The October War of 1973 saw the superpowers frantically airlifting large quantities of weapons to their proxies and threatening each other more directly than before.

The trend was not encouraging. American officials soon set to work trying to reverse it.

Chapter 5

Over a Barrel: 1973–1980

1. THE NEW WEAPON

An unspoken concern of the Nixon administration during the early part of the October War was that the Israelis, frightened at the setbacks they were suffering, might feel obliged to go nuclear. Although the Israeli government steadfastly refused to confirm that Israel had developed nuclear weapons, many observers believed it had. Few doubted that if Israel felt its security seriously threatened, it would use everything it had against its attackers. Luckily for all concerned, Israel never felt sufficiently threatened to demonstrate that it really did have the big bombs.

In fact, the unleashing of a new and powerful weapon in Middle Eastern affairs fell to the Arabs. During the second week of the war, following the commencement of the American resupply of Israel's arms, the Arab members of the Organization of Petroleum Exporting Countries announced their intention to cut oil production 5 percent per month until the Israelis withdrew from the territories occupied in the 1967 war and the rights of Palestinians were restored. A few days later, when Nixon asked Congress for more than $2 billion to pay for the weapons and equipment going to Israel, the Arab OPEC members proclaimed a complete embargo of oil to the United States.

Since the late 1940s, American leaders had lain awake nights fretting that someone might shut off the Middle Eastern oil spigot. For most of the postwar period, American concern had centered on the vulnerability of the United States' allies to an oil shortfall. The Europeans and Japan possessed next to no petroleum of their own. (None that they could produce at reasonable cost, anyway—the British and

Norwegian North Sea fields wouldn't pay their way until after the large price rises of the post-October War period.) If the oil stopped flowing in, the economies of the allies would seize up. Under such circumstances, holding the alliance together might become extremely difficult.

As for the United States itself, imported oil amounted to a relatively small portion of the energy picture through the mid-1950s. In 1954, imports totaled less than one-sixth of domestic production; in 1957, they came to slightly less than one-fifth, where they remained for a decade. Yet even this modest rise in imports worried American domestic producers, who lobbied for import quotas. (Companies with major operations overseas viewed the rise in imports with greater equanimity.) The domestic producers' efforts paid off: in March 1959, Eisenhower announced a schedule of quotas designed to curtail imports. The chief ostensible aim of the quotas was the enhancement of American security against the threat of dependence on foreign sources; the most obvious result was an artificial inflation of the price of the oil the domestic producers pumped.

The quota system, which lasted until the early 1970s, witnessed an increase in domestic production, but it couldn't deal with the enormous expansion of American demand for petroleum. By 1972, American demand had tripled from that of the early postwar period to a level of more than 16 million barrels per day. The principal cause of the boom in demand for oil was the sustained growth of the American economy, especially that portion relating to the automobile industry. By 1972, Americans drove nearly 120 million cars and trucks, and they drove them millions of miles farther than at any previous period in their history—many of those miles on the new and growing interstate highway system. Because gasoline and diesel fuel were relatively cheap, fuel efficiency hardly existed as a concept of motor-vehicle design.

Equally significant for the petroleum politics of the 1970s, energy consumption in Western Europe and Japan expanded even faster than in the United States. The Europeans switched from economies based on coal to economies fired by oil; Japan's economy simply grew at an astonishing rate.

The consequence was that by the early 1970s world petroleum production barely managed to stay ahead of consumption. American producers were stretched to their limit, pumping at nearly full capacity. In March 1971, the Texas Railroad Commission, the body that for decades had set production quotas for Texas oil fields, and thereby indirectly set prices for American oil generally, authorized production at 100 percent of capacity for the first time since World War II. The Nixon administration responded to the pressure on supplies by relaxing, and then abolishing, the import quotas. By 1973, Americans were importing 6 million barrels per day, or more than one-third of total consumption.

The United States' unaccustomed dependence on imported oil rendered it especially susceptible to the manipulation of oil exports by countries that had lots of oil to sell. Of such countries, by far the most important were in the Middle East, and the most important of the Middle Eastern oil exporters was Saudi Arabia. What gave the Saudis, who controlled one-fifth of world oil exports, and to a lesser extent the other Middle Eastern producers, such leverage against the oil-consuming countries was that they could fairly easily adjust their production to suit their political or economic tastes. If they wanted to expand output, they could do so; if they chose to leave the oil in the ground, they could do that almost as easily.

This flexibility in production was what had led to the birth of OPEC in the first place: producers hoped to curtail output and thereby raise prices. Yet from its founding in 1960 until the early 1970s, efforts by the cartel to increase members' income had usually gotten tangled up in the slack in the world oil market. If OPEC trimmed production, non-OPEC countries such as the United States could boost production, negating the upward pressure on prices. So toothless was the cartel during this early phase that the producing countries had to negotiate, as more or less equal business partners, with the companies that purchased their oil. Dictating terms remained beyond OPEC's reach.

As the oil market stretched tight in the early 1970s, however, OPEC came into its own. Prices edged up during the first years of the decade, and when OPEC members gathered in Vienna in the autumn of 1973, they expected to push prices higher still. The fortuitous outbreak of the October War, just as the Vienna meeting commenced, intensified the upward pressure on prices all the more. It also added a political dimension to the negotiations, at least for the Arab members of OPEC, who responded to the U.S. resupply of Israel with the progressive cutbacks in production and the anti-American embargo.

Between the tight supply situation, the shock of another Middle Eastern war (which raised insurance rates and other transportation costs, and potentially threatened the oil fields with destruction), and the politically induced curtailment of output, petroleum prices went through the roof. An oil company executive, confronting the specter of a winter of short supplies, described the atmosphere that drove his firm to bid prices up: "We weren't bidding just for oil. We were bidding for our life." The Arab OPEC members announced a 70 percent increase in the posted price of their oil, to just over $5 per barrel. The sensitive spot market, where buyers scrambled for oil to top off tanks, showed still greater jumps. In November, nervous buyers signed short-term contracts for oil at $16 and $17 per barrel. One Japanese firm went as high as $22.[1]

The price rises and supply shortfalls immediately manifested themselves in the United States, most conspicuously at gas stations around the country. The price of a gallon of gas shot up, reflecting both the increase in petroleum prices already experienced by refiners and distributors and the further increases they anticipated. Worse than the ballooning of prices was the widespread unavailability of gasoline at any price. Suppliers rationed what they had among the stations they dealt with; when the stations ran out, their operators shut off the pumps and went home. Drivers, seeing some gas stations closed at midday, joined the long lines at those still open, even when they didn't really need the gas. Such preemptive purchasing exacerbated the shortages, blistering tempers in the process, and souring the national mood.

Had Americans maintained their composure, they could have ridden out the oil embargo with minor discomfort. World oil supplies fell less than 10 percent in the wake of the October War, as Iran and other non-Arab producers boosted output (and raked in windfall profits). But so central had oil become to the economic well-being of the industrialized nations that the slightest hint of a disruption in supplies could trigger a panic.

It could also contribute to a broader rise in the prices of goods throughout the industrialized world. Modern economies run on energy, and when the price of a principal source of energy goes up, the price of nearly everything else goes up too. For years afterward, economists would debate the relative contribution of the leap in oil prices to the sharp increase in inflation in the United States and elsewhere

[1] Daniel Yergin, *The Prize: The Epic Quest for Oil, Money, and Power* (New York, 1991), p. 615.

during the latter half of the 1970s. (Government deficits and easy-money policies were also prime suspects in the United States.) But no one denied that the rising cost of oil contributed significantly. And when people spent more money on oil, they had less to spend on other items. (Oil prices rose much faster than wages and most other prices.) The result was that factories and businesses of all kinds laid off workers. Interest rates climbed as depositors demanded an inflation hedge; high interest rates crimped the automobile and construction industries and generally discouraged investment. By the end of the decade, the United States was suffering from an unprecedented combination of inflation and economic stagnation, summarized in the newly coined term "stagflation."

Yet for all the difficulties it caused Americans, the oil embargo had relatively little effect on the United States' Middle East policy. To some extent, in fact, the embargo backfired. Americans were already disposed to view Israel as the gutsy underdog, surrounded by greater numbers of hostile forces—and, in the most recent case, the victim of a sneak attack, on the holiest of Jewish holidays. They tended to view the Arab embargo as blackmail, which of course it was. While U.S. leaders worked harder than ever for a settlement of the problems that underlay the Arab-Israeli dispute, and the American public generally applauded these efforts, there was no massive defection from support for Israel. Indeed, the connection between the United States and Israel grew even stronger during the several years after the October War.

2. BY THE TURKISH SWORD

The tightening of the Washington-Tel Aviv connection (the Israelis would have made it a Washington-Jerusalem connection, but the U.S. government refused to accept the legitimacy of Israel's switch of capitals to the older city after the June War) would take its most conspicuous form in the 1978 Camp David accords. Before then, though, American leaders had to deal with a crisis unrelated to the Arab-Israeli struggle. In the summer of 1974, the long-running troubles on Cyprus flared anew, after nearly ten years of comparative calm on the island. The Greek Cypriots and Turkish Cypriots had tired of shooting at each other after the close brush with war in 1964, and had mostly stopped. A military coup in Athens in 1967 momentarily raised the level of tension back to 1964 levels, as the Turks, fearing that the Greek colonels would seek a military solution to the Cyprus problem, prepared to preempt. Johnson sent his favorite fixer, Cyrus Vance, to Ankara to tell the Turks they really didn't have anything to worry about, and then to Athens to make sure he wasn't spreading untruths. Vance accomplished the feat, largely because the colonels really did *not* want to take over Cyprus at this point. After several days of bated breath in the interested capitals and on the ground in Cyprus, the tension meters in the area fell to their normal background level.

For the next seven years, Americans worried more about Greece than about Turkey or Cyprus. The regime of the Greek colonels was brutal, even by the thuggish standards applied to military juntas, and though Washington accepted the favors the colonels offered—bases for U.S. ships, for instance—American officials had to hold their noses and fend off probing questions from human rights advocates in Congress and the media.

While the colonels were tough, they weren't very prudent, at least on the evidence of the summer of 1974. For reasons not obvious, even to their diminishing number of defenders, the colonels devised a plot to assassinate Cyprus's president-archbishop Makarios and re-place him with a figure more amenable to persuasion toward *enosis* or a variant thereof. Makarios sensed that he was about to be hit—in-creased Greek-sponsored terrorist activity helped give the plot away—and he loudly proclaimed the fact to the world, hoping there-by to avert the blow. "I have more than once so far felt," he declared melodramatically, "and in some cases I have touched, a hand invisibly extending from Athens and seeking to liquidate my human exis-tence."[2]

Makarios's warning failed, and on July 15 disaffected troops of the Greek-Cypriot national guard began shelling the presidential palace. Makarios narrowly escaped with his life. Shortly thereafter, the rebels, acting in conjunction with the junta in Athens, announced the instal-lation of Nikos Sampson as president in Makarios's place.

In Ankara, the Turks could hardly believe the colonels' foolishness and their own good luck. By overthrowing Makarios, the Athens junta had provided Turkey with the pretext it had been seeking since at least 1964, to invade Cyprus and take over the northern portion of the island. Until now, whenever Ankara contemplated such a move, it had

[2]Christopher Hitchens, *Cyprus* (London, 1984), p. 81.

to factor in the diplomatic costs of being seen as subverting the sovereignty and independence of Cyprus. By their anti-Makarios blunder, the Greek colonels had brought on themselves the onus of subversion. It was doubtless with self-satisfied glee—and confidence that the demand wouldn't be met—that Ankara demanded the restoration of Makarios and legitimate government in Cyprus. Otherwise, Turkey would be forced to intervene.

As had happened in 1964 and again in 1967, Washington responded to the threat of Turkish invasion by mobilizing the bureaucracy. Joseph Sisco, who occupied George Ball's old post as undersecretary of state for political affairs, jetted off to Ankara to determine whether the Turks could be dissuaded from moving militarily.

Sisco discovered that they couldn't be, at least not by means within the reasonable reach of the Nixon administration. In July 1974, the administration's reach was shorter than ever. The president had his back to the Watergate wall; he had holed up at his house in San Clemente, California, where he had all he could do to stay abreast of events in Washington, let alone Turkey. Under the circumstances, Nixon was in no position to hurl Johnson-like thunderbolts at the Turkish government. Besides, any American thunderbolts might well have bounced off. The Turks were fed up with the United States' insistence on restraint. As the Turkish prime minister, Bulent Ecevit, told Sisco, "The United States and Turkey both have made mistakes—the United States by preventing Turkish military action, and Turkey by accepting. We should not make the same mistakes again." Ecevit added, "We have done it your way for ten years, and now we are going to do it our way."[3]

As good as his word, Ecevit gave the order to invade. Within a few days, Turkish forces occupied the northern part of Cyprus—roughly the part of the island they would have received under the 1964 Acheson plan.

With this backfiring of its scheme to settle the Cyprus dispute, the already-tottering junta in Athens collapsed, making the job of the Turks considerably easier than it might have been. The colonels gave way to civilian leaders, a development that lessened the pain for Greeks most of seeing Cyprus partitioned by the Turkish military.

Without congratulating the Turks on a job well done, the Nixon administration—which at this time, regarding foreign affairs, essen-

---

[3]Laurence Stern, *The Wrong Horse* (New York, 1977), pp. 119–120.

tially meant Henry Kissinger—indicated its satisfaction at what seemed a more or less definitive solution to the Cyprus problem. From the distance of Washington, anything relatively permanent looked better than what had obtained during the years since Cypriot independence. Turkish Cypriots would be safe under Turkish protection. Greek Cypriots could go about their business in what was left of their country, without the distraction of civil war. Turkey had what it had long wanted. Greece would learn to live with the situation. For such an outcome, the abrogation of Cyprus's sovereignty seemed a modest price to pay.

Not all Americans agreed with Kissinger's calculations. Greek-Americans and others dismayed at the administration's acquiescence in Turkey's action demanded at least a cutoff of U.S. military aid to Ankara. Kissinger tried unsuccessfully to block the blockade, on the grounds that American aid provided needed leverage to keep Turkey from going even further than it had gone. As he muttered after he failed, "A freewheeling Congress destroyed the equilibrium between the parties we had precariously maintained; it legislated a heavy-handed arms embargo against Turkey that destroyed all possibility of American mediation."[4]

Notwithstanding Congress's belated indication of American displeasure, the deed was done. Negotiations at Geneva failed to reverse the partition of Cyprus, which became a fact of international life during subsequent years. In keeping with the longstanding U.S. approach to Cyprus, that country's visibility in American foreign policy lessened as its volatility in regional affairs diminished.

3. PERSISTENCE PAYS: THE CAMP DAVID ACCORDS

The Arab-Israeli dispute was as visible as ever, and almost as volatile. When the shooting in the 1973 war ended, Israeli troops remained locked at close quarters with Egyptian forces near the Suez Canal, and with Syrian units in the vicinity of the Golan Heights. During the several months that followed, the Nixon administration—again, chiefly Henry Kissinger—spared no effort to separate the combatants and prevent further hostilities. Kissinger concentrated on Egypt as

[4]Henry Kissinger, *Years of Upheaval* (Boston, 1982), p. 1192.

both the most important Arab party to the dispute with Israel and the Arab state that seemed most likely to come to peace terms. Although Kissinger took a broad view of international relations and thought in terms of a grand strategy for U.S. foreign policy—revealed most obviously in the policy of detente toward the Soviet Union and China—his tactical approach to diplomatic affairs was decidedly incrementalist. He believed that when deep suspicion characterized relations between countries, as between Israel and the Arab states, successful negotiation required proceeding by a series of small steps. Only as each side discovered that minor compromises wouldn't produce disaster, and in fact might yield positive benefits, would each gain sufficient confidence to take larger steps. Kissinger believed that the important thing was steady progress, even if the progress was slow.

The secretary of state focused first on disengaging the Egyptian and Israeli forces near the Suez Canal. The disengagement came in stages, and required time and constant American reassurance to the two parties that neither was giving up more than it was getting. The Israelis initially insisted that their forces be allowed to retain control of the strategic Mitla and Gidi passes; Egypt demanded withdrawal. The Israelis rejected anything more than a symbolic Egyptian force on the east bank of the Suez Canal; the Egyptians wanted two infantry divisions and two hundred tanks. Kissinger gradually managed to narrow the gap between the two sides by shuttling between their capitals and chipping away at each's resistance. Eventually, at the beginning of 1974, Egypt agreed to let Israel keep control of the passes, while Israel accepted a modest but more-than-token Egyptian force on the canal's east bank. As a reward to the Americans, President Sadat declared that he would work to end the Arab oil embargo. The Nixon administration promised to support full implementation of Security Council Resolution 242, pleasing the Egyptians, and it forgave $1 billion in debts Israel owed for American weapons, pleasing the Israelis.

For reasons having to do partly with Sadat's persuasive skills and partly with their own desire to avoid driving the United States permanently to alternative suppliers, the Arab oil producers in March 1974 lifted the anti-American embargo. This move encouraged Kissinger to redouble his efforts toward further disengagement of Israeli and Arab forces. So far, he had gotten nowhere with the Syrians; in fact, fighting intermittently broke out between Israeli and Syrian troops. The basic problem was the close proximity in which Israel and Syria existed. While the large and sparsely populated Sinai served as a buffer between Israelis and Egyptians, nothing so big or empty separated Israelis from Syrians. But again Kissinger's determination paid off. In May 1974, Israel and Syria, both weary of constant mobilization, agreed to terms of disengagement.

Further steps came harder. Although Egypt and Israel hinted at the possibility of deescalating still more, other players in the Middle East weren't sure they liked the idea. The Syrians worried that if Israel and Egypt made up, the Israelis could turn the full force of their guns on Syria, should matters again come to blows. The Soviet Union preferred to keep the Arab-Israeli pot bubbling, since such bubbling inclined the enemies of the United States' client, Israel, to look to Moscow for help and advice. Detente or no detente, the Kremlin sought to conserve, and if possible expand, its influence in the Middle East—just as Washington did.

But Egypt and Israel wanted a deal more than they wanted to please those who didn't. Through the end of 1974, and into the following year, Kissinger continued his bouncing back and forth between the two countries. Especially in Israel, he became an unwelcome guest, at least in the eyes of that vocal portion of the populace that desired no compromise with the enemy. The better-controlled Egyptian people offered somewhat greater hospitality, but Egyptian supporters of the Palestinians decried anything that diminished Egypt's ardor for the Palestinian cause.

Finally, though, in September 1975, Egypt and Israel reached a second agreement. Egypt committed itself to the peaceful resolution of disputes with Israel—a significant retreat from Cairo's earlier insistence that Israel was an outlaw state that might rightly be treated with force. Israel consented to withdraw from the Sinai passes, as well as to relinquish control of oil fields in the Sinai.

The United States sweetened the deal significantly for both parties. To the Israelis, who had required the more convincing, or at least proved the better bargainers, Washington promised additional economic and military aid. It also promised to make up for the oil Israel was handing back to the Egyptians, and it pledged prompt consultation in the event the Soviets started acting obnoxious. Finally, in a commitment that would prove sticky later, the United States agreed not to recognize or negotiate with the Palestine Liberation Organization until the PLO accepted Israel's right to exist and endorsed United Nations Resolutions 242 and 338. (The latter was the resolution that set the framework for ending the 1973 war; it also reiterated 242 and called for peace negotiations among the warring parties.) To Egypt, Washington declared that it would facilitate discussions between Israel and Syria (Egypt preferred not to be the only Arab state at peace with the Zionists), that it would assist Cairo in the development of a military early-warning system in the Sinai, and that it would consult with Egypt in the event of alleged Israeli violations of the agreement. In addition, to keep an eye on everyone, the United States would place a team of civilian truce monitors in the Sinai.

For a time, Kissinger hoped to keep these U.S. guarantees to Israel and Egypt secret. But word leaked out, upsetting both those legislators and members of the American public who thought the United States was doing too much for Egypt, and the smaller number who thought it was doing too much for Israel. The controversy didn't help the political fortunes of Gerald Ford, now president following Nixon's August 1974 resignation. Ford was an easy target for Democrats, especially after his pardon of Nixon for Watergate-related crimes Nixon said he never committed. Kissinger, by this time, was very controversial too: liberals despised him for his and Nixon's Vietnam policies, conservatives hated him for detente, and nearly everybody distrusted him for his deceptive style. Under the circumstances, the best Ford and Kissinger could hope for regarding the Middle East was to defend the gains they had made. Any further initiatives would have to await a new administration.

The new administration turned out to be headed by Jimmy Carter. More than any president before or after him, Carter took a personal interest in the conflict between Israel and its neighbors, especially Egypt. At Carter's insistence, the United States government strove mightily to devise a peace settlement both the Israelis and the Egyptians could accept. Carter achieved his goal, and the 1978 Camp David accords, which led to a 1979 peace treaty between Israel and Egypt, provided the diplomatic high point of an otherwise flat four years in office.

Carter's success in bringing Israel and Egypt to an agreement resulted from a fortunate coincidence of personalities and national interests. Carter's particular concern for the Arab-Israeli dispute reflected his religious background: as a self-styled "born-again" Southern Baptist, he felt very deeply the significance of Jerusalem and the lands of the Bible. Carter didn't interpret the politics of the Middle East in quite such an explicitly religious fashion as some Christian fundamentalists—who saw the regathering of the Jews in Zion as evidence of the imminent Second Coming of Jesus—but he couldn't help thinking that he ought to do whatever he could to bring peace to the Holy Land. In addition, being a politician, Carter recognized that if he could produce a peace treaty between Israel and the largest of the Arab states—something Truman, Eisenhower, Kennedy, Johnson, Nixon, and Ford had failed to accomplish—he might reap sizable political benefits.

Israel's prime minister, Menachem Begin, came to the Camp David negotiations from an entirely different direction than Carter. Begin had been born in Poland; most of his family perished in Hitler's anti-Jewish holocaust. During the struggle for the creation of the Zionist state, Begin had led the Irgun, a guerrilla organization that resorted to terrorism against British officials and Palestinians. After independence, Begin had carried his hardline views into parliamentary politics, pushing within the Knesset (Israel's parliament) for the expansion of Israel into Judea and Samaria—the terms he and others of like mind used for the West Bank. In 1970, Begin resigned from Golda Meir's cabinet upon the cabinet's decision to accept Resolution 242. To Begin, this decision seemed to portend giving up Judea and Samaria. Begin's views remained those of an outsider until June 1977, when Israelis rejected the long-ruling Labor party in favor of Begin's Likud coalition.

To American thinking, Begin's election was half a blessing, half a curse. On one hand, he seemed far less amenable to a compromise with the Arabs than his Labor predecessors had been, on account of both his expansionist ideology and his personal stubbornness. On the other hand, if he *could* be persuaded to cut a deal with the Egyptians, he would have less difficulty delivering Knesset approval than an Israeli leader with a reputation for softness. In the 1970s, it was a commonplace of American political analysis that only someone like Richard Nixon, a person with a name for anticommunist vigilance, could get away with opening relations with Communist China. Begin filled an analogous role in Israeli relations with the Arabs. Of additional significance was the fact that although Eretz Israel—the greater Israel Begin and others hoped to restore—included land recently held by Jordan, it didn't infringe on Egyptian territory. When the Hebrews of Moses' day had ended their forty-year wandering in the Sinai desert, they crossed over into the Promised Land and didn't look back.

The third partner to the Camp David agreements was Sadat of Egypt. Of the three men, the Egyptian president risked the most. Within influential circles both in Egypt and among Arabs generally, the notion of a peace with Israel, certainly one that failed to provide satisfaction on the Palestinian question, was anathema. Yet unlike his predecessor Nasser, Sadat was an Egyptian before he was an Arab, and he determined to retrieve the Sinai for his country, even at the cost of recognizing the Zionists as legitimate neighbors. Where Carter brought persistence and determination to the Camp David negotiations, and Begin brought stubbornness and an impeccable record of anti-appeasement of anti-Zionists, Sadat brought boldness and a willingness to hazard the wrath of his enemies.

For the three countries involved, the Camp David negotiations came at a propitious moment. During the mid-1970s, the United States was at a foreign-policy crossroads. The disheartening outcome of the Vietnam War disillusioned many Americans on the idea of continuing the Cold War, which in any case had lost much of its obvious motivation amid detente. At the same time, the United States' vulnerability on the energy question, highlighted by the Arab oil embargo, suggested that a reordering of priorities would be wise. Rather than focus on the global balance of power, perhaps the United States should address regional issues with a direct impact on American jobs and standard of living—such as the Arab-Israeli conflict.

For Israel, the 1973 war had shattered the sense of invulnerability that the previous bouts with the Arabs had nurtured. Although the fighting ended with the Israelis firmly in control of the military situation, the severe—for them—losses they suffered in the war's early going demonstrated the necessity of preventing another such conflict. The Nixon administration had come to the rescue in Israel's moment of testing, but Moscow had shown that it was able to counter U.S. aid to Israel with Soviet aid to Egypt and Syria. Continuation of the Middle Eastern arms race would make future wars all the more dangerous. Besides, after Vietnam, who could rely on the steadfastness of the United States? A peace agreement with Egypt offered an alternative to the economy-crushing, psyche-draining, eternal watchfulness that permanent preparation for war required. Finally, because Sinai possessed only strategic, rather than religious and ideological, significance, swapping territory for peace in that region could make sense.

Egypt likewise was ready to consider putting down the cudgels. The 1973 war had accomplished its purpose of vindicating Arab pride, and while the Israelis had eventually gained the upper hand on the battlefield, Egyptians could and did interpret this as the result primarily of U.S. intervention. It damaged no Egyptian's self-respect to lose to the world's greatest superpower. As for the Palestinians, although some Egyptians still insisted on solidarity with the refugees, many had decided that Egypt had other matters to tend to, such as the persistent poverty of Egypt's rapidly growing population. For twenty-five years, Egypt had championed the Palestinian cause; the time had come for Egyptians to take care of Egypt. The fact that Egypt's western and southern neighbors, Libya and Sudan, were experiencing and causing unrest on Egypt's borders additionally disposed Cairo to mend fences on its eastern frontier.

The American initiative that eventually produced the Camp David accord commenced in the latter half of 1977. Carter launched the initiative in the face of much conventional wisdom. Before starting his major effort with Begin and Sadat, the president summoned the Democratic "wise men"—retired veterans of previous administrations—to the White House. The old-timers, having lived through the Arab-Israeli battles from the start, warned Carter to keep clear. Middle East negotiations, they said, were a losing proposition for the United States; the president would proceed at America's peril and his own.[5]

Yet Carter went ahead, unwilling to admit defeat before trying. After careful soundings and months-long preparation, much of it shrouded in secrecy, Carter invited Begin and Sadat to join him at the presidential retreat in the Maryland mountains. The three met at Camp David in September 1978 for a three-day conference that stretched into nearly two weeks. The conference lasted as long as it did, and produced the results it did, chiefly because of Carter's refusal to let Begin and Sadat go home without coming to terms.

Carter was not particularly hopeful when the conference started. Begin had mellowed only slightly since his election in June 1977, and the policies he had enunciated then—policies Carter described in his diary as "frightening"—hadn't softened a lot either. Begin still refused to budge on the West Bank, asserting that Israel owned Judea and Samaria by moral and historical right. Sadat had shown greater flexibility, in particular by traveling to Jerusalem in November 1977. Sadat

[5]Jimmy Carter, *Keeping Faith* (New York, 1982), p. 315.

hadn't given away any of the Arab position on that trip, but the simple fact that he made the trip and addressed the Knesset showed his willingness to take forthright steps toward peace. (It also branded him a traitor in the eyes of many Arabs.) Even so, on the opening day of the Camp David conference, Sadat spoke in terms so uncompromising that that some observers thought he was trying to torpedo the meeting. Describing his reaction to Sadat's speech, Carter recalled afterward, "My heart sank. It was extremely harsh and filled with all the unacceptable Arab rhetoric." Sadat's opener blamed the Israelis for the wars between the Arabs and Israel and insisted that Israel give up the Old City of Jerusalem, allow the creation of a Palestinian state, and compensate owners for land Israel had occupied since 1967.[6]

In inviting Begin and Sadat to Camp David, Carter had intended that the three of them sit down together and work out a formula for peace between Israel and Egypt. For two days, the trio did indeed meet as a group. But so contentious and unproductive did the meetings become—to the point where the Israelis started packing to leave—that Carter junked the Begin-Sadat face-to-face approach in favor of some short-distance shuttle diplomacy. For the last week of the conference, the president met separately with the Israeli and Egyptian leaders, endlessly carrying the most recent offer from one to the other, looking for language and concessions that would bring the two sides to terms.

Carter wisely excluded reporters from the conference—an easy matter, given Camp David's secluded location and tight security. As a result, the three parties could hope to keep any accord under wraps until they had tied up all the loose ends. Both Sadat and Begin soon indicated more give in their positions than their public posturings had revealed. Sadat, whom Carter came to admire and respect greatly, told the president that Egypt's initial hard line was a bargaining tactic. Sadat suggested that Carter propose modifications, which Egypt would accept, thereby encouraging Israel likewise to soften its stance.

Begin was somewhat more difficult. The Israeli prime minister was personally pricklier than Sadat—a trait probably not mitigated by his hotly contested after-hours chess matches with Carter's national security adviser, Zbigniew Brzezinski, a fellow Polish emigré. Begin insisted that the West Bank was an integral part of Israel; the Pales-

[6]Ibid., pp. 288, 340.

tinians living there would never have a state of their own. To emphasize his determination, he refused to halt the establishment of Jewish
settlements on the West Bank. Begin also rejected a statement offered by Carter acknowledging the inadmissability of taking territory
by war. When Carter pointed out that such a statement formed the
preamble to Resolution 242, which Israel had endorsed, Begin merely responded that he was reiterating what had been Israel's policy for
eleven years. Carter, at patience's end, retorted, "Maybe that's why
you haven't had peace for eleven years."[7]

By this stage of the negotiations, everyone involved could see that
Sadat cared much more about the Sinai, which was a piece of Egypt's
traditional territory, than about the West Bank and Gaza. As an Arab
leader, the Egyptian president was obliged to register protests at Israel's occupation of the lands claimed by the Palestinians; but his
heart lay in the Sinai, Egypt's own. Carter saw the possibility of sepa-
rating the issue of the Sinai from that of the other occupied territories. Sadat agreed to the separation, which Begin had supported all
along. This division of diplomatic labor turned out to be a summit-
saver.

Yet there remained a lot of tough slogging. Although the Israelis
had more or less adjusted to the thought that they might eventually
hand the Sinai back to Egypt, they had a hard time actually accepting
that they might have to remove the settlements they had established
there. "We don't dismantle settlements," Begin said adamantly. "We
don't plow them up or demolish them." But gradually Begin eased his
opposition, declaring that he would leave the matter to the Knesset to
decide. Sadat accepted this solution, though the Egyptian president
added that if the Knesset insisted on holding on to the settlements,
then Egypt wouldn't feel bound to honor its part of any Camp David
bargain.[8]

After some eleventh-hour door-slamming—the product of both
calculation and exhaustion—the two sides reached an accord. The
heart of the agreement was an Egyptian pledge to sign a peace treaty
with Israel and extend diplomatic recognition to the Zionist state, in
exchange for Israel's evacuation of the Sinai and dismantling of the
Sinai settlements.

---

[7]Steven L. Spiegel, *The Other Arab-Israeli Conflict: Making America's Middle East
Policy, from Truman to Reagan* (Chicago, 1985), p. 355.

[8]Ezer Weizmann, *The Battle for Peace* (New York, 1981), p. 364.

On the issue of the West Bank and Gaza—that is, the Palestinian issue—nothing so clear-cut emerged. The Camp David accord called for additional negotiations on the future of the territories, negotiations to include Egypt, Israel, Jordan, and "the representatives of the Palestinian people." The negotiations should create "new arrangements" giving "due consideration both to the principle of self-government by the inhabitants of these territories and to the legitimate security concerns of the parties involved." This was language only diplomats could love: it would keep them wrangling for years.[9]

The Camp David accord of September 1978 led to the promised peace treaty between Egypt and Israel the following March, and to Israel's phased return of the Sinai to Egypt. It led to no such resolution of the Palestinian question, as the loose wording ("the representatives of the Palestinian people"—Who were they, and how would they be chosen? What would be the nature of the "new arrangements"?) and implicit contradictions (between Palestinian "self-government" and Israel's "legitimate security concerns") allowed both sides to wiggle out of whatever others thought they might have committed to. The Arab states besides Egypt blasted the Camp David accords as a betrayal of the Palestinians and declared Egypt a pariah. Hardliners in Israel dug foxholes against any further retreat from what they saw as Israel's defense needs.

As a way of getting Begin and Sadat past the criticism, Carter enhanced the attractiveness of the Camp David package by including big increases in U.S. aid to both parties. On the signing of the Egypt-Israel peace treaty, the American secretary of defense, Harold Brown, wrote a letter to his Israeli counterpart promising $3 billion in new American military assistance. The Carter administration also informed the Israelis that it would expedite approval of several arms requests that had been held up—conspicuously—during the negotiations. Finally, Washington reaffirmed the earlier guarantee of a supply of oil to Israel. Brown wrote to the Egyptian defense minister as well, pledging the United States to $1.5 billion in aid to Egypt. American help for Israel and Egypt soon became a regular affair, and within a short while those two countries were receiving the largest portion of American foreign assistance.

[9]T. G. Fraser, *The Middle East 1914–1979* (New York, 1980), pp. 171–176.

4. THE FALL OF THE SHAH, THE RISE OF THE AYATOLLAH

Not far behind was Iran. Though Tehran got less from Washington per year than Israel or Egypt, it had been on the payroll much longer. The first large post-Mossadeq installment of U.S. help—$400 million between August 1953 and late 1956—laid the groundwork for a regular program of military and economic assistance from Washington. The shah got another several hundred million by the end of the 1950s. In addition, the oil settlement Tehran worked out with foreign companies after Mossadeq's ouster poured hundreds of millions more each year into the shah's coffers.

Washington occasionally thought that the shah, flush as he was, might consider spreading the wealth a bit. A little more democracy wouldn't have hurt either. In the immediate aftermath of Mossadeq's overthrow, when the Tudeh-Soviet threat seemed particularly real and imminent, the U.S. government had winked at, even encouraged, strong measures by the previously ineffectual monarch. But the shah got carried away, and before long his security forces, especially SAVAK, the secret police, were intimidating the political opposition. Because the United States had tied itself closely to the shah's regime, it came in for the kind of criticism Iranian nationalists had leveled at Britain earlier. An Iranian critic of the shah, Abol Hassan Ebtehaj, described the situation in 1961, from the safe distance (he hoped—mistakenly; he was arrested a few months later on returning to Iran) of San Francisco. "Not so very many years ago in Iran," Ebtehaj said, "the United States was loved and respected as no other country, and without having given a penny of aid. Now, after more than $1 billion of loans and grants, America is neither loved nor respected; she is distrusted by most people, and hated by many."[10]

John Kennedy tried to cure the shah of the worst of his autocratic ways. In line with Kennedy's general emphasis on economic development and political reform as the most effective long-term means for keeping Third World countries out of communist clutches, Kennedy encouraged the shah to devote fewer resources to the military and more to the economy. As a carrot, the president offered increased American economic aid. As a stick, he threatened cutbacks in military assistance.

[10]James A. Bill, *The Eagle and the Lion: The Tragedy of American-Iranian Relations* (New Haven, Conn., 1988), p. 130.

The shah accepted the advice, after a fashion. He expressed interest in reform, but demonstrated that he intended to keep the pace and direction of reform firmly under his control. He launched what he called a "white revolution"—as opposed to a communist "red revolution"—involving educational improvements, land redistribution, and curbs on corruption at various levels.

While the reforms succeeded in appeasing Washington, they did less well in improving the lot of Iran's poor. At the same time, they antagonized two groups that would grow increasingly influential during the next two decades. Members of the urban middle class thought the shah was going too slowly: these westernized, educated, relatively well-off folks wanted more say in the government. Islamic fundamentalists thought the shah was going too fast: the mullahs and their followers decried the undermining of traditional Islamic values and demanded closer adherence to the teachings of the Prophet.

Lyndon Johnson had problems other than Iran to worry about—Vietnam and the Great Society, not to mention the June War—and under Johnson, the American pressure for reform substantially diminished. Nor did the pressure increase after Johnson left office. The geopoliticians in the Nixon administration let the shah know that so long as he remained a staunch pro-Western ally, they wouldn't inquire too closely into his handling of Iran's internal affairs. Under Nixon and then Ford, Washington made certain that the shah got all the weapons he needed, or thought he needed. Direct U.S. aid no longer represented such a large portion of Iran's national budget as before, but the booming oil prices of the 1970s kept the shah well supplied with cash to purchase the latest gear for his army, navy, air force, and secret police.

While the primary American objective in selling arms to Iran was strategic—to maintain friendly and stable governments in the Persian Gulf in the wake of the British withdrawal—two secondary objectives were also significant. The first was the recycling of petrodollars. With money draining out of the United States to pay inflated prices for oil, American leaders sought ways to repatriate some of that money and close the current-account deficit that resulted. Selling high-ticket items like F-5 fighter planes, C-130 transports, and helicopter gunships to Iran didn't close the deficit entirely, but it helped.

The second objective was ensuring the survival of the American defense industry. In the aftermath of Vietnam, the Pentagon was scaling back purchases of all manner of items, with consequent ill effects on the profit margins of major weapons contractors. Finding foreign customers like Iran for American arms served to keep profits up, weapons workers employed, defense-dependent communities solvent, and—the political bottom line—legislators from sensitive dis-tricts in office.

From this combination of causes, the arms flowed to Iran at rapid rate—more than $10 billion worth between 1971 and 1977. Recalling the atmosphere in Tehran during the period, the chief of the U.S. military advisory group there declared, "It was a salesman's dream."[11]

American solicitude encouraged the shah to think grandly of himself. In 1971, he hosted an extravagant festival celebrating 2,500 years of the Persian monarchy. Estimates of the cost of the affair ran to $200 million, a part of which was offset by U.S. aid. Some shah-watchers thought the celebration, during which Pahlavi linked himself to Cyrus the Great and other Persian demigods, pushed him off the deep end. In its wake, he showed a tendency toward megalomania and growing disconnectedness from the lives of ordinary Iranians. He tightened his security apparatus, further alienating the middle classes, even as he proceeded with the secularizing reforms that infuriated the radically conservative religious groups.

It helped neither the shah nor the United States that large numbers of Americans—technicians, advisers, support staff—accompanied the American weapons and equipment delivered to Iran. By the end of 1976, Americans in Iran numbered nearly 25,000. Even if they had been exemplary guests, and some were, they would have tried the patience of the millions of Iranians who knew that the shah was spending money on them that he might have been spending on projects more essential to the well-being of the Iranian people. Earlier, Iranians had learned to distrust the West while watching British officials, soldiers, and capitalists pull the strings of the Iranian government; now their distrust focused on the Americans.

When Jimmy Carter reached the White House in 1977, the situation in Iran was heading toward a crisis. Carter placed great store in respect for human rights by governments allied to the United States; in this area, the shah wasn't doing well. The Iranian SAVAK had become notorious for its repressiveness, including its common use of torture, and its long reach, even to the United States, where its agents kept tabs on Iranian students and other expatriates. Amnesty Interna-

---

[11] Barry Rubin, *Paved with Good Intentions* (New York, 1980), p. 135.

tional and other human rights monitoring organizations regularly excoriated the shah's government for its abuses. The secretary-general of Amnesty International put the indictment bluntly: "No country in the world has a worse record in human rights than Iran."[12]

Carter also winced at the U.S. policy of arming Iran to the teeth. As a Democratic candidate, Carter had lashed the Ford administration for pursuing policies that fueled an arms race in the Middle East. As president, Carter had to listen to all the reasons for those policies, including the perennial clincher: that if American companies didn't sell Iran the weapons, then the French or someone else would. Knowing the cutthroat nature of the international arms market, it was a difficult argument to dispute.

In shaping his own policy toward Iran, Carter found himself pulled two ways. On one side were the administration's hawks, led by National Security Adviser Brzezinski, who took whichever part of a debate was the most anti-Soviet. Regarding Iran, Brzezinski pointed out that for twenty-five years the shah had been a good ally of the United States. If he didn't run Iran quite according to the preferences of the American Civil Liberties Union, his failure to do so simply showed that Iran wasn't Massachusetts. Brzezinski contended that in the post-Vietnam era, American allies were watching the United States more closely than ever. Would Washington honor its commitments, or cut and run when the going toughened? Perhaps backing the shah would produce less than optimal results for the people of Iran. But the American president had a whole world to worry about. Credibility counted. As an aside, Brzezinski could note that many Republicans and other conservatives were already rebuking the president for insufficient steadfastness against radical change. To waffle on Iran would open the administration to additional pummeling.

On the other side were the administration's doves, led by Secretary of State Cyrus Vance. The doves hoped for a continuation of detente and for concentration on issues, such as human rights, that in the past had often been subordinated to the perceived geopolitical demands of the Cold War. On the subject of Iran, the doves emphasized the growing instability in that country and the need for the United States to accommodate itself to the forces for change, lest they get out of control and totally shatter the U.S. position in Iran. Henry Precht, the State Department's country director for Iran, spoke for the doves

[12]Bill, op. cit., p. 187.

when he contended that American expressions of unwavering support for the shah simply exacerbated the revolutionary tendencies in Iran. Such expressions lulled the shah into thinking change was unnecessary, thereby cutting the ground from under moderate reformers and driving the country into the arms of the radicals.

At first, Carter sided with the doves on most issues, including Iran. The president attempted to apply his thinking on human rights to the shah's government. He sent Vance to Tehran in the spring of 1977 to explain to the shah how the new administration felt about human rights. "I stressed their importance as a key element of our foreign policy," the secretary recalled later. "I emphasized that the president was committed to reaffirming the primacy of human rights as a national goal."

But the shah wasn't interested. "He said that his regime was under attack from within by Communists and assorted fellow travelers," Vance reported, "and that there were limits on how far he could go in restraining his security forces. He warned that if Iran were to slip into civil strife, only the Soviet Union would stand to gain." Vance had just informed the shah that the administration had approved the sale to Iran of 160 top-of-the-line F-16 fighter planes and was planning to press Congress to authorize the delivery of several flying radar stations (AWACs). Without batting an eye, the shah asked for 140 F-16s beyond those already approved.[13]

Though Carter expostulated with the shah about human rights, the monarch stood firm. Carter, unsure of himself in a region as volatile as the Persian Gulf, declined to press the matter. The president refused to invoke the kind of sanctions—a suspension of arms sales, for instance—that would really have gotten Tehran's attention. The shah concluded that the Americans weren't serious about reform in his country.

He was largely correct. As the administration prepared for a November 1977 Iranian royal visit to the United States, U.S. officials set down three objectives for the visit (as Vance described them): "to convince the shah of the president's firm commitment to the U.S.-Iranian special relationship; to secure the shah's agreement to a systematic arrangement for projecting Iran's defense needs and our ability to meet them; and to elicit a commitment from the shah that he would take a moderate and sympathetic position on oil prices at the

[13]Cyrus Vance, *Hard Choices* (New York, 1983), pp. 318–319.

December OPEC meeting." Promoting human rights in Iran didn't make the short list.[14]

The item about the OPEC meeting reflected the administration's, and America's, continuing sensitivity on the oil issue—a sensitivity that further undermined the administration's will to push for human rights reform. Though the gas lines of 1973 and early 1974 had disappeared, prices remained far above what Americans had long been used to. The administration hoped the shah would restrain others in OPEC from driving prices higher still. To this end—among others, such as spreading the cost of production of American weapons—the administration decided to go on trying to satisfy the shah's craving for arms. When the shah arrived in Washington, Carter reported success in gaining congressional approval for the AWACs, and when the shah added 70 F-14s to his request for the extra 140 F-16s, the president said he would see what he could do.

The shah's visit included one embarrassing moment. Anti-shah protesters demonstrated beyond the fence as Carter and his guest posed for cameras on the White House lawn; when the crowd grew particularly troublesome, police lobbed tear-gas grenades to disperse the rowdies. Unexpectedly, the wind carried the gas into the faces of the Carter-Pahlavi entourage, producing tight throats and runny eyes. The president thought little of the affair at the time, but later saw it as an omen. "That day—November 15, 1977—was an augury," he wrote. "The tear gas had created the semblance of grief. Almost two years later, and for fourteen months afterward, there would be real grief in our country because of Iran."[15]

But the visit pleased the monarch. "The shah left Washington encouraged by his conversations with the president," Vance recalled, "and we received from the embassy in Tehran glowing reports of a new mood of confidence and satisfaction."[16]

The confidence was misplaced. Even as the shah hobnobbed in Washington, his regime was crumbling. To his credit, the shah recognized some of the symptoms of decay and made modest efforts to treat them. He released a number of political prisoners; he shuffled his cabinet; he eased restrictions on the press; he expanded, albeit slightly, the scope for political opposition. But without giving away far

[14]Ibid., p. 321.

[15]Carter, op. cit., p. 434

[16]Vance, op. cit., pp. 321–323.

more power than he ever intended, he couldn't satisfy the increasingly radical demands of those who agitated against him.

The demands and the agitation both escalated early in 1978.
Shortly after a Carter trip to Tehran, during which the president ef-
fused over the shah's "great leadership," pronounced Iran "an island
of stability in one of the most troubled regions of the world," and
praised the "respect, admiration, and love" the Iranian people held
for their royal leader, the country erupted. Demonstrations in the
holy city of Qom led to police attacks on theology students; two dozen
died and many more were wounded. Riots in Tabriz caused hundreds
more deaths. Tehran exploded in May, Meshed in July, Isfahan and
Abadan in August. In September, army troops fired on a large crowd
gathered in Tehran's Jaleh Square, killing or wounding as many as
2000.

Despite the spiraling violence, the Carter administration held to
the line that the shah could contain the challenge to his regime. This
underestimate of the true nature of what was fast becoming a revolution had a variety of sources. In the first place, the trauma in Iran occurred simultaneously with the Carter administration's all-out push
toward an Israeli-Egyptian settlement; the Jaleh Square incident took
place while Carter and his Middle East specialists were secluded at
Camp David with the Israelis and Egyptians. Second, U.S. intelligence on Iran had never been very good. American relations with
Iran hadn't been sufficiently important to induce many American officials to devote careers to mastering the Farsi language and otherwise
immersing themselves in Iranian politics and culture; consequently,
U.S. analysts looking at Iran misgauged the proportions between the
unrest they could see and that which they couldn't see. They assumed
that the riots and other demonstrations indicated the alienation of a
comparatively small group of people rather than the disaffection of
huge segments of the population. Third, because U.S. policy backed
the shah, the American bureaucracy tended to filter out reports challenging the wisdom of that policy.

The filtering process worked particularly well—that is, poorly—
when the U.S. ambassador in Tehran, William Sullivan, submitted a
report entitled "Thinking the Unthinkable." Sullivan, a no-nonsense
foreign service officer who had done stints in Vietnam and Laos before being posted to the Philippines of Ferdinand Marcos, initially
believed that those persons agitating against the shah were the political equivalent of horseflies: distracting and occasionally painful,

but hardly life-threatening. The events of the first nine months of
1978, however, caused him to reconsider. In his report to Washington, Sullivan noted that popular support for the shah had nearly
vanished. The contest for control of the country had come down to
the military against the mullahs. The latter, of whom the outstand-
ing figure was the exiled Ayatollah Ruhollah Khomeini, were calling
for strikes and other forms of broad-based resistance against the
regime. The generals would have to decide whether to break up
the strikes by force or let Khomeini and the fundamentalists carry
the day.

Sullivan didn't know how matters would turn out, and he accepted
that for the present the United States should stick by the shah. But
Washington should prepare alternatives in case this policy failed and
the shah jumped ship. "If it should fail and the shah should abdicate,"
Sullivan wrote, "we need to think the unthinkable at this time in
order to give our thoughts some precision should the unthinkable
contingency arise."[17]

But the Carter administration was falling increasingly under the
sway of the Brzezinski school of hardball geopolitics, partly as a result
of Soviet misbehavior in places like Angola, partly as a result of the
carping from the American right, and partly as a result of Brzezinski's
mastery of the art of bureaucratic warfare. Washington chose not to
think the unthinkable. The administration stuck to its policy of unwavering support for the shah.

And the turmoil in Iran mounted daily. Strikes paralyzed large
sectors of the economy; inflation and hoarding-induced shortages
pinched the middle class and ravaged the poor; once-radical political
factions came to appear moderate. The power of Khomeini grew, although he remained in France. The ayatollah, sensing that he had the
shah on the run, pressed harder than ever. He refused to temper his
demands. He insisted that the shah relinquish power and that the
shah's secular, modernizing Iran be remade at once into an Islamic
theocracy. When an associate suggested that a gradual transition to Islamic rule might be better, Khomeini retorted, "No gradualism, no
waiting." He added, "We must not lose a day, not a minute. The people demand an immediate revolution. Now or never."[18]

---

[17]Gary Sick, *All Fall Down: America's Tragic Encounter with Iran* (New York, 1985),
pp. 81–83.

[18]Rubin, op. cit., p. 222.

Washington still backed the shah. As late as December 12, Carter declared, "I fully expect the shah to maintain power in Iran, and for the present problems in Iran to be solved." To prevent the slightest confusion, Carter continued, "The shah has our support and he also has our confidence."[19]

But the shah couldn't get a handle on his troubles. "He doesn't know what to do next," an unnamed U.S. official told the *Washington Post*, before adding, "Neither do we." Part of the shah's difficulty was that he was slowly dying of cancer, and realized it. Whether a healthy shah would have reacted more vigorously to the challenges he faced is impossible to tell; this sick one couldn't summon the energy. Another part of the shah's problem was that he didn't know how far to trust his army to carry out orders anymore. Would the generals relay orders to fire on civilians? Would the rank and file obey such orders?[20]

In the end, the shah chose not to test the army's loyalty. At the end of December 1978, he handed power to a new prime minister, Shahpour Bakhtiar. Two weeks later, he left the country.

The shah's departure only accelerated the pace of the revolution. Millions of people took to the streets. Many carried weapons and used them against landlords, employers, creditors, and sundry others they had it in for. Surging crowds attacked symbols of the Pahlavi regime and its erstwhile supporters: military and police headquarters, government offices, foreign banks and hotels, the U.S. embassy. Islamic fundamentalists destroyed liquor stores and movie houses. Bakhtiar's government lasted only a month, soon swept away by the flood of emotion that accompanied the triumphal return of Khomeini to Tehran at the beginning of February 1979.

The United States exercised almost no control over the events of this period, although the Carter administration did try to steer things in a direction that favored American interests. Shortly after the shah exited Iran, Washington dispatched General Robert Huyser, the number two man at the United States' European command headquarters and a person who had close personal and professional ties to members of the Iranian military. Huyser's mission aimed to keep Khomeini, whom Washington correctly perceived as being bitterly anti-American, out of power. The plan was to tie Iran's armed forces to Bakhtiar or to encourage the generals to take power into their

[19]*Public Papers of the Presidents,* 1978, p. 2226.
[20]Rubin, op. cit., p. 225.

own hands if Bakhtiar couldn't hold it. The mission failed: Bakhtiar lost his grip, and the army refused to fire on the millions who came out in support of Khomeini.

But the American machinations, such as they were, reinforced the widespread belief that the United States was plotting a restoration of the shah, on the pattern of the 1953 CIA operation against Mossadeq. These suspicions caused many Iranians to view every American move as a possible precursor to an effort to return the shah to power.

American relations with Iran quickly declined to a condition of almost complete counterproductivity. The Carter administration carefully sought to encourage moderate elements in Iran, but by the very act of meeting with representatives of the Bakhtiar government and that of Bakhtiar's successor, Mehdi Bazargan, U.S. officials tended to discredit those governments in the eyes of the many Iranians who had come to see the United States as irrevocably and diabolically manipulative. The U.S. Senate didn't help matters by passing a measure condemning the summary execution of individuals associated with the shah's regime. Whatever the moral justification for such a statement, the radicals in Iran denounced the condemnation as intrusive and hypocritical. Where was the Senate when Pahlavi's goons were killing innocent Iranians, with American-supplied weapons?

To a degree that Washington insufficiently appreciated at this time, Khomeini and the radicals actively encouraged bad feelings between Iran and the United States. When some associates voiced concern that the American-Iranian relationship was being seriously endangered, Khomeini answered, "May God cause it to be endangered. Our relations with the United States are the relations of the oppressed with the oppressor; they are the relations of the plundered with the plunderer." Khomeini went on to ask, "What need have we of the United States?"[21]

In fact, Khomeini did need the United States, or at least found it handy. America became a blunt instrument for beating the moderates who hoped to halt the Iranian revolution short of the establishment of an Islamic theocracy. As in many revolutions, the radicals enjoyed the advantage of appearing more dedicated than the moderates to the principles from which the revolution arose—in this case, hatred for the shah and all he stood for, including close ties between Iran and

[21]Ibid., p. 290.

the United States. Yet the moderates weren't without resources. In particular, many members of the Iranian middle class desired to preserve the advantages of living in a modern, secular society. For this reason, the revolution progressed more slowly than Khomeini had thought it would. To speed the pace of change, the radicals felt obliged to try to polarize conditions in the country.

An obvious target for the polarizers was the U.S. embassy in Tehran. In February 1979, just two weeks after Khomeini's triumphal return from exile, an armed crowd attacked the embassy. The American ambassador, Sullivan, recognized that a spirited defense of the embassy by the marine guards would produce large numbers of casualties and enormous quantities of bad blood; consequently, he surrendered the building to the attackers. They shot and killed an Iranian employee at the embassy and wounded a U.S. marine. They also took Sullivan and some one hundred other persons hostage.

On this occasion, the Khomeinists opposed such direct action. The hostage-takers, it turned out, were leftists who hoped to push the revolution in a Marxist direction. The Khomeinists had accepted the leftists' cooperation in ousting the shah, but they didn't want to let the leftists in on the spoils of the ouster. Within hours of the embassy takeover, the Khomeinists disavowed it, allowing representatives of the still-moderate government to negotiate with the hostage-takers and free the captives.

By the autumn of 1979, however, the situation had changed. The leftists were no longer a threat, and the Khomeinists had only the moderates to contend with. Since the moderates continued to retard the progress of the revolution, the Khomeinists wanted an issue to galvanize public support for their program. The Carter administration provided the issue by allowing Pahlavi to enter the United States for medical treatment.

Certain U.S. officials had warned against giving the shah a visa. The state department's Henry Precht thought it was a very bad idea. "Should the Shah come to the U.S.," Precht wrote in March, "it would be a disaster for U.S.-Iranian relations, for the Western position in the region, and would create a severe security problem for our personnel in Tehran." In September, the embassy in Tehran filed a situation report declaring of the shah, "Any decision to allow him or his family to visit the U.S. would almost certainly result in an immediate and violent reaction." This report added that the strength of such a reaction might exceed the ability of the Iranian government to contain it.[22]

Yet Carter went ahead and let the shah enter the United States. To some degree, the president responded to the simple humanitarian appeal of a dying man for the best possible medical treatment. To some degree, Carter responded to political pressure from critics who held that the least the United States owed an ally of such long standing was sympathy in his final days—and that a president who refused to show such sympathy, in order to appease revolutionaries in Iran, didn't deserve reelection in 1980.

Officials at the U.S. embassy in Tehran reacted with instant dismay to the news that the Carter administration had issued Pahlavi a visa. One person later taken hostage recalled the moment when the American chargé d'affaires, Bruce Laingen, relayed the news: "Total silence followed. In time it was broken by a faint groan. Faces literally went white. I put my hands over my own face and had a good think—not about policy or professional duties, but how much I wanted to go home."[23]

The wish to go home only increased during the next ten days. The Khomeinists derided the American statement that medical reasons accounted for the shah's visit to New York; the Americans, they said, were plotting a reversal of the revolution. As additional evidence, they cited a recent meeting in Algeria between National Security Adviser Brzezinski and Bazargan. Huge crowds demonstrated outside the U.S. embassy, encouraged by Khomeini's demands that the United States return the shah to Iran to face revolutionary justice. On November 4, hundreds of particularly committed demonstrators, apparently having planned their action for some time, climbed the walls of the embassy compound, overwhelmed the guards, and seized more than seventy hostages.

At first, the Carter administration hoped for a quick resolution, like that of the hostage incident of the previous February. But events soon blasted this hope. Khomeini applauded the action of the hostage-takers, transforming them into heroes of the revolution. The ayatollah used the hostages against Bazargan: when the hostage-takers, with Khomeini's blessing, ignored Bazargan's efforts to free the Americans, the hapless prime minister was forced to resign. Power

[22]Bill, op. cit., pp. 323–324.
[23]Ibid., p. 326.

passed to the hardline Revolutionary Council. Within weeks, the Khomeinists achieved their goal of reconstitutionalizing Iran as an Islamic state.

But the struggle for control of the revolution continued, and the hostages became a football between the weakening moderates and the strengthening radicals. The latter sought a continuing confrontation with the United States, now officially styled the "Great Satan" of the West, in order to prove their devotion to Iranian nationalism and the teachings of the Koran. The hostages provided the surest means of keeping the confrontation going. Several days after the takeover of the embassy, Khomeini ordered the release of the African-Americans and women held; several months later, the captors let a sick hostage go. But the remaining fifty-two had too much value as guarantors of bad relations with the United States to be given up. They stayed in custody.

The Carter administration tried various means to get the hostages back. It halted the shipment of military spare parts to Iran; it deported Iranian students; it barred oil imports from Iran; it froze Iranian financial assets; it applied legal and diplomatic pressure through the United Nations and the International Court of Justice; it packed the shah off to Panama as soon as reasonably possible (whence he traveled to Egypt, where he died in July 1980); it broke diplomatic relations with Iran; it declared an economic embargo against Iran. In April 1980, Carter ordered a military rescue attempt, but the effort failed when two helicopters collided, killing eight members of the rescue team.

5. WHEN IT RAINS, IT POURS:
THE SOVIET INVASION OF AFGHANISTAN

Carter's inability to get the hostages back seemed to many Americans to epitomize the sad state to which America had fallen by the late 1970s, and it injured Carter grievously in the presidential election campaign of that year. Carter didn't make matters easier for himself by virtually imprisoning himself in the White House to concentrate on Iran. The news media, capitalizing on the drama of the situation, picked up on the theme of "America held hostage" and played it back endlessly.

More significant in a strategic sense, however, than the holding of the fifty-two hostages were events happening next door to Iran in

Afghanistan. For more than a century, Afghanistan had served as center court in the "great game" between Britain and Russia, in which the Russians tried to push south toward Persia and India, while the British tried to keep the Russians back. Neither side ever controlled Afghanistan for long, largely because the Afghans ferociously resisted dictation from outside infidels. After 1945, the game changed, most notably in the withdrawal of Britain from India. The United States didn't immediately pick up where the British left off: Afghanistan was very far away, and Americans had more pressing matters to contend with. Besides, the Soviets just after World War II showed relatively little interest in Afghanistan—far less than in Eastern Europe, Turkey, or Iran. The Eisenhower administration considered sending military aid to Afghanistan, but the Pakistanis, allies Washington judged more important than the nonaligned Afghans, objected, and the administration confined itself to a modest amount of economic aid.

Gradually, however, Moscow moved closer to Kabul. The Soviet Union began providing weapons to the Afghans, and although Afghanistan never abandoned its allegiance to the principle of nonalignment, by the late 1970s the Soviets were on cozy terms with the government of Mohammad Daoud Khan. Unfortunately for Moscow and for Daoud, the Afghan leader had lots of enemies, some of whom combined to overthrow him in April 1978, massacring the entire Daoud family and those of his primary associates to emphasize their point. The *good* news, from Moscow's angle, was that Afghanistan's new strong men, Nur Mohammad Taraki and Hafizullah Amin, didn't object to extending Daoud's pro-Soviet policies.

But some of those policies stepped on the toes of Islamic fundamentalists in Afghanistan, who were taking heart from the success of the fundamentalists across the border in Iran. Some of these Afghan fundamentalists raised the flag of revolt against the Taraki government. Amid the fighting, terrorists kidnapped and killed the U.S. ambassador in Kabul. In September 1979—while the revolution in Iran continued to gain momentum—Taraki himself went down, although not at the hands of the rebels. He was done in by Amin, who preferred sole power to sharing.

The Soviets gave Amin a few months to stem the insurgency, but he did no better than Taraki. Moscow grew increasingly nervous, especially after the Iranian students seized the U.S. embassy and the Revolutionary Council took control of Iranian politics. The Kremlin feared that the rampaging fundamentalism sweeping Iran would spill over into Afghanistan and—much worse—into the largely Islamic provinces of Soviet Central Asia.

In the final week of December, the Kremlin decided that Amin wasn't up to the job of quashing the revolt. Moscow ordered a massive airlift of troops over the mountains into Afghanistan; tanks and other support soon followed. Although the Soviets asserted that Amin had invited them in, he became one of the first casualties of the intervention. His replacement, Babrak Karmal, announced that Amin had not been what he claimed to be. Rather, he was an "oppressor and dictator," a "murderer," a "bloodthirsty agent of American imperialism," and a "charlatan of history"—whatever that was. The Soviet newspaper *Pravda* reported the verdict at the beginning of 1980: "Overthrown by a wave of popular indignation, the treacherous scoundrel was tried and shot."[24]

The Carter administration didn't shed any tears for Amin, but it worried plenty about what the Soviet invasion of Afghanistan portended. At the minimum, it indicated serious trouble for Carter's re-election prospects. Carter had premised his foreign policy on a comparatively benign view—compared with that of his conservative critics, that is—of Soviet intentions. The Democratic president contended that the United States shouldn't let an inordinate fear of communism place American policy in a straightjacket. Carter's emphasis on human rights, in those areas where he in fact emphasized them, reflected his desire to move beyond the Cold War; so did his willingness to devote great energy to such regional initiatives as the Camp David negotiations. But Carter's demotion of the Soviet threat opened him to criticism from rightists, who held that the communist danger was as mortal as ever. Before the Soviets invaded Afghanistan, the president could brush off much of the criticism as partisan belly-aching and Cold War–mongering; afterward, he couldn't.

Exacerbating Carter's political troubles was the recent steep rise in petroleum prices. This latest jolt to the world oil economy—the "second oil shock"—had begun during Pahlavi's last months in Tehran, when strikes by Persian Gulf oil workers cut Iranian exports from around 4.5 million barrels per day to less than 1 million. By the time the shah fled Iran, the strikers had closed down the oil industry in the country almost entirely. Since Iran had lately been the world's second largest oil exporter, the loss of Iranian oil put a severe crimp

---

[24]H. W. Brands, *India and the United States* (Boston, 1990), p. 166.

on international supplies. It also put a fright into purchasing agents, who bid oil prices sharply up, from $13 per barrel to $34 before relative calm returned to the markets. In the United States, gas lines reappeared, provoking violence in some neighborhoods, annoyance in all. Although prices moderated during the first half of 1979, as the oil strikers returned to work upon the shah's departure, the November seizure of the U.S. embassy, followed by the Soviet invasion of Afghanistan, sent another sharp tremor through the system. Spot-market cargoes of oil sold for as much as $45 per barrel. As Americans examined their record heating bills and waited in line for gas, they had plenty of time to consider whether Carter was the person to lead their country into the new decade.

Politics aside, the Soviet invasion convinced Carter that there really *was* something to this geopolitics business. In particular, he had to ponder the possibility that the Soviet invasion of Afghanistan foreshadowed a major move toward the Persian Gulf. In 1946, during the Iran crisis that had done much to trigger the Cold War, Loy Henderson and others in the State Department had warned against a possible Soviet thrust toward the oil fields of the gulf. At that time, the Truman administration had warned Moscow against such a thrust, and the Russians shelved whatever plans they might have been concocting.

Now Carter felt obliged to issue a similar warning. In January 1980, the president declared the Soviet invasion of Afghanistan to be "the greatest threat to peace since the Second World War." Enunciating what came to be called the Carter Doctrine, he pledged that the United States would oppose further advances by the Soviets. "Let our position be absolutely clear," he said. "An attempt by any outside force to gain control of the Persian Gulf region will be regarded as an assault on the vital interests of the United States of America, and such an assault will be repelled by any means necessary, including military force." To put steel into his warning, Carter announced the creation of a special military unit, the Rapid Deployment Force, designed to respond on short notice to threats to the peace of the gulf.[25]

✿   ✿   ✿

[25]*Weekly Compilation of Presidential Documents*, Jan. 14, 1980, and Jan. 28, 1980.

Of the three issues that persistently preoccupied American leaders with respect to the Middle East—oil, Israel, and the Soviet Union—the first gained tremendously in importance during the 1970s, the second receded somewhat during the last half of the decade, and the third roared to the forefront of American concerns at the decade's end.

Oil became a powerful weapon, its effectiveness enhanced by the tightness of world oil markets. Although attempts by the Arab OPEC members to force a shift in U.S. policy on the Arab-Israeli question failed, the quadrupling (and more) of oil prices during the 1970s had a huge effect on the lives of Americans. The price rises disrupted the American economy, contributing to unprecedented inflation and other kinds of dislocation. If no change in U.S. Middle East policy could be directly attributed to the oil shocks of the decade, the shocks certainly contributed to the sensitivity of American leaders to events in the Persian Gulf. Not that Washington really required sensitizing: the Iranian revolution and the Soviet invasion of Afghanistan were sufficient to have caught any administration's attention.

Israel receded in American policy because of Carter's success in getting the Israelis and Egyptians to sign a peace accord, and also because of the excitement in Iran and Afghanistan. American leaders hadn't forgotten Israel—Israel's friends in the United States made sure of that—but with the likelihood of war between Israelis and Arabs apparently lower than it had been for years, Washington could worry about other things for a while.

Things such as the Soviet Union. The Nixon-Kissinger policy of detente had been disintegrating for some time under the combined weight of unrealistic expectations and continuing superpower jockeying in the Third World. But it was the Soviet invasion of Afghanistan that killed detente. Carter went over completely to Brzezinski and the hawks, leaving Vance and the doves behind. (Vance took the occasion of the failed Iran hostage rescue mission, which he had advised against, to quit.) The Carter Doctrine of January 1980 signaled that the Cold War was on again. Carter now had to convince American voters that he was the right person to direct the renewed offensive.

Chapter 6

Full Immersion: 1980–1992

1. BOMBED IN BEIRUT

As things turned out, Carter's conversion to anti-Soviet orthodoxy came too late to save his chances for reelection. If anything, his harping on the Soviet threat to the Persian Gulf made matters worse, since it reminded voters of the continuing deadlock with Iran over the hostages. In fact, voters didn't need the president to remind them: the evening news reports kept count of how many days the hostages had been held, and every trip to the gas station drove home the point that something was upsetting the oil neighborhoods of the Middle East. Carter's Republican opponent in the election, Ronald Reagan, made much of the Persian Gulf troubles. Patriotic propriety prevented Reagan from explaining just how *he* would free the fifty-two Americans, but he conveyed the distinct impression that he wouldn't stand still and watch Iranian fanatics humiliate the United States.

Possibly, members of Reagan's campaign organization let the Iranians know more in private than the candidate let the American people know in public. The Republicans worried that Carter would spring an "October surprise"—an eleventh-hour deal with Iran that would release the hostages. Rumors at the time and somewhat more substantial reports that surfaced several years later indicated that William Casey, then Reagan's campaign manager and subsequently CIA director and mastermind of the Iran-contra operation, tried to prevent such a deal by negotiating an agreement, tacit perhaps, with influential persons in Iran to hang on to the American hostages until after the election. In exchange, a Reagan administration would let

Iran receive, probably through Israel, American weapons and spare parts. This was a particularly tempting enticement, since Iran had just been attacked by Iraq, and the huge arsenal the shah had built up required a constant stream of American spare parts to stay in operation. Apparently as evidence of its good faith, the Reagan team nodded at Israel to fly a load of F-4 spare tires to Iran; the shipment arrived in late October.

Whether or not the Reaganites and the Iranians explicitly cut a deal, many observers found it curious that the hostages were released the day Reagan took office, just minutes after the new president's swearing in. The observers' curiosity would have increased had they known that Israel very shortly began a major resupply operation, delivering hundreds of millions of dollars' worth of American equipment to Iran. Israeli diplomat Moshe Arens asserted afterward that Israel coordinated its activities in this matter with U.S. officials "at almost the highest of levels."[1]

Whatever shenanigans the Reagan team was up to regarding the hostages, Reagan presented himself as better able to deal with the Soviet threat than Carter, and most Americans agreed. The new Republican administration moved quickly to revive enthusiasm in the West for the Cold War. Reagan railed against what he called the "evil empire" of the Soviets, and he summoned his compatriots to the ramparts of freedom—wherever the ramparts happened to be at a given moment. During the early and middle 1980s, Central America seemed especially under siege; Reagan sent hundreds of millions of dollars in economic and military aid to the rightist government of El Salvador, which was fighting a leftist insurgency, and to a rightist insurgency in Nicaragua, which was fighting the leftist government. The Reagan administration provided smaller amounts of assistance to anticommunist rebels in Angola and Cambodia.

The administration also sent weapons and supplies to the anti-Soviet *mujahideen* in Afghanistan. Like the aid to the Nicaraguan contras (at this stage, at least), aid to the Afghan rebels was nominally covert. This didn't mean the aid was secret—everyone who cared knew about it—but it did mean that the administration didn't officially acknowledge the program. Acknowledgment would have made life more difficult for the Pakistanis, who served as the channel for most of the aid. As matters were, the Soviets had a hard time resisting the

[1]*New York Times,* April 15, 1991.

temptation to chase the Afghan rebels across the border into Pakistan; had Pakistan taken a high profile in the Afghan war, Moscow might have found the temptation irresistible. So the Reagan administration kept officially mum about the Afghan aid program, and the Pakistanis managed to stay out of the war.

Largely because Carter initially had refused to view the world in narrowly anti-Soviet terms, the Democratic president had managed to summon the attention and energy necessary for a breakthrough in Middle Eastern diplomacy; at least partly because Reagan *did* adopt such a narrow perspective, the Republican president didn't produce anything like the Camp David agreement between Israel and Egypt. To some degree, of course, Carter had caught Israel and Egypt at a propitious moment; Reagan had no such luck.

In fact, Carter's good luck became Reagan's bad luck (which was only fitting, given that in other areas—oil prices, Iran, Afghanistan— Carter's bad luck had become Reagan's good luck, at least to the point of Reagan's getting elected). To a greater extent than Anwar Sadat himself had probably realized it would, the Egyptian leader's decision to settle with Israel poisoned the well for would-be Arab peacemakers. If the nearly unanimous hostility shown to Egypt by other countries of the Arab world hadn't scared off those who might have followed Sadat's example, the Egyptian president's assassination in 1981 by Muslim zealots did. The ruling regime in Saudi Arabia, to cite one case, was still shaking following a 1979 takeover of the Grand Mosque in Mecca by hardline fundamentalists; though Saudi security forces had eventually rooted out the rebels, the incident erased whatever fleeting thoughts the Saudi ruling family might have had about warming to the Zionists. And like Sadat's subsequent murder, the attack on the Grand Mosque frightened compromising types throughout the Middle East. While none of the Arab states was particularly eager to start another round of war with Israel, neither did any besides Egypt show much interest in real peace.

For this reason, the likelihood of significant movement toward a larger reconciliation between Israel and its neighbors was quite small during the early years of Reagan's presidency—which didn't much bother Reagan, intent as he was on the Soviet menace. If anything, Israel and the neighboring Arab states other than Egypt were moving closer to war than to peace.

The trouble at this stage centered on Lebanon. Although the American intervention of 1958 had stabilized the political situation in that country, U.S. troops couldn't deal with the underlying source of turbulence: the imbalance among the various religious groups, particularly the Christians, mostly Maronite Catholics, who held the bulk of the political and economic power, and the Muslims, especially the Shiite Muslims, who had the larger population. The existence of smaller communities such as the Druze, who, like the Muslims, felt short-changed by current power-sharing arrangements, complicated the picture. So did the ideological divide between the mostly conservative Christians and many radical Muslims.

The arrival of thousands of Palestinian guerrillas after the 1970 Jordan uprising complicated things still further. The PLO fighters used southern Lebanon as a base for operations against Israel; at the same time, they sided with the radical Muslims, who took a strong anti-Israel stance, against the conservative Christians, who didn't. In 1975, the situation blew up, and Lebanon, once an oasis of cosmopolitan moderation in the Middle East, disintegrated into civil war. By early 1976, the government had lost control of most of the country to rival Christian and Muslim militia groups.

As the opposing factions hammered away at each other, Lebanon's neighbors got worried. Syria, whose leaders had long considered Lebanon legitimately part of their own country, or at least a country within their sphere of influence, had nonetheless refrained from overt involvement in Lebanese affairs until the civil war began. A variety of more pressing problems, relating mainly to Israel, prevented Damascus from concentrating on Lebanon. But the prospective dissolution of Lebanon caused the Syrian government of Hafiz al-Asad to redirect its thoughts. Nominally, Syria supported the PLO and its radical friends in Lebanon; as the leader (with the looming defection of Egypt) of the anti-Israel front, Syria could hardly do otherwise. But Asad didn't relish the idea of a PLO-dominated Lebanon any more than he had relished the idea of an autonomous PLO in Syria. In either case, the Palestinians might goad the Israelis into a war the Syrians didn't want to fight. To prevent this happening, during the spring and summer of 1976 Asad sent 13,000 Syrian troops and 400 Syrian tanks into Lebanon. The Syrian forces fought on behalf of the Christians against the PLO and the Muslim militias. Yet rather than seeking a clear-cut victory for either side, the Syrians sought primarily to avert a collapse of the status quo.

Israel took longer to become directly involved in the Lebanese civil war, although Israeli trigger fingers got itchy when Syria went in.

While the conservative Christians had controlled Lebanon, Israel experienced little difficulty getting along with them. But after the June War of 1967, and especially after the expulsion of the PLO from Jordan in 1970, the border between Israel and Lebanon heated up. PLO guerrillas lobbed mortar shells into northern Israel; in response to these attacks, and in retaliation for such terrorist operations as a 1968 assault on an Israeli airliner in Athens, Israeli forces struck at PLO bases and associated sites—and some not quite so associated, such as the Beirut airport—in Lebanon. In most cases, the Israelis struck quickly and retired back across the border. Occasionally, however, they stayed longer, as in 1978 during the so-called Litani operation. In this instance, Israeli infantry and armor drove deeper than usual into southern Lebanon, pushing the PLO units north beyond the Litani River.

But the gains of the Litani offensive proved temporary, and by 1982 the Israelis had determined that their country's security required more sweeping measures. In June of that year, Israeli armed forces invaded Lebanon in large numbers. What the Israelis initially intended has remained a subject of considerable dispute. The official government line described "Operation Peace for Galilee" as similar to the Litani campaign, with the aim of securing a PLO-free zone contiguous to Israel's northern border. But subsequent events indicated that at least some Israeli military leaders—Ariel Sharon, the defense minister, for one—had more ambitious aims, notably the annihilation of the PLO in Lebanon and the expulsion of Syrian forces from that country.

The Reagan administration viewed developments in Lebanon with ambivalence. Certain persons within the administration, particularly Secretary of State Alexander Haig, interpreted the contest between Syria and Israel chiefly in terms of the Cold War. The salient fact for Haig was that Syria was a Soviet client, while Israel was a U.S. client. Therefore an Israeli victory over the Syrians would be an American victory over the Soviets. On this account, Washington ought to encourage, or at least not *dis*courage, Israel from doing what the Israelis deemed necessary in Lebanon.

Others in Washington, including Vice President George Bush and Defense Secretary Caspar Weinberger, took a contradictory view. Though Bush and Weinberger agreed with Haig on the fundamental importance of the Cold War, they differed with him regarding what the Cold War implied for U.S. policy in the Middle East. They worried that a major Israeli offensive in Lebanon would destroy the possibility of retrieving stability in that country. A chronically unstable Lebanon would constitute an open invitation for further Soviet meddling in the Middle East.

In the days just after the Israeli invasion began, Reagan refused to make his own position clear. Other Western leaders condemned the massive Israeli violation of Lebanese sovereignty, but the American president kept quiet. Because the Israelis were using lots of American-supplied weapons, silence readily conveyed the impression of approval. Although the Reagan administration at first supported a United Nations resolution insisting that Israel withdraw from Lebanon, a short while later Haig talked the president into vetoing a stronger measure calling for sanctions against Israel.

After several days of heavy fighting, it grew increasingly evident that Israeli ambitions extended beyond the securing of a PLO-free zone in southern Lebanon. Israeli forces drove deeper and deeper into Lebanon until they arrived at the outskirts of Beirut. There they undertook to crush the several thousand PLO guerrillas holed up in the mostly Muslim western portion of the city. Meanwhile, Israel's soldiers handled the Syrians roughly, driving some Syrian troops back into the Bekaa Valley and trapping others in Beirut, while blitzing the Syrian air force with almost no Israeli aircraft losses.

Haig applauded the unfolding Israeli victory as the portent of a diplomatic breakthrough. It represented, he asserted, a "great opportunity to make peace." The secretary of state believed that with the Syrians on the run and the PLO cornered, the Israelis could enforce a settlement in Lebanon that would terminate that country's civil war on terms conducive to regional stability.[2]

The members of the Bush-Weinberger camp disagreed. They contended that the United States couldn't allow the Israelis to continue ravaging Lebanon without risking the alienation of much of the world. American estimates indicated a casualty count among the Palestinians and Lebanese already in five figures; many of the dead and wounded had fallen to arms supplied by the United States. Washington had to take active measures to distance itself from the carnage.

Reagan sided with Bush and Weinberger, provoking Haig, who was huffy about other matters as well, to quit the administration. The

---

[2]Alexander M. Haig, Jr., *Caveat: Realism, Reagan, and Foreign Policy* (New York, 1984), p. 342.

president wrote to Begin to urge the Israeli prime minister to rein in his troops; he reiterated the message when Begin visited Washington at the end of June.

Although Reagan's expostulations had little immediate effect on Israel's actions, a diplomatic initiative launched a short while later yielded greater results. By the beginning of July, anyone at all familiar with the course of the fighting in Lebanon could see that a building-to-building battle for Beirut would drench the streets of that city in blood. Many Israelis were already questioning the cost of the war; not many wished to see hundreds more troops come home dead or maimed. As for the PLO, while some of the guerrillas might have welcomed a hero's death, more seemed content at the showing they had made thus far and preferred to live to fight another day. The Israelis insisted on getting the PLO out of Lebanon; the PLO insisted on leaving alive.

American troubleshooter Philip Habib recognized the reconcilability between the Israeli and Palestinian demands and worked hard to get them to recognize it also. Eventually they did. The PLO agreed to leave Lebanon for Algeria, Tunisia, and other radical parts of the Arab world, while the Israelis—after considerable last-minute pounding of PLO positions—agreed to let the guerrillas go. The United States provided a small peacekeeping force to help supervise the evacuation.

This second American intervention in Lebanon (the first since 1958) proceeded smoothly. By mid-September, more than 8000 PLO fighters had left Beirut. Several thousand Syrian soldiers took the opportunity to return to Syria. The American peacekeepers left shortly afterward. The success of the operation and the ease with which the U.S. troops extricated themselves allayed the concern of many in the United States who worried that the Reagan administration was getting the country into another Vietnam or worse.

But subsequent events almost immediately revived that concern. During the third week of September, assassins murdered the Christian president of Lebanon, Bashir Gemayel. Christian militiamen responded to the deed by entering two Palestinian refugee camps near Beirut and massacring some 800 Palestinians, including hundreds of women, children, and old people. Israeli troops occupying the area stood by and let the killing proceed.

The massacre at the Sabra and Shatila camps fulfilled the worst fears of Palestinian civilians in Lebanon, who had watched with trepidation while the PLO fighters, their only reliable defenders, left the country. It also brought demands that U.S. troops return to Beirut to prevent further score-settling. The Reagan administration, anxious to deflect charges that its preoccupation with avoiding another Vietnam had caused it to pull U.S. troops out prematurely, agreed to reintroduce them.

The trouble was that this time the American marines had only a very ill-defined goal, and one that possessed no obvious termination point. They would assist the Lebanese government to assert its authority over the country, against the various groups currently fighting there. Just what this meant, how long it would take, and whether it was even possible, no one could say for certain.

The work went slowly for the first few months. Then things turned bad. Rebels began firing on American soldiers and American positions; in April 1983, a Shiite Muslim suicide bomber attacked the U.S. embassy in Beirut, killing seventeen Americans and twenty-three other persons. Among the dead were the CIA station chief in Beirut and the CIA's top Middle East analyst.

The embassy bombing raised new questions in the United States regarding the role of the American marines in Beirut. With the 1984 elections on the horizon, the Reagan administration sought to assure voters that it wasn't entering any quagmires; Democrats in Congress and elsewhere were happy to suggest that such was precisely what the administration was doing. Continuing artillery attacks, especially by Druze forces in the mountains outside Beirut, against U.S. troops stationed at the Beirut airport lent credibility to the predictions of the administration's critics. This credibility increased as the American marines engaged their attackers in firefights, as American carrier-based planes overflew Lebanon, and as the big guns of American warships shelled Druze positions. The escalation of U.S. involvement alarmed congressional Democrats, who at the end of September compelled the president to accept an eighteen-month time limit on the deployment of American troops to Lebanon.

A new and newly tragic twist in the tangled plot of Lebanese affairs shortened the American stay. On October 23, a Shiite terrorist-martyr drove a truck filled with explosives into the American zone at the Beirut airport; when the truck exploded, it killed 241 American marines and 58 French soldiers.

Had most Americans discerned any significant worthy purpose in the marines' presence in Lebanon, this latest bombing might have produced a remember-Pearl-Harbor reaction. But most Americans found politics in Lebanon nearly incomprehensible, and few understood why American soldiers ought to get themselves killed there. After trying to put a brave face on the matter, the Reagan administration announced early in 1984 that it was planning to "redeploy" the American troops from the Beirut airport to U.S. naval vessels offshore. Reagan contended that the shift didn't indicate an abandonment of previous American objectives in Lebanon. "We're not bugging out," the president told reporters. "We're just going to a little more defensible position."[3]

2. LIBYA AND THE SPECTER OF TERRORISM

However the Reagan administration sought to explain the departure of the U.S. troops, the world could see that the terrorists had won. They had killed a couple hundred American soldiers, and the rest had fled. During the 1980 campaign, candidate Reagan had vowed never to give in to terrorism. Doubtless, he meant it, at the time. But Reagan as president came to understand the difficulties of adhering to such a policy. The most important of these difficulties followed from the fact that in nearly any encounter with the United States, the terrorists had less to lose than the American president did. To be sure, they might lose their lives, but the fact that some of them were willing to commit suicide for their cause indicated that they had higher priorities than just continuing to breathe. Unlike the president, they weren't responsible for the safety and well-being of hundreds of millions of people; nor did they have the moral reputation of a great country to uphold. When terrorists bombed the U.S. embassy in Lebanon or the U.S. marines' position at the Beirut airport, Reagan might have responded by ordering reprisals against the closest reasonably plausible target—more or less as the Israelis did in such circumstances. But where the Israelis, surrounded by enemies and fighting for their national existence, accepted the principle of collective punishment, Americans didn't—not sufficiently, at any rate, for Reagan to feel free to adopt a policy based on that principle.

Yet Reagan wasn't so hamstrung as to be entirely without recourse to terrorist attack, as he demonstrated in relations with Libya. Since

[3]*American Foreign Policy: Current Documents, 1984*, p. 581.

the 1969 coup that had vaulted Qaddafi to power, the Libyan leader had championed the cause of revolutionary groups against the United States and pro-Western regimes in the Middle East. Beyond the required excoriation of Israel—against which he declared a fight to the death—he denounced the governments of Egypt, Jordan, Morocco, and Tunisia. On a number of occasions he went beyond verbal assaults to active support of insurgents conspiring to overthrow those governments. He provided sanctuary to Palestinian terrorists of the Black September movement who killed eleven Israeli athletes at the 1972 Munich Olympic games, and he was widely suspected of complicity in a number of other terrorist incidents against Israel and countries of the West.

Publicly, Qaddafi had trouble making up his mind whether to embrace terrorism explicitly or not. Libya signed a number of United Nations conventions against terrorism, but Qaddafi consistently expressed sympathy for those driven to extreme measures. Moreover, he judged the West—the United States in particular—to be hopelessly hypocritical on the terrorist question. The United States, by virtue (vice, rather) of being a superpower, practiced terrorism daily. "Foreign bases, nuclear weapons, starvation, economic warfare, naval fleets"—all these, he claimed, were "acts of terrorism." Addressing himself specifically to the issue of Palestinian terrorism, Qaddafi said, "Why do Americans forget that the Palestinians have been expelled from their homeland and that the U.S. is helping the occupier keep hold of the land of the Palestinians? But when a Palestinian hijacks a plane to express his despair, the U.S. shakes the world by saying that this is terrorism and an end should be put to it."[4]

Such sentiments scarcely endeared Qaddafi to Americans. The fact that he established close ties to the Soviet Union didn't help his case. By the late 1970s, he had become America's favorite villain. The Carter administration singled Libya out as guilty of aiding and abetting international terrorism. The Reagan administration went further. Beyond using American aid to bolster governments Qaddafi was attacking, the Republicans employed the CIA to train and support anti-Qaddafi Libyan exiles. A specific plan to topple Qaddafi may or may not have existed; the exile army never mounted a seri-

[4]Mahmoud G. El-Warfally, *Imagery and Ideology in U.S. Policy toward Libya, 1969–1982* (Pittsburgh, 1988), p. 72.

ous effort to do so. But at the minimum, Washington wanted to spoil Qaddafi's sleep.

It was (and still is) unclear how much responsibility Qaddafi actually had for the terrorist activities that grew increasingly frequent and bloody during the 1980s. He almost certainly provided logistical assistance to groups and individuals who perpetrated some nasty deeds, and he made no apparent effort to distance himself from the terrorists. On the other hand, he evidently believed, as he said, that he was simply doing as he was being done to. After a contingent of the Libyan exiles assaulted a Libyan army barracks, Qaddafi blamed the United States, and offered a warning. "We are capable of exporting terrorism to the heart of America," he declared. "We are also capable of physical liquidation, destruction, and arson inside America." Americans had inflicted terrorism on Libya. "We will respond likewise." Several months later, he said, "We are always wronged; therefore we have the right to fight Zionism, we have the right to fight America, and we have the right to export terrorism to them because they have done everything to us."[5]

By statements like these, Qaddafi made himself an easy political target for the Reagan administration. Especially after the bombing of the U.S. marines at the Beirut airport, the administration was looking for targets. When 1985 brought the hijacking of an American TWA airliner and murderous shooting sprees at the Rome and Vienna airports, administration officials decided to take strong measures. Although Libya's part in the recent actions was uncertain, Reagan in January 1986 declared a national emergency with respect to Libya, blocking American trade with that country and freezing Libyan assets in the United States. Justifying these measures, Reagan described the Rome and Vienna massacres as "the latest in a series of atrocities which have shocked the conscience of the world." The president added, "Qaddafi's longstanding involvement in terrorism is well documented, and there's irrefutable evidence of his role in these attacks." (When a reporter asked how the administration could be so sure of Qaddafi's involvement, the president declined to reveal his sources of information.) Reagan asserted that Qaddafi deserved to be treated "as a pariah in the world community." He concluded, "If these steps do not end Qaddafi's terrorism, I promise you that further steps will be taken."[6]

[5]Brian L. Davis, *Qaddafi, Terrorism, and the Origins of the U.S. Attack on Libya* (New York, 1990), pp. 66, 185.

[6]*American Foreign Policy 1986*, pp. 446–447.

Further steps came soon. In March 1986, the president ordered the U.S. Sixth Fleet to engage in maneuvers in the Mediterranean just off the Libyan coast. Libya had long claimed sovereignty over the Gulf of Sidra; the United States had equally long rejected the claim. In 1981, this difference of opinion had led to an aerial dogfight in which U.S. planes had shot down two Libyan aircraft. In 1986, the administration evidently hoped for another tussle. On the record, the administration contended that it was merely exercising its right of free passage in international waters; on background, one unnamed U.S. official admitted, "Of course we're aching for a go at Qaddafi." Another said, "If he sticks his head up, we'll clobber him. We're looking for an excuse."[7]

On March 24, Libyan shore batteries commenced missile fire against the U.S. task force. The latter responded by blasting Libyan radar installations and sinking or crippling several Libyan patrol boats. Libyan casualties numbered in the dozens.

The encounter in the Gulf of Sidra only whetted Washington's appetite. "The next act of terrorism will bring the hammer down," an anonymous but senior administration official told *Newsweek* magazine.[8]

The next act happened at the beginning of April. In the wee hours of a Saturday morning, a bomb ripped apart a night club in West Berlin, killing one American soldier outright, mortally injuring a second, and wounding more than two hundred other persons, including scores of American soldiers.

The administration quickly leaped to the conclusion that Libya lay behind the bombing. The leap resulted partly from some intercepted cable traffic between Tripoli and East Berlin and partly from the Reagan administration's predisposition to hit Qaddafi. Although subsequent information indicated that Syria at least shared responsibility for the bombing, with some reports putting primary blame on Damascus and Asad, the administration apparently took the view that Qaddafi deserved punishment for plenty of crimes, if not necessarily for this one. Reagan expressed no doubt of the link between Qaddafi and the Berlin bombing. "Our evidence is direct," the president said. "It is precise; it is irrefutable."[9]

As punishment, Reagan ordered a brief but intense air assault against Libya and Qaddafi. On April 15, U.S. F-111s based in

[7]Davis, op. cit. p. 104.

[8]*Newsweek*, April 7, 1986.

[9]*Weekly Compilation of Presidential Documents*, April 21, 1986.

Britain joined A-6s, A-7s, and F/A-18s from American aircraft carriers in the Mediterranean for a coordinated series of raids against Tripoli and Benghazi. Whether the administration was trying specifically to kill Qaddafi remains a matter of dispute; certainly American leaders would have shed few tears had one of the bombs dispatched him. None did. Yet the U.S. planes inflicted severe damage on several Libyan military sites; at the same time, they killed dozens of Libyans. Qaddafi claimed that the dead included his adopted daughter, but skeptical Qaddafi-watchers didn't rule out posthumous adoption.

The American bombing of a country with which the United States wasn't at war sparked considerable outcry around the world (which in turn triggered a backlash in the United States against the critics, especially "Eurowimps" like the French, who had refused to let the U.S. planes from Britain fly through French airspace on the way to Libya). The bombing also elicited predictions of a wave of terrorist counteractions. Events of the first few weeks after the raids bore out the predictions. Gunmen gravely wounded a U.S. diplomat in Sudan; another American diplomat took two bullets in Yemen; the body of an American hostage shot through the head turned up in Beirut; two Libyans carrying grenades were arrested near an American officers' club in Ankara; somebody angry at the United States fired rockets at the U.S. embassy in Indonesia. No one could say with any assurance what Qaddafi had to do with these incidents, although Radio Tripoli definitely encouraged reprisals against the United States with violent denunciations of "the mad terrorist Reagan" and advice that "he who kills an American enters heaven; he who slaughters an American creates a new glory for the Arab nation with blood."[10]

After several weeks, though, things began to settle down, and in the longer term, terrorist activities declined. While the Reagan administration predictably claimed a chastening effect for the bombing of Libya, an overall tightening up of security in sensitive spots around the world probably contributed as much to curtailing the atrocities. The Europeans especially, both from concern for their own safety and to keep Washington from taking matters into its own hands again, deported suspicious-looking Libyans and other foreign nationals and adopted a variety of measures to make bombings, hijackings, and the like more difficult.

[10]Davis, op. cit., p. 189.

3. IMPLAUSIBLE DENIABILITY, OR ARMS FOR THE AYATOLLAH

Whether or not the attack on Libya diminished the terrorist threat from Tripoli's direction, it did little to deter terrorists operating on behalf of Iran. In the wake of the 1982 Israeli invasion of Lebanon and the introduction of U.S. troops into that country, radical Lebanese Shiites belonging to such groups as Hezbollah (Party of God) and Islamic Jihad continued the anti-American offensive that already included the bombing attacks on the American embassy and the American marine post at the Beirut airport. In January 1984, assassins murdered the president of the American University of Beirut, Malcolm Kerr; shortly thereafter, Americans began disappearing off the streets of the Lebanese capital. Kidnappers took three American hostages during 1984, including William Buckley, the new CIA station chief in Beirut, who died in captivity, evidently after torture. Kidnappers seized four more Americans in 1985, including the director of Catholic Relief Services in Beirut and the head of the American University hospital. Meanwhile, terrorists bombed the U.S. embassy in Kuwait.

The precise motives of the kidnappers and bombers were impossible to tell, but Hezbollah, the dominant force among the hostage-takers, was avowedly attempting to further the aims of the Islamic revolution in Iran, and strong indications were that the group operated with Iran's support, if not entirely under Iran's control. Shortly after the killing of Malcolm Kerr, the Reagan administration listed Iran as a sponsor of international terrorism. The kidnappings that followed did nothing to change Washington's view.

For public consumption, the administration adopted the position that it didn't and wouldn't negotiate with the hostage-takers. "The United States gives terrorists no rewards," Reagan declared in June 1985. "We make no concessions. We make no deals."[11]

The truth was otherwise. For several months before the president made this statement, the staff of Reagan's National Security Council had been investigating the possibility of improving relations with Iran. In principle, the idea made sense: whether Americans liked it or not, Iran remained the largest power of the Persian Gulf region, and U.S.

[11]*The New York Times,* July 1, 1985.

interests would probably suffer if Iran long continued to be estranged from the United States. In practice, though, there was serious doubt whether Iran was ready to reciprocate the American desire for improved relations, and whether American efforts at improvement wouldn't simply explode in Washington's face. The State and Defense departments took the skeptical view: the professional diplomats and the Pentagon held that in trying to cultivate Iran, the administration would be walking into a trap. The CIA thought improvement was possible, but the intelligence agency wanted to see some concrete demonstrations of Iran's good faith, such as the release of the American hostages held by Hezbollah in Lebanon, including the CIA's own William Buckley, still alive at this time.

Despite the skepticism, there *was* some reason to believe that Tehran also wanted better U.S.-Iranian relations. In September 1980, Iraq had attacked Iran, starting a war that would last for eight years. Although Iran had thrown over most vestiges of Pahlavi's rule, it hadn't traded in the shah's American-built weapons, and as the fighting against Iraq proceeded, the Iranians found themselves running low on ammunition and spare parts. During the first years of the war, Tehran had circumvented the U.S. arms embargo—initially imposed after the seizure of the American embassy, and extended (and applied to Iraq as well) after the outbreak of the Iran-Iraq war—by purchasing required supplies in the always-active international arms bazaar. But recently the Reagan administration had been pressing Washington's allies and clients to cut off third-party shipments to Iran. A State Department release in May 1985 explained the administration's position: "The U.S. does not permit U.S. arms and munitions to be shipped to either belligerent and has discouraged all free-world arms shipments to Iran because, unlike Iraq, Iran is adamantly opposed to negotiations or a mediated end to the conflict."[12]

One third party that didn't like the idea of cutting off weapons to Iran was Israel. Although the Khomeini regime constantly breathed fire at the Zionist state, the Israelis considered Iran the less threatening of the two antagonists in the Persian Gulf war. For one thing, Iran was farther away than Iraq; for another, Iranians felt scant kinship for the Palestinians, with whom they shared neither language nor much history. (They broadly shared religion with the Muslims

[12]*Report of the Congressional Committees Investigating the Iran-Contra Affair* (Washington, 1987), p. 159.

among the Palestinians, but most Muslim Palestinians were Sunnis, as opposed to Shiite Muslims, of whom the Iranians composed the largest national group. Anyway, shared Islam hadn't prevented the war between Iran and Iraq.) Israel had enjoyed reasonably good relations with Iran during the years of the shah's rule, and it hoped to enjoy good relations with Iran under a successor regime to that of Khomeini, who wouldn't live forever. In the meantime, Israel didn't mind helping even the radicals currently running Iran, if such help meant keeping Iraq's Saddam Hussein occupied away from Israel's borders.

When the Israelis got wind that Washington, or at least some groups within the Reagan administration, were seeking a means of opening doors to Iran, they offered their services. They said they would be pleased to sell military equipment to Iran, if the U.S. government approved.

This suggestion appealed to Robert McFarlane, Reagan's national security adviser, and William Casey, the director of the CIA. McFarlane circulated a draft directive recommending that the administration seek a rapprochement with anti-Khomeini elements in Iran by encouraging U.S. allies and friends to "help Iran meet its import requirements," including "provision of selected military equipment."[13]

Secretary of State George Shultz and Defense Secretary Weinberger objected strongly. Shultz asserted that the proposal to permit or encourage the flow of Western arms to Iran was "contrary to our interest both in containing Khomeinism and in ending the excesses of this regime." Weinberger blasted McFarlane's draft as "almost too absurd to comment on." The defense secretary added, "It's like asking Qadaffi to Washington for a cozy lunch." Weinberger expanded on his reasons for opposing the pro-Iran initiative, saying that a reversal of the administration's policy on arms sales "would be seen as inexplicably inconsistent by those nations whom we have urged to refrain from such sales" and might well lead to an "alteration of the strategic balance in favor of Iran while Khomeini is still the controlling influence."[14]

One might have thought that the opposition of the secretaries of state and defense would have blocked a major foreign-policy reversal.

[13]Ibid., p. 165.
[14]Idem.; Caspar W. Weinberger, *Fighting for Peace: Seven Critical Years in the Pentagon* (New York, 1990), pp. 363–364.

In most presidential administrations, it would have. But McFarlane and his deputies on the NSC were persistent, and devious, and Shultz and Weinberger didn't keep as close an eye on them as they should have. With McFarlane's blessing, Israeli officials met with Iranian officials to talk weapons; the latter indicated a desire to receive U.S. TOW antitank missiles—perhaps 100 or so for starters.

McFarlane raised the issue with the president in August 1985, or slightly before. (The after-the-fact reconstruction of these events relied on some fuzzy memories.) Reagan had recently met with the families of the American hostages and took to heart the families' pleas for action to release their loved ones. When McFarlane said that the sale of the missiles could lead to the release of the hostages, the president overruled Shultz's and Weinberger's objections, and (according to McFarlane's later testimony, and to the balance of evidence, despite Reagan's self-claimed absence of recollection of doing so) authorized the sale. On the morning of August 20, a plane left Israel with ninety-six TOWs; it landed its load in Tehran several hours later.

But no hostages were freed. The middleman in the exchange was a shady character named Manucher Ghorbanifar, an Iranian expatriate whose reported ties to Pahlavi's SAVAK and whose apparent complicity in an unsuccessful 1980 anti-Khomeini coup didn't prevent him from thinking he could broker a deal between Washington and the revolutionary regime in Tehran. Ghorbanifar explained to his U.S. contacts that in a mixup the TOW missiles had gone to the wrong people. The commander of the most militant wing of the revolution, the Iranian Revolutionary Guards, had grabbed the weapons before the moderates they were intended for could take delivery. Yet Ghorbanifar refused to give up the game (and the fat commission he was deriving from it). He argued that another shipment of missiles ought to convince the Iranians to spring at least some of the hostages.

Reagan's disappointment at the failure to get the hostages out on the first try apparently only increased his desire to see the captives free. Persuasive evidence (although again not Reagan's memory) indicates that when McFarlane presented Ghorbanifar's argument to the president, Reagan approved the delivery of a second batch of TOW missiles. A shipment of 408 TOWs left Israel and landed in Tabriz—beyond the reach, Ghorbanifar contended, of the Revolutionary Guards—on September 14. The following day, one of the American hostages, Benjamin Weir, surfaced safely near the U.S. embassy in Beirut.

One hostage seemed niggardly for over 500 missiles, even to those pushing the initiative. At this point, the arms-for-hostages effort might have halted were it not for two facts. First, the principal opponents of the effort, Weinberger and Shultz, didn't know what was going on. McFarlane, figuring that they couldn't stop what they didn't know about, declined to inform them of the arms transfer, and they didn't exert themselves to find out.

Second, by this time the shipments of arms to Iran had acquired a justification beyond the president's desire to free the hostages. Throughout this period the administration was locked in a battle with Congress over U.S. aid to the contra rebels in Nicaragua. In 1984, Congress had approved an amendment (the Boland amendment) to the fiscal 1985 appropriations bill, blocking funds for the contras' military operations, and the president had signed the bill into law. But imaginative go-getters on the NSC staff, especially Oliver North, decided to seek funding by extra-congressional methods. They solicited donations from contra-friendly individuals and governments, and they began diverting profits from the sale of weapons to Iran to the contras.

This combination of factors kept the secret sale of weapons to Iran alive. Through Ghorbanifar, the Iranians asked for American Hawk anti-aircraft missiles. In October 1985, Michael Ledeen, an NSC consultant, met in Geneva with Iranian representatives to discuss the terms of a transfer of Hawks. There Ledeen discovered that the Iranians were raising their price: in addition to 150 Hawks, they demanded 200 Sidewinder missiles and 30 to 50 Phoenix missiles.

This was higher than the administration was willing to go, especially since Tehran had failed to follow through on the earlier agreements—as McFarlane and other Americans in the know interpreted them—to release several hostages. By the third week in November, Oliver North and his associates had devised a counteroffer. The administration would authorize taking eighty Hawks from Israel's armory and delivering them to Iran; if the Iranians then arranged the release of five American hostages and perhaps a French hostage, Iran would receive forty more Hawks from Israel. Israel would be compensated with missiles from the United States. After considerable difficulty determining whose planes would fly the Hawks to Iran and what route they would follow, the CIA sent an aircraft to pick up the first eighteen missiles. On the night of November 24–25, the CIA plane flew from Tel Aviv to Tehran.

But the Iranians didn't like what they received. They complained that these were the wrong kind of Hawks (in fact, the Iranians had entertained mistaken notions of the Hawks' capabilities), and that anyway the missiles had Israeli markings. The Iranians evidently felt that having their missile corps learn that the Islamic republic required the help of the Zionists in defending the homeland entailed too many risks. Ghorbanifar passed along a message from the Iranians: "We have done everything we said we were going to do, and you are now cheating us, and you must act quickly to remedy this situation." The Iranians made plain that no American hostages would be released until the United States had effected the required remedies.[15]

Remarkably, even this turn of events failed to kill the arms-for-hostages initiative. Oliver North argued—and he could be very convincing, as millions of American television watchers discovered during the subsequent congressional investigation of the Iran-contra affair—that the administration had gone too far to back out. The disappointed hostage holders might vent their disappointment on the captive Americans. "If we do not make at least one more good try at this point," North wrote, "we stand a good chance of condemning some or all to death." The United States might also encounter a renewed wave of terrorism. "While the risks of proceeding are significant," North concluded, "the risks of not trying one last time are even greater." (North evidently didn't feel it necessary or appropriate to add that the Iranians might blow the whistle on the affair, to the chagrin of the Reagan administration.)[16]

Besides, the arms sales to Iran were generating sizable sums of money for the contras and promised to generate far more. As matters eventually transpired, the reality fell short of the promise, and the contras got only between about $4 million and $16 million—with the figure varying according to who was counting the money and telling the story to the congressional committee. But at the time, North and friends had reason to think the numbers would be much higher.

By this stage of the operation, any doubt that the Reagan administration was bartering arms for hostages—as opposed to pursuing some grander strategic purpose—had largely disappeared. North went so far in the direction of frankness as to write out an elaborate formula for the exchange:

[15]*Report,* p. 187.
[16]Ibid., p. 194.

H-hour: 1 707 w/300 TOWs = 1 AMCIT
H + 10 hrs: 1 707 (same A/C) w/300 TOWs = 1 AMCIT
H + 16 hrs: 1 747 w/50 HAWKS & 400 TOWs = 2 AMCITs
H + 20 hrs: 1 707 w/300 TOWs = 1 AMCIT
H + 24 hrs: 1 747 w/2000 TOWs = 1 French hostage

(Translation: At zero-hostage-hour, one Boeing 707 jet would deliver 300 TOW missiles, and one American citizen would be freed; ten hours later, the same kind of aircraft would deliver 300 more TOWs, and a American hostage would be released; and so forth.)[17]

Getting the Iranians to accept this schedule required effort. McFarlane traveled to London early in December 1985 to meet with Ghorbanifar and some representatives of the Israeli government. The negotiations bogged down, partly because McFarlane was learning to distrust Ghorbanifar's talents (he had always distrusted Ghorbanifar's motives, although not enough not to use him). McFarlane left the meeting convinced, as he later remarked, that the Iranian deal-maker was a "borderline moron." Problems with Israel over replenishing the weapons stocks raided for the arms-for-hostages program, as well as over other procedural details, caused the Israelis to reconsider their participation in the program. So did an opinion by Reagan's lawyers that allowing Israel to resell American weapons to Iran might violate U.S. law (presumably jeopardizing Israel's own supply line).[18]

To avoid some of the problems, the White House decided to deal directly, or at least more directly, with Iran. On January 17, 1986, Reagan signed a top-secret paper affirming that the sale of arms from the United States to Iran served the U.S. national interest and authorizing such sales. The following month the administration sold 1000 TOW missiles to Iran. As an additional enticement, American intelligence agencies provided Iran with military intelligence about Iraq and that country's position and prospects in the Iran-Iraq war.

North and John Poindexter, Reagan's new national security adviser, argued that Iran intended to secure the release of all the American hostages upon the delivery of the intelligence information and the missiles. Other American officials weren't so sure. As one CIA analyst later told the congressional investigating committee:

[17] Idem.
[18] Ibid., p. 199.

"Under no conditions would the government of Iran ever allow all the hostages to be released. . . . The only leverage that those who held the hostages have is the hostages, so why would they give them up?" Another CIA official, Deputy Director John McMahon, thought delivering order-of-battle and related information to Iran was downright stupid. McMahon warned William Casey that the information the United States was providing "could cause the Iranians to have a successful offensive against the Iraqis with cataclysmic results."[19]

The doubters were right, at least about the hostages. Iran took the information and the missiles, and the hostages stayed in captivity. But this latest failure didn't prevent further efforts in the same direction, since the contra side of the operation was going slowly but comparatively well. The February missile sale yielded a $10 million payment to Richard Secord, the American go-between handling the financial aspects of the arms deals. Secord in turn paid $3.7 million to the CIA, the nominal owner of the missiles before Iran got them. This left more than $6 million—less Secord's commission, the size of which remained a matter of dispute throughout the whole congressional investigation—for the contras and perhaps other worthy, but legally unfundable, covert activities.

In May, the Poindexter-North team tried again. The president approved a trip by McFarlane, no longer officially attached to the White House but still vitally interested in the Iran initiative, to Tehran. McFarlane would arrive with the first installment of a new shipment of arms, this of parts for Hawk missiles. He hoped to return with guarantees of the release of the hostages, if not with the hostages themselves. To celebrate the triumphal end of a long and trying process, McFarlane took a chocolate cake with him to Tehran. (Presumably, champagne would offend the devout Muslims he would be dealing with.)

But this episode proved as disappointing as the rest. When McFarlane got to Tehran, his Iranian interlocutors insisted that they had to receive *all* the Hawk parts before they could turn any captives loose. McFarlane insisted back that the hostages had to come out first. For four days the two sides went round and round—with the cake presumably getting stale. Finally McFarlane packed up and left, although the first planeload of parts stayed in Iran.

[19]Ibid., pp. 218, 228.

Perhaps thinking they had bargained too hard, the Iranians several weeks later arranged the release of hostage Lawrence Jenco, who became the second hostage freed since the arms dealing had begun. Though McFarlane had rejected a more attractive offer just before leaving Tehran—two hostages then, two more when the rest of the Hawk parts arrived—the administration responded to the release of Jenco by delivering the balance of the parts.

During the autumn of 1986, North and Poindexter tried to discover a new, more reliable channel for dealing with the Iranian government. They found some different Iranians to talk to, but these persons turned out to represent the same decision makers in Tehran and had the same aim as their predecessors: to acquire American weapons for use in the war against Iraq, by releasing just enough hostages to keep the weapons coming. In October, the White House agreed to ship another 500 TOW missiles. On October 27, the missiles arrived in Iran, where they were snatched up by the Revolutionary Guards. On November 2, a third American hostage, David Jacobsen, was released.

The next day the arms-for-hostages scheme came to a screeching halt. A Lebanese magazine broke the story, and all involved ran for cover. The Reagan administration initially denied the reports that the U.S. government, contrary to the repeated professions of its officials, had been selling weapons to Iran in order to obtain the release of American hostages. But too many people knew about the operation to keep it quiet, and within weeks the general outlines were clear. The plot thickened at the end of November as word of the contra connection got out. When Congress reconvened at the beginning of January 1987, the Democratic leadership, along with some indignant Republicans, demanded an investigation of the whole business.

The investigation produced some moments of melodrama, featuring Oliver North wrapped in the American flag and proclaiming his devotion to the principles that made America strong—not including the rule of law. The investigation also produced evidence of a singular forgetfulness at the highest levels of the administration. But it failed to produce the proverbial smoking gun: irrefutable proof that the president himself had ordered illegal activities.

Smoking gun or not, the Reagan administration scurried to distance itself from Iran. The administration thereby added to the momentum that was putting the United States on the side of Iraq in the Iran-Iraq war. The government of Iran was hardly less embarrassed than Washington. Tehran reasserted its passion for the objectives of the Islamic revolution, and denounced the American Great Satan in terms more sulfurous than ever.

4. WHEN SADDAM HUSSEIN WAS ONE OF THE GOOD GUYS: THE FIRST GULF WAR

An observer convinced of the subtlety and acuteness of the Reagan administration's foreign policy might have judged the arms-for-hostages deal to be a diplomatic reinsurance scheme: a hedging of American bets in the Persian Gulf. Less charitable types interpreted it as a prime example of bureaucratic bungling, an instance of policy making by the zealous ignorant, who couldn't keep straight what the United States was trying to accomplish between Iran and Iraq.

The unkind critics had the better case, since for most of the 1980s Washington had leaned toward Iraq in that country's war with Iran. The Iran-Iraq war began when Iraq's Saddam Hussein took the opportunity of Iran's revolutionary turmoil to renew the age-old struggle between Mesopotamia and Persia. The Iraqi government had initially greeted the fall of Pahlavi with satisfaction, not least because Baghdad had never thought much of the U.S. strategy of arming the shah as an agent of pro-Westernism in the gulf. But when Khomeini started preaching Islamic revolution not only for Iran but for other Muslim countries as well, the Iraqi regime reconsidered its position. When Iran began supporting insurrectionary activities by Iraq's Kurdish and Shiite communities, culminating in assassination attempts against various Iraqi leaders, Baghdad decided to teach the Iranians a lesson. Border skirmishes and artillery exchanges escalated until the end of September 1980, when Saddam Hussein ordered Iraqi troops across the frontier into Iran.

Americans, still preoccupied by Tehran's holding of the American hostages, had trouble sympathizing with Iran. Nor did American sympathy increase in the first two years of the war, during which Iraq generally got the better of the fighting. As the balance shifted in Iran's favor after 1982, American leaders fretted that Khomeini might actually have his way in toppling Saddam Hussein and the Baathists in Baghdad and replacing them with folks more to his liking. The Reagan administration responded with a tilt in the direction of Iraq, strengthening U.S. representation in Baghdad and organizing a blockade of weapons to Iran (which it violated itself in the arms-for-hostages deal).

Yet, for the most part, the Reagan administration kept the United States out of what became an enormously bloody but indecisive stalemate. In Washington's view, so long as neither side seemed about to deliver a knockout blow to the other, and thereby threaten to dominate the region, there was no percentage in getting deeply involved.

The percentages changed toward the end of 1986, when Iran stepped up attacks on shipping in the Persian Gulf. Iranian gunboats particularly targeted vessels calling at Kuwait, the oil-rich Arab emirate at the head of the gulf, which had been helping to underwrite Iraq's war effort. Partly because they were so wealthy, and partly because they often flaunted their wealth, the Kuwaitis counted few friends, even among their fellow Arabs. But countries that have oil don't need friends; they have customers, who tend to be more reliable. The Kuwaitis appealed for assistance to the international community, shrewdly including both the Soviet Union and the United States. When Moscow said it would oblige, the Reagan administration felt it could do no less. Caspar Weinberger explained the reasoning afterward: "If we did not assist in the movement of the oil shipments through the Gulf, the Soviet Union would be more than happy to become the sole guarantor of the security of the small Gulf states." At the moment, the Soviet presence in the gulf was miniscule. Washington intended to keep it that way. "I was quite sure," Weinberger said, "that if we did not respond positively to the Kuwaitis, the USSR would quickly fill the vacuum, and that the Gulf states, already concerned for a number of reasons [especially the fall of the shah] about American reliability, would not be able to deny basing and port facilities to their new protectors."[20]

What the Kuwaitis had in mind was the reflagging of Kuwaiti ships under U.S. registry and U.S. protection. The Reagan administration quickly approved the plan. The Soviets had already agreed to a similar scheme, but when Washington gave its okay, it strongly encouraged the Kuwaitis to back out of their arrangement with Moscow. Kuwait partially complied, chartering a few Soviet ships for oil-carrying work rather than reflagging their own under the banner of the hammer and sickle.

[20]Weinberger, op. cit., pp. 389–390.

The Reagan administration presented the reflagging operation as entirely in keeping with its official neutrality in the gulf war. Kuwait, after all, was neutral, even if the Kuwaitis' oil income—which Tehran was trying to cut off—benefited their fellow Arabs in Iraq and hurt the Persians in Iran. But no one watching at this time had much difficulty determining where Washington's good wishes lay.

That small difficulty diminished further in May 1987, when an Iraqi fighter plane patrolling the gulf fired on a U.S. warship, the *Stark.* The attack severely damaged the *Stark* and killed thirty-seven American sailors. The Iraqis claimed mistaken identity, and the administration chose to accept the excuse, if only because no one in Washington could come up with a compelling reason why the Iraqis would have hit the U.S. ship deliberately. (Later, when Saddam Hussein became a bad guy, some people would look—not very successfully—for a deeper motive behind the *Stark* affair.)

The accident, if such it was, had two consequences. First, it convinced Iran that the United States remained the Great Satan, ready to side with almost anyone against the Islamic republic. Second, it warned the U.S. Congress of the hazards of war duty in the Persian Gulf. The attack on the *Stark* came even before U.S. warships began convoying the reflagged Kuwaiti tankers down the gulf; what those warships would encounter once they got in the thick of the tanker war was anyone's guess. Democrats and a few Republicans on Capitol Hill mumbled about invoking the War Powers Act of 1973, which was designed to limit the president's ability to put the United States at war without the consent of Congress. Reagan quieted some of the mumbling by reassuring the American people that the United States wasn't taking sides in the war between Iran and Iraq; the reflagging and convoying operation simply had the purpose of ensuring the freedom of the seas, and, in particular, of guaranteeing the free flow of Kuwaiti oil to world markets.

The oil-escorting operation turned out to be less eventful than the critics had feared. The Western Europeans, led by Britain and France, sent naval vessels to the gulf to help out; this expanded Iran's target list, in case the Iranians decided to start shooting at ships defending the tanker traffic. It also alleviated complaints in the United States about American sailors defending oil destined for European automobiles. In September 1987, a U.S. ship seized an Iranian craft caught in the act of laying mines; a month later, U.S. forces retaliated for an Iranian missile attack on one of the reflagged tankers by destroying an Iranian communications post on an offshore oil platform. But neither the Reagan administration nor the Iranian government particularly wanted these skirmishes to expand into a real war.

Reagan had the 1988 elections to worry about—not for himself, but for the Republican party and his heir apparent, George Bush. And although Iran continued to top the American list of disliked foreign countries, almost no voters looked favorably on a war against the Iranians.

As for the Iranians, they had a full plate dealing with Iraq. The Iranian economy was slumping drastically after seven years of war; public enthusiasm for the war likewise was sagging. Starting early in 1988 and continuing into the spring, Iraq bombarded Iranian cities with missiles, which didn't do much for Iranian morale either. In April, Iraqi troops recaptured the strategic Faw peninsula, reversing one of the principal Iranian gains in the war to date.

Yet radical elements in Iran still saw hostility against the United States as a device for preventing more moderate types from sidetracking the revolution. The Iranian Revolutionary Guards stepped up mine-laying activities, which resulted in an explosion against the U.S. destroyer *Roberts*. Washington ordered reprisals against a pair of Iranian oil platforms in the gulf.

The American policy of tit-for-tat continued into the early summer of 1988. During that time, it occasioned relatively little controversy outside Iran. In July, however, a tragic accident (according to the Reagan administration) or mass murder (according to Tehran) produced a new round of questioning of American actions in the Persian Gulf. On July 3, the U.S. destroyer *Vincennes* spotted an aircraft on radar, flying out of Iran on what seemed a threatening route. The American ship had just engaged Iranian gunboats, and the officers and crew were nervous. The captain ordered rockets fired, and watched them destroy the plane—only to discover that it was an Iranian airliner carrying nearly 300 passengers. All aboard died. The Iranian government condemned the Americans as barbaric warmongers.

The incident would have produced greater repercussions than it did, had the Iranian government not decided at this time that enough was enough in the war against Iraq. On July 18, after nearly eight years of one of the most futile conflicts of the twentieth century, Iran accepted a United Nations ceasefire resolution, and the first Persian Gulf war ended.

5. HUSSEIN BECOMES A BAD GUY: THE SECOND GULF WAR

Getting from the ceasefire to a permanent peace accord took two years and the prospect of another war in the Persian Gulf, over another country. For nearly thirty years, Iraq had coveted the territory and oil of Kuwait: the territory because it controlled Iraq's outlet to the gulf, the oil for the obvious reasons of wealth and power. On more than one occasion, Baghdad had waved swords in Kuwait's direction, but each time it had stopped short of invasion and annexation. After fighting much larger Iran to a draw, however, Saddam Hussein was feeling his oats, and he decided to revive his country's claims against Kuwait. In July 1990, he accused Kuwait (and other oil producers) of conspiring to hold down oil prices, thereby depriving Iraq of revenues required to pay for the recent war with Iran. He also alleged that Kuwait was stealing oil from the Rumaila oilfield, which straddled the border between Iraq and Kuwait. To lend emphasis to his complaints, Hussein sent 100,000 Iraqi troops to the border region.

Because Iraq had huffed and puffed against Kuwait before, with no grave consequence, because bluster seemed to characterize Hussein's style on most political issues, and because U.S. analysts thought it would be a few years before the Iraqi army was up to whatever gulf-dominating schemes Hussein was hatching, the United States didn't take Baghdad's threats against Kuwait especially seriously. The American ambassador to Iraq, April Glaspie, met with Hussein on July 25, her first direct conversation with the Iraqi president since she had arrived in Baghdad two years before. Hussein, ignoring the American tilt in his favor during the war with Iran, blasted the United States for joining the ranks of Iraq's enemies—for plotting with Kuwait, he said, to keep oil prices down and Iraq impoverished.

Depending on whose story was true, Glaspie either warned Hussein in no uncertain terms to keep his hands off Kuwait (her story) or indicated that Iraq's troubles with Kuwait were a matter for the Arabs to solve, without U.S. involvement (his story). Whatever Glaspie really told Hussein on July 25, Washington definitely did *not* adopt a highly visible stance on the Iraq-Kuwait dispute before the beginning of August. Had the U.S. government believed that Hussein was about to order his troops into Kuwait, President Bush could have warned him that such a move would bring down on his head the wrath of the United States. But U.S. intelligence analysts thought Hussein would settle for something less than all of Kuwait: an agreement to curtail oil production and raise prices, perhaps, or forgiveness of the war debts Iraq owed Kuwait, or a lease or transfer of the two Kuwaiti islands that blocked Iraqi access to the Persian Gulf, or cession to Iraq of Kuwait's corner of the Rumaila oilfield. Already Baghdad had consented to discuss its differences with Kuwait. The troop movements might well be just a bargaining tactic.

On August 2, however, Saddam Hussein demonstrated the wishfulness of this thinking. Probably believing that the United States would do no more than slap his wrist, or at worst impose trade restrictions, he ordered his troops into Kuwait. The Kuwaitis were in no position to defend themselves. Since the petrodollars had begun gushing in during the 1970s, the Kuwaitis had fallen into the habit of hiring foreign workers—Palestinians, Pakistanis, Filipinos—to do their menial labor. But foreigners who dug ditches drew the line at digging tank traps. The Iraqi forces required less than a day to capture Kuwait City and establish control over the country. Kuwait's ruler, Emir Jabir al-Ahmad Al Sabah, flew away to Saudi Arabia one step ahead of the Iraqi tanks.

Catching U.S. officials by surprise, the Iraqi offensive required the Bush administration to guess what else Hussein might have in store. The CIA, embarrassed by its failure to forecast the most potentially destabilizing development in the Middle East since World War II, now leaned to the side of predicting too much. According to accounts published later, CIA director William Webster warned Bush that Hussein had his eyes on Saudi Arabia—if not the whole kingdom, at least the country's oilfields. Webster also estimated that the Saudis wouldn't put up much of a fight against an Iraqi invading force.

This left the Bush administration in a quandary. The world, or that large part of it that consumed oil, could live with a merged Iraq-Kuwait. Such a merged entity would be an important player in the international energy market, but as long as Saudi Arabia, the largest exporter of Middle Eastern oil, remained independent, Hussein would lack a stranglehold over supplies and prices. An Iraqi seizure of Saudi Arabia, on the other hand, might turn the global oil picture on its head. Where the price of a barrel of oil (already soaring on news of the invasion of Kuwait) would stop, none could tell. In addition, an Iraqi takeover of Saudi Arabia would afford Hussein enormous financial power, potentially convertible to military power. This prospect alone was enough to sober anyone.

The Bush administration deemed it imperative to prevent Iraq's tanks from continuing into Saudi Arabia, but the Saudis initially seemed ambivalent about the idea. Though they had no desire to be Hussein's next victims, they evidently had some doubts regarding the United States' steadfastness as a protector. They remembered how quickly the Americans had fled Lebanon after suffering a mere few hundred casualties. By nearly all predictions, a tangle with Hussein would produce a great many more than a few hundred casualties; and the last thing the Saudis desired was to provoke Hussein by appealing to the United States for protection, only to have the Americans turn tail and leave Saudi Arabia undefended.

To allay the Saudis' fears, Bush called King Fahd and asked if he could send the U.S. defense secretary, Dick Cheney, to Riyadh. The king had to be convinced before he would see such a high-level American official; even talking to Americans might prove dangerous. But in the end, he told Bush to send Cheney.

The Pentagon chief succeeded in persuading Fahd to invite U.S. troops into Saudi Arabia. Cheney conveyed Bush's assurance that the United States wouldn't employ half-measures in dealing with Hussein. If the Iraqi strongman wanted a fight, he'd get one. Fahd reportedly demanded a commitment that if war broke out, Hussein would "not get up again." Precisely what Cheney said in response, neither U.S. nor Saudi officials chose to divulge.[21]

While working on the Saudi government to accept American military help, the Bush administration sought to convince other governments to take diplomatic and economic action against Iraq. The British needed no convincing whatsoever; indeed, reports indicated that it was British Prime Minister Margaret Thatcher who convinced Bush of the need to send troops to the Persian Gulf, and right away. The French were less demonstratively bellicose than the British, but Paris joined Washington and London in freezing Iraqi and Kuwaiti assets (the latter to prevent financial looting by the Iraqis) and in condemning Baghdad's aggression.

The key to the international united front, however, was the Soviet Union. Since the accession to power of Mikhail Gorbachev in 1985, the Soviets had been busy liquidating their participation in the Cold War, the better to concentrate on domestic reforms—what they called *perestroika* (restructuring) and *glasnost* (openness). In 1988, they

---

[21]*Newsweek,* Jan. 28, 1991.

agreed to pull out of Afghanistan, where they had failed to subdue the mujahideen. In 1989 and 1990, they took the much larger step of pulling back from Eastern Europe. Generally, the Kremlin followed a much less confrontational line toward the West—which, not coincidentally, was the obvious source of the foreign aid and investment Moscow would need to revive its sickly economy.

Where previous crises in the Middle East had usually found the United States and the Soviet Union on opposite sides, the 1990 crisis in the Persian Gulf found them on the same side. On August 2, the Kremlin suspended deliveries of military equipment to Iraq. This was no small sacrifice, since Iraq had been a good customer, and the Soviet Union couldn't easily afford the loss of the hard currency the weapons sales provided. Also on August 2, the Soviet representative on the United Nations Security Council not only didn't veto an anti-Iraq measure, as he most likely would have done in the past, but voted with the other fourteen members to condemn the invasion of Kuwait and demand Iraq's withdrawal. On August 6, the Soviet delegate voted with twelve other members (Cuba and Yemen abstaining) to impose economic sanctions against Iraq. On August 9, following Baghdad's announcement that it was annexing Kuwait, Moscow sided with the rest of the Security Council in declaring the annexation void. Two weeks later, the Soviets voted to authorize the United States and like-minded countries to use military means to enforce the United Nations sanctions.

Not having to worry about Soviet counterintervention, the Bush administration moved quickly to place U.S. troops on the ground in the Persian Gulf area. At first, the American deployment was "wholly defensive," in the words of the president. The administration was responding to an emergency—the possibility that the Iraqi army would keep going past Kuwait into Saudi Arabia—and it initially acted to deal with that emergency. The president ordered the dispatch of 125,000 U.S. troops, scores of ships, and hundreds of aircraft to Saudi Arabia and the waters nearby.[22]

Before long, however, American officials began thinking about doing more than defending Saudi Arabia. With each passing week, an Iraqi invasion of Saudi Arabia seemed less likely. Logic said that if Hussein had been planning such an invasion, he would have launched it before all the American forces started arriving. On the other hand,

[22]*Weekly Compilation*, Aug. 13, 1990.

the passing weeks showed no sign of an Iraqi withdrawal from Kuwait. Indeed, where Hussein formerly had hinted at leaving Kuwait after installing a friendly government there, now he described Kuwait as Iraq's nineteenth province.

The United Nations sanctions were supposed to supply pressure that would compel Hussein to leave Kuwait. From the first, though, many observers doubted that the sanctions would do the trick. During the eight-year war against Iran, Hussein had shown his ability to tighten his compatriots' belts; odds were that he would be able to tighten them again. Besides, as a self-made dictator, he didn't have to retain the active support of the Iraqi people. So long as the army—especially the elite Republican Guards—stayed happy, he could probably stay in power. And past experience indicated that he wouldn't hesitate to starve the civilian population to keep the soldiers happy. At the best, economic sanctions would take a long time to work.

Washington worried that it wouldn't have a long time. For the moment, the world stood nearly united against Iraq; but whether the disparate anti-Iraq coalition of Westerners and Asians and Africans, capitalists and communists, Christians and Muslims and Jews and Buddhists could hold together, was anybody's guess. Petroleum consumers would be tempted to cut a deal with Baghdad for cheap oil (Baghdad quickly slashed its prices). Arabs and Muslims would get fidgety in a group that included Israel (even though Israel, with strong U.S. encouragement, kept its head low). Third World countries would gravitate back toward their natural anti-Americanism (not least because the governments of coalition states were often more staunch against Saddam Hussein than many people in those states, who saw Hussein as a hero challenging the hegemony of the U.S. imperialists).

Hearing the clock ticking, the Bush administration pondered tougher measures to eject Iraq from Kuwait. The administration publicly adduced a variety of reasons in support of ejection. The obvious one, the one given greatest emphasis by the president, was that Hussein had committed an outrage against international law and morality by invading a foreign country; unless the United States and other right-minded nations acted to undo the outrage, the world would slide dangerously toward global chaos. This argument combined American idealism with American self-interest. The idealism came from the belief that action to free Kuwait from Hussein's grasp would be good for the Kuwaitis, who quite evidently were suffering under the Iraqi occupation—although, as postwar investigations showed, not as badly as the Kuwaiti government-in-exile let on. The self-interest arose from the judgment that if the world descended into anarchy, the United States couldn't avoid the ill consequences. When Bush spoke of a "new world order"—an international system in which small states as well as large could live in peace and freedom from fear—he had in mind a security framework of benefit to the United States as well as to the small countries.

The new-world-order argument didn't persuade everyone. Skeptics asked why Washington hadn't demanded that Israel be ejected from the West Bank, Gaza, and the Golan Heights; or Turkey from northern Cyprus; or, for that matter, the Soviet Union from the Baltic republics; or China from Tibet. Did the new world order apply only to minor and middling countries not allied to the United States? American defenders of Israel immediately responded that there was no comparison between Israel's position in the occupied territories and Iraq's seizure of Kuwait. After all, Israel was surrounded by avowed enemies, against whom the Israelis had fought several wars. What had Kuwait ever done to Iraq? (Turkey, the Soviet Union, and China had far fewer defenders in the United States than Israel did.) As with most arguments about the Arab-Israeli dispute, this one chiefly convinced those who didn't need convincing and left others cold. But the fact that the skeptics drew parallels to occupations Washington didn't much object to indicated that the case for a new world order wasn't as self-evident as Bush hoped.

The second reason, in the view of the Bush administration, why Iraq had to give up Kuwait was that Hussein's control of a large portion of the world's oil supply would endanger American prosperity. Secretary of State James Baker summed up this aspect of the argument in a single word: "Jobs." America's economic health depended, as it had since early in the century, on a stable and reasonably priced supply of oil. Iraq's seizure of Kuwait's oil had already sent prices zooming and threatened to do worse. The exposure of the Europeans and the Japanese, who relied more on imports than the United States did, was even greater than America's. Given the interconnected nature of the world economy, a recession in Europe or Japan couldn't help but damage America's chances of avoiding or mitigating the recession in the United States that economists had been forecasting for some time.

This part of the argument wasn't completely airtight either. OPEC-watchers noted that Iraq's seizure of Kuwait's oil changed the economics of supply and demand only slightly. The international oil business had never been especially competitive, and it certainly hadn't been since the emergence of OPEC during the 1970s. The elimination of Kuwait as an independent producer would make the business only marginally less competitive. The key to the situation—the swing producer who more than any other could determine prices—was Saudi Arabia, which now seemed safe. As to the recent jump in oil prices, that said less about events already past than about fears for the future. It wasn't entirely unreasonable to contend that a Hussein who controlled Kuwait's oil would be a more responsible Hussein, one with a greater stake in the long-term stability of prices and supplies. The Saudis had learned during the late 1970s that too-high oil prices pushed consumers to alternative sources of energy and to conservation; this, rather than any solicitousness for the welfare of their customers, had kept the Saudis from ratcheting the price higher than it was. Presumably, Hussein was as shrewd as the Saudis.

To the argument that, whatever the economics of the matter, Baghdad would subordinate economics to politics and might embargo oil to countries whose politics it didn't like, doubters responded that the Arab producers had done precisely this in 1973. In other words, an independent Kuwait was hardly a guarantee against disruptions of supply.

Additional reasons for wresting Kuwait back from Iraq had more to do with the character of Hussein and his regime than with the hijacking of his neighbor state. Hussein made no secret of his desire to develop nuclear weapons to match those almost certainly possessed by Israel. He was scary enough armed with conventional (including chemical) weapons; armed with nukes, he would be far more frightening. Further, letting Hussein get stronger would grievously tempt the Israelis to go after him before he became too much to handle. In 1981, Israel had bombed an Iraqi nuclear facility in order to set Hussein's nuclear program back a few years. Since then, Iraq had acquired new military capabilities, including chemical weapons and ballistic missiles. Hussein just recently had vowed to burn Israel to a crisp if it attacked again. Whether his capacities matched his boast was something the world would be better off not finding out.

Armed with these reasons, and with a growing military force in the area, the Bush administration moved increasingly toward war with Iraq during the autumn of 1990. The final decision for war didn't come until the beginning of 1991; yet even before then, preparations for war constituted the best device for achieving a diplomatic solution to the crisis. Although the first installment of U.S. troops had sufficed to deter an Iraqi attack on Saudi Arabia—assuming Hussein had been planning something along those lines—rooting the Iraqis out of Kuwait would require a considerably larger force. In late October, following a meeting in Saudi Arabia between the chairman of the U.S. Joint Chiefs of Staff, Colin Powell, and the American commander for the Middle East, Norman Schwarzkopf, Bush decided to double the size of the U.S. force. This decision didn't commit the United States to an offensive war against Iraq, but it made an offensive war possible. And it made Hussein think seriously about whether he really wanted to keep Kuwait.

It also made the American people think seriously about whether they really wanted to go to war to free Kuwait. Many decided they didn't. Opponents of war included veterans of the anti-Vietnam movement, who considered the Middle East potentially as treacherous underfoot as Southeast Asia; critics of big business, who saw a war for Kuwait as a device to secure the bottom lines of multinational oil companies and large weapons-producers; Pentagon-tamers, who interpreted the Defense Department's apparent enthusiasm for war (Defense Secretary Cheney openly questioned whether economic sanctions would do the job against Hussein) as a means of averting the post-Cold War cuts that looked otherwise inevitable; partisan Democrats, who believed they might make Republican trigger-happiness into an issue for the 1990 and 1992 elections; and Bush-bashers, who detected a sinister influence in the president's career ties to the oil industry and wondered whether he was using the Persian Gulf crisis to distract voters from a scandal involving his son, from an ongoing comedy of errors surrounding the federal budget, and from the "wimp" image that had tailed him through the 1988 campaign.

Caught between domestic critics, who charged him with being too fast to go to war, and Saddam Hussein, who apparently didn't believe he would, Bush walked a narrow line. To increase the credibility of the war option without thoroughly alarming the American public, the president lobbied the United Nations for what amounted to an international declaration of war against Iraq. Members of the Security Council generally judged that a resolution allowing the use of force to free Kuwait was a logical extension of the measures they had approved already. For some of the smaller members, approval came cheap, since they were voting other countries' soldiers, rather than their own, into battle. Yet it also came dearly, since none of the countries on the Security Council wished to delegate the authority to make war in the name of the United Nations to Washington (or London or Paris or whatever capitals accepted the council's invitation to fight against Hussein).

The Soviet Union had particular reasons to weigh carefully a vote for the use of military power. In the first place, Iraq had been a Kremlin client for years, and Moscow's ties to Baghdad had given the Soviets much of their influence in the Middle East. To sell Iraq out would do little for the confidence of Moscow's present and future allies elsewhere. Second, though the Iraqis looked likely to put up a good fight, against a U.S.-led coalition they would be badly overmatched. The reputation of Soviet arms could only suffer as a consequence. Third, by 1990 the Soviet Union possessed only a marginal claim to superpowerdom. To tag along in the wake of the United States and meekly grant approval to a U.S.-promoted resolution would further undermine Moscow's prestige. Finally, such approval might politically undermine Gorbachev, who confronted increasing pressure at home from conservatives. Already they charged him with losing Afghanistan and Eastern Europe; now he seemed to be losing the Middle East. It hardly appeared coincidental that Soviet Foreign Minister Eduard Shevardnadze, the architect of the policy of cooperation with Washington against Hussein, felt so beset by attacks from the right that he resigned just as the crisis in the Persian Gulf was getting really hot.

Chiefly to save face, the Soviet government offered its own version of a use-of-force resolution, one that specified a date before which the United Nations would not countenance military action. But in other respects, the Kremlin held to its earlier backing for a unified front. Although the Bush administration haggled a bit over when open season on Hussein should begin, by the end of November all the details and all fifteen Security Council votes were in place. Hussein had until January 15, 1991, to clear out of Kuwait. After that, member countries of the United Nations had the Security Council's authorization to use "all means necessary" to effect Iraq's withdrawal.

Obtaining world approval for the use of force, or whatever approximation to world approval a unanimous Security Council resolution implied, was the easy part. Persuading Congress to go along proved much harder. The Bush administration had to deal with the constitutional question of whether it needed the legislature's assent to wage war, as the Constitution seemed to say, or whether the president could commit U.S. troops to battle on his own authority as commander-in-chief, as the post-1945 examples of Korea and Vietnam (and, more recently though less dramatically, Grenada and Panama) appeared to indicate. The administration also had to deal with the issue of whether it was allowing economic sanctions enough time to work. Almost no one expected a war to be as nearly casualty-free as it turned out; few wished to send American soldiers to die if the trade squeeze might accomplish the same end. Those advocating patience, led by Georgia Democrat Sam Nunn, the chairman of the Senate Armed Services Committee, bolstered their case by bringing to Capitol Hill a succession of former defense secretaries and chairmen of the Joint Chiefs of Staff, who recommended holding off on the use of force a while longer.

In addition, the administration had to contend with some diplomatic dickering by Saddam Hussein. The Iraqi invasion of Kuwait had caught thousands of Americans and other Westerners inside Kuwait and Iraq. As protection against efforts to undo the invasion, Hussein ordered the detention of most of these foreigners, sending some to sensitive installations around Iraq to act as human shields against air or other attack. Hussein probably thought little about the morality of holding foreigners as hostages; he had done far worse to the Kurds in Iraq, and was doing worse to the Kuwaitis. But this aspect of the crisis particularly antagonized many Americans, for whom the mere idea of hostages symbolized the humiliation of their country at the hands of Middle Eastern madmen and terrorists. Eventually Hussein recognized the damage he was doing to himself by keeping the foreigners, and he decided to let them go.

Hussein announced the release not long after the United Nations vote on the use of force, and just after Bush proposed direct high-level discussions between Washington and Baghdad. Hussein accepted Bush's invitation to send the Iraqi foreign minister, Tariq Aziz, to the United States, but he dithered on a reciprocal visit by Secretary Baker to Iraq. Finally, when he agreed to receive Baker, he said the visit couldn't take place until just before the deadline set by the Security Council. The Bush administration interpreted this as a subterfuge designed to erode the resolve of the anti-Iraq coalition, and told Hussein to keep his invitation.

Amid this maneuvering, Congress took up the issue of whether to authorize the president to use military force against Hussein. Few legislators wished to rule out the use of force entirely; pacifists have never done well in American politics. Nor did any lawmakers care to be seen as unpatriotic in failing to back the president in a moment of peril. Yet at the same time, the Democrats who controlled the Senate and the House of Representatives didn't propose to surrender war-making power to the executive branch. They decried what Hussein had done in Kuwait; they avowed their support for measures designed to make him disgorge what he was trying to swallow. But many weren't convinced that the time for war had come. The administration ought to have more patience and give sanctions longer to work.

In the end, though, the delayers lost. The Republicans garnered enough Democratic support for the use-of-force resolution to squeak through; in the Senate, the measure passed by only five votes.

6. THE UNITED STATES' FIRST MIDDLE EASTERN WAR

The two use-of-force measures—the one in the United Nations and the other in the U.S. Congress—shifted the momentum in the Persian Gulf crisis decisively toward war. The United Nations measure placed the prestige of the international organization on the line. Admittedly, the United Nations' prestige hadn't been very great for some time, but it was reviving as the paralysis induced by the Cold War wore off. To set a deadline and not enforce it might fatally short-circuit the revival. The congressional measure placed the prestige of the president on the line. For Bush to declare Hussein an international outlaw, to liken him to Hitler (one of Bush's more provocative analogies), to declare that his seizure of Kuwait must not stand, to request authorization from Congress for the use of force, to get that authorization, and then to not use force, would be anticlimactic at best, politically fatal at worst.

As the January 15 deadline approached, the key to averting war lay with Hussein. But by this time, the key fit the lock poorly. Hussein almost certainly had underestimated what the American response to his takeover of Kuwait would be; he was in good company in his underestimation, since no one had been guessing on August 1, 1990, that there would be nearly half a million U.S. troops in Saudi Arabia five months later. Had he known what the Americans would do, and had he recognized the readiness of other countries to accept American leadership on the issue of Kuwait, he almost surely would have figured out another way to settle Iraq's problems with its neighbor. Subsequently, had he not made such a big deal of declaring Kuwait an inalienable part of Iraq, he might have managed a pullout without unacceptably embarrassing himself. Most obviously, had he known what devastation the U.S.-led offensive against Iraq would produce, he would have reconsidered the whole question of Kuwait. But he didn't know all this in advance, just as American officials didn't know on August 1 that Hussein would invade Kuwait. And by January 1, he was as entrenched politically in the position he had dug for himself as Bush was in *his* position. From neither side did compromise come easily.

From neither side, in fact, did compromise come at all, and hours after the United Nations deadline passed, the war began. American naval vessels fired the first shots: Tomahawk missiles that skimmed the desert en route to Baghdad. While the Tomahawks approached their targets, U.S. electronic-warfare aircraft blinded and overloaded Iraqi radar, allowing American bombers access to military installations, communications centers, and assorted other targets in Iraq and Kuwait.

Further complicating the Iraqis' job of air defense was the deployment of revolutionary new "stealth" technology, which made U.S. F-117As virtually invisible to radar. And when the planes neared their destinations, many of them dropped laser-guided bombs that found their targets with a degree of precision unprecedented in history. The Pentagon treated American television viewers to videotapes of bombs riding their electronic rails down the camera's crosshairs to the roof of the Iraqi air force headquarters and to similar high-value sites.

At first, a few brave Iraqi fighter pilots scrambled to intercept the attackers, but they quickly got themselves shot down, leaving the Americans and the other coalition members, chiefly the British, in control of the air over Iraq and Kuwait. Many of the Iraqi planes not destroyed at the outset of the war wound up in Iran, to which their pilots had flown them—and themselves—for safety.

Iraq's only important counterthrust in the first phase of the war was its launching of Scud missiles at Israel and Saudi Arabia. American analysts had feared that Iraq would mount chemical warheads (a few real doomsayers thought perhaps even a rudimentary nuclear bomb or two) on the Scuds, which would cause massive casualties wherever they hit. As matters turned out, the Scuds carried no chemical or nuclear warheads; evidently Hussein had been talking through his hat about singeing Israel. But even armed with ordinary explosives, the Scuds put a scare into the coalition.

The less worrisome were those Scuds that hit Saudi Arabia, since the Saudis were already involved in the war against Hussein up to their necks; the more worrisome were those that hit Israel. From the beginning of the crisis, Washington had feared that Hussein would try to transform the Iraq-Kuwait quarrel, a fight among Arabs, into a fight between Arabs and Israelis. To this end, Hussein rhetorically championed the cause of the Palestinians—even as his ravaging of the Kuwaiti economy threw hundreds of thousands of Palestinians out of work—and cast his challenge to the West as a blow against the American-Zionist conspiracy. He fooled the Palestinians, or rather the leadership of the PLO, which voiced strong support for Hussein against the filthy rich Kuwaitis.

But he didn't fool many other people, at least not among those who ran the governments of countries with particular interest in the affairs of the Persian Gulf. His failure to do so owed especially to Israel's forbearance in not being provoked by the Scud attacks to retaliate against Iraq. Israel's forbearance in turn owed a great deal to Washington's rapid delivery of Patriot antimissile missiles, which provided psychological insurance, if not much physical protection. (How effective the Patriots were in intercepting the Scuds remained a matter of debate for many months after the war. Even those Patriots that did hit Scuds allowed debris to rain down on the cities targeted.) Israel's forbearance also reflected the billions of dollars in aid Washington had supplied over the years.

With Israel agreeing to lie low, holding the rest of the coalition together proved comparatively simple. It helped that the war went exceedingly well from the allies' standpoint. American and British planes flew thousands of sorties per day, aided by French, Saudi, and Kuwaiti aircraft. Together, the allies succeeded in destroying much of that which might conceivably contribute to Iraq's ability to sustain its occupation of Kuwait. In the process, they suffered exceedingly modest casualties, numbering only in the low hundreds.

After five weeks of the air war, Bush gave the order for U.S. ground forces to take the offensive. Troops from other anti-Iraq coalition members joined the Americans in a multipronged assault across the border from Saudi Arabia into Kuwait and Iraq. While helicopter-

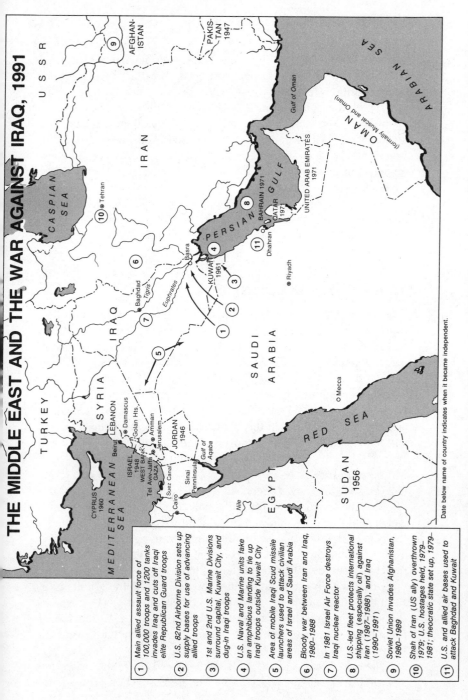

THE MIDDLE EAST AND THE WAR AGAINST IRAQ, 1991

Date below name of country indicates when it became independent.

1. Main allied assault force of 100,000 troops and 1200 tanks invades Iraq and cuts off Iraqi elite Republican Guard troops

2. U.S. 82nd Airborne Division sets up supply bases for use of advancing allied troops

3. 1st and 2nd U.S. Marine Divisions surround capital, Kuwait City, and dug-in Iraqi troops

4. U.S. Naval and Marine units fake an amphibious landing to tie up Iraqi troops outside Kuwait City

5. Area of mobile Iraqi Scud missile launchers used to attack civilian areas of Israel and Saudi Arabia

6. Bloody war between Iran and Iraq, 1980–1988

7. In 1991 Israeli Air Force destroys Iraqi nuclear reactor

8. U.S.-led fleet protects international shipping (especially oil) against Iran (1987–1988), and Iraq (1990–1991)

9. Soviet Union invades Afghanistan, 1980–1989

10. Shah of Iran (US ally) overthrown 1979; U.S. hostages held, 1979–1981; theocratic state set up, 1979—

11. U.S. and allied air bases used to attack Baghdad and Kuwait

borne U.S. units landed fifty miles inside Iraq, far behind the Iraqi lines, allied tanks and personnel carriers raced around the Iraqi defensive positions to sever retreat routes. Feared poison-gas counterattacks and bitter-end resistance by Hussein's Republican Guards never materialized; the Guards apparently found the air bombardment very demoralizing. With a rapidity that surprised even the most hopeful American forecasters, Iraqi resistance collapsed. Hussein's troops surrendered in groups of several thousand at a time; perhaps 100,000 Iraqi soldiers were killed.

On February 27, six weeks after the war began, coalition forces liberated Kuwait City. Hours later, with allied troops occupying a sizable portion of southern Iraq, Bush called off the attack.

7. UNFINISHED BUSINESS

The Persian Gulf War of 1991 marked the culmination of a trend toward greater American involvement in the Middle East, a trend that had been under way since 1945. During the late 1940s, Washington had gotten involved in the region politically, warning the Soviet Union out of Iran and backing the Zionist drive for a Jewish state in Palestine, and economically, sending a big package of aid to Turkey and Greece. In the early 1950s, the United States intensified its political and economic activities in the Middle East, promoting alliances with and among America-friendly governments like those of Turkey and Iraq, and helping topple America-unfriendly governments like that of Mossadeq in Iran.

The 1956 Suez crisis deepened American involvement in the Middle East and led to the addition of a military element in American regional policy. The Eisenhower Doctrine represented an attempt to fill the gap left by the collapse of British power, using U.S. troops, such as those Eisenhower sent to Lebanon in 1958, as the filler. The 1960s saw the closer identification of the United States with Israel, a development that drew the United States still deeper into the Middle East. Both the June War of 1967 and the October War of 1973 set American presidents and their advisers working overtime as Washington attempted alternately to restrain the Israelis and protect them, especially from Soviet growling.

The closer American ties to Israel produced a greater sense of responsibility for seeking peace in the Middle East. The Carter administration got part way to peace with the Camp David accord of 1978. The Reagan administration lost ground in Lebanon, when its peacekeeping force wandered to one side in the Lebanese civil war and suffered consequences including the deaths of hundreds of American soldiers.

The Iranian revolution of 1979 and the seizure of the American hostages in Tehran brought events of the Persian Gulf into tens of millions of American living rooms, pulling Americans emotionally into the Middle East in a way they had never experienced. The first Gulf war, between Iran and Iraq, endangered oil shipments to the West, leading Washington to strengthen the U.S. naval presence in the gulf and to hit back at Iranians hitting oil tankers—and, tragically, at some Iranians who were merely riding an airliner.

George Bush's 1991 decision to wage war against Iraq followed logically, if not quite inexorably, from what had gone before. Since 1945, American leaders had identified the Middle East as a region critical to American security. The one thing that, more than anything else, made the region critical was its oil, and for the whole period after World War II, Washington bent every effort to guarantee the free flow of Middle Eastern oil to the West. Saddam Hussein, by grabbing control of Kuwait and making himself master of a large portion of Middle Eastern oil and threatening to seize Saudi Arabia's oil as well, threw himself squarely in the path of forty-five years of American policy. A different president than George Bush might have adopted a different strategy for breaking Hussein's grip, but any American president would have sought essentially the same objective.

In this respect, the Gulf war of 1991, although representing a major quantitative change in U.S. involvement in the Middle East, didn't signify any real qualitative change. The aftermath of the war suggested as much. For a few weeks following the Iraqi surrender, Americans celebrated a brilliant victory, but the heady feeling soon evaporated, and they began asking themselves just what they had won. Kuwait was free, but would require many months, or even years, to restore its oil production to prewar levels. Saddam Hussein wasn't the regional threat he had been, but he continued to hold power in Baghdad and to thumb his nose at the United States and the West.

Of the three factors that had long caused American leaders such concern regarding the Middle East—oil, Israel, and the Soviet Union— the first two remained much as before. The United States and most other Western countries were nearly as dependent on imported oil as ever. As before, the Middle East was the largest exporter of oil. So long as this was the case, the United States would be very sensitive to political and other instability in the region. Washington would also be sensitive to issues touching Israel. The Iraqi invasion of Kuwait and the resulting war had sobered various parties in the Middle East sufficiently that the major disputants in the Arab-Israeli quarrel agreed for the first time to attend a general peace conference. The conference took place in Madrid in the autumn of 1991. By then, however, the sobering effect of the war had largely worn off, and the momentum toward peace diminished considerably. The conferees agreed only to talk further, elsewhere, and they agreed to this grudgingly. Desultory talks took place in Washington at various times during 1992. On the central issue—the future of the territories occupied by Israel and the fate of the Palestinians residing there—the disputants were somewhat closer to an accord than they had been. At least the Israelis were meeting face to face with the Palestinians. But by most other evidence—including the continuing Palestinian *intifadah* (uprising) and the Israeli government's insistence on building new settlements in the territories—a peace arrangement all could live with seemed far off.

Only regarding the third factor—the Soviet Union—had there been real change. Five years of reform under Gorbachev had thoroughly alarmed Soviet hardliners; in August 1991, they arrested Gorbachev in an effort to seize the government and reverse his policies. But the coup soon unraveled, and power passed to the governments of the separate Soviet republics. One by one, they defected from the Soviet Union, which by the end of the year had ceased to exist.

This was good news for U.S. Middle East policy, but not entirely good news. For more than forty years, American leaders had worked tirelessly to limit Soviet influence in the Middle East, on the reasoning that the United States' foremost rival would use that influence to American detriment. Now the Soviet threat had disappeared, along with the Soviet Union. American policy makers could relax a little.

But not too much, as the Gulf war of 1991 demonstrated. Although the end of the Cold War had made possible the solid United Nations front against Iraq, it also removed a sometimes-important source of relative order in the Middle East. During the Cold War both Washington and Moscow had had an incentive to keep the Middle East from dissolving into anarchy. Each side realized that conflicts

in the Middle East might escalate into conflicts between the superpowers, which neither wanted. Because each side had clients in the
region, each could exert, through those clients, a restraining effect on
regional quarrels. As long as Israel looked to Washington for weapons,
and Egypt and Syria to Moscow, the Israelis, Egyptians, and Syrians
had to pay attention to the concerns of their sponsors. The dependence of the superpowers' clients on their sponsors had been most
evident during the October War of 1973, when only resupplies from
the United States and the Soviet Union kept the opposing armies in
the field, and when Washington and Moscow exerted strong pressure
for a ceasefire. But the dependence existed, if sometimes in attenuat-
ed form, throughout most of the Cold War. And it helped prevent difficulties in the Middle East from becoming more difficult than they
already were.

The demise of the Soviet Union meant the end of this occasionally
beneficent influence. (Sometimes the influence had been detrimen-
tal, at least from Washington's point of view—as, for example, prior to
the Suez crisis of 1956, when Moscow began supplying weapons to
Nasser.) It likely wasn't an accident that the United States' first Middle Eastern war, in the Persian Gulf in 1991, came in the wake of
Moscow's withdrawal from the region. As long as the Soviets had
been active in the area, they never would have meekly allowed the
Americans to send half a million troops to pummel one of their
clients. To prevent this, they would have leaned hard on someone like
Saddam Hussein, who appeared to be making such American action
necessary. This isn't to say that Hussein necessarily wouldn't have attacked Kuwait if the Cold War had still been going. Maybe he would
have. But, in doing so, he would have had a few more things to think
about. And these few more might well have changed his mind. As
matters turned out, in the absence of Soviet influence, changing his
mind required the largest single U.S. military operation since World
War II.

What all this demonstrated was that the situation in the Middle
East at the end of the Cold War wasn't tremendously different from
what it had been previously and that the American role in the region
probably wouldn't decrease dramatically. Soviet Union or no Soviet
Union, the Middle East remained crucially important to Americans.
They needed its oil as much as before; they cared about Israel just as
much. This being so, odds were that the region would keep them
awake nights far into the future.

For Further Study

The following selection of books isn't exhaustive. It is designed to introduce the interested reader to other works useful to an understanding of American relations with the Middle East. A more thorough bibliography on the Middle East (and not just on U.S. relations with the region) can be found in Ritchie Ovendale, *The Middle East since 1914* (London, 1992).

1. OVERVIEWS AND BACKGROUND

There aren't many books that deal with U.S. relations with the Middle East as a whole. Most authors concentrate on one facet or another: the Arab-Israeli dispute, the Iranian revolution, oil, or something else. Most books that have taken a comprehensive approach have been bypassed by quickly moving events. Those that have worn well have generally dealt with events at some distance in the past. For background on the post-1945 period, the reader can refer to William R. Polk, *The United States and the Arab World* (Cambridge, Mass., 1975); John S. Badeau, *The American Approach to the Arab World* (New York, 1968); Robert W. Stookey, *America and the Arab States* (New York, 1975); Seth P. Tillman, *The United States in the Middle East* (Bloomington, Ind., 1982); Philip L. Groisser, *The United States and the Middle East* (Albany, N.Y., 1982); Thomas A. Bryson, *American Diplomatic Relations with the Middle East, 1784–1975: A Survey* (Metuchen, N.J., 1977); William Stivers, *America's Confrontation with Revolutionary Change in the Middle East, 1948–1983* (New York, 1986); John C. Campbell, *Defense of the Middle East* (New York, 1960); and Willard A. Beling, ed., *The Middle East: Quest for an American Policy* (Albany, N.Y., 1973).

Additional pre-World War II background can be found in James A. Field, Jr., *America and the Mediterranean World, 1776–1882* (Princeton, N.J., 1969); David H. Finnie, *Pioneers East: The Early American Experience in the Middle East* (Cambridge, Mass., 1967); John A. DeNovo, *American Interests and Politics in the Middle East, 1900–1939* (Minneapolis, 1963); and Phillip J.

Baram, *The Department of State in the Middle East, 1919–1945* (Philadelphia, 1978).

Several authors have taken the Middle East as a whole, but focused on particular aspects of U.S. policy making. Two solid studies are George Lenczowski, *American Presidents and the Middle East* (Durham, N.C., 1990), and Alan Dowty, *Middle East Crisis: U.S. Decision-Making in 1958, 1970, and 1973* (Berkeley, 1984). On U.S. naval policy in the Middle East, there is Thomas A. Bryson, *Tars, Turks, and Tankers: The Role of the U.S. Navy in the Middle East, 1800–1979* (Metuchen, N.J., 1980).

2. ISRAEL AND THE ARABS

The Arab-Israeli dispute has generated the largest amount of literature pertaining to American policy. T. G. Fraser, *The USA and the Middle East Since World War 2* (New York, 1989), is succinct and relatively up-to-date. Steven Spiegel, *The Other Arab-Israeli Conflict: Making America's Middle East Policy from Truman to Reagan* (Chicago, 1985), gives the best coverage of the pulling and hauling within the U.S. government. Mordechai Gazit, *President Kennedy's Policies toward the Arab States and Israel* (Tel Aviv, 1983), concentrates on the early 1960s. For the late 1960s through the late 1970s, the most authoritative works are two by William Quandt: *Decade of Decisions: American Foreign Policy and the Arab-Israeli Conflict, 1967–1976* (Berkeley, 1977), and *Camp David: Peacemaking and Politics* (Washington, 1986). More on peacemaking can be found in Saadia Touval, *The Peace Brokers: Mediators in the Arab-Israeli Conflict, 1948–1979* (Princeton, N.J., 1982), which depicts both American and other diplomats, and Dan Tschirgi, *The American Search for Mideast Peace* (New York, 1989).

Persons wishing to focus on the Israeli part of the U.S. Middle East equation should start with Peter Grose, *Israel in the Mind of America* (New York, 1983), an appraisal sympathetic toward Israel; and George W. Ball and Douglas B. Bell, *The Passionate Attachment* (New York, 1993), a critical view. From there they can proceed to John Snetsinger, *Truman, the Jewish Vote, and the Creation of Israel* (Stanford, 1974); Zvi Ganin, *Truman, American Jewry, and Israel* (New York, 1979); and Kenneth Ray Bain, *The March to Zion: United States Policy and the Founding of Israel* (College Station, Tex., 1979), which cover the period leading to the establishment of Israel. Evan M. Wilson, *Decision on Palestine: How the U.S. Came to Recognize Israel* (Stanford, Cal., 1979), is a combination analysis-memoir by a State Department official. H. W. Brands, *Inside the Cold War: Loy Henderson and the Rise of the American Empire, 1918–1961* (New York, 1991), has a long chapter on the Palestine-Israel question, as well as several chapters on other aspects of U.S.-Middle East relations. Bernard Reich, *Quest for Peace: United States-Israel*

Relations and the Arab-Israeli Conflict (New Brunswick, N.J., 1977), illuminates the late 1960s and 1970s. Alfred M. Lilienthal, *The Zionist Connection*
(New York, 1978); Isaiah L. Kenen, *Israel's Defense Line: Her Friends and
Foes in Washington* (Buffalo, N.Y., 1981); and Edward Tivnan, *The Lobby:
Jewish Political Power and American Foreign Policy* (New York, 1987), scruti-
nize the politics of U.S. relations with Israel. Cheryl Rubenberg, *Israel and
the American National Interest* (Urbana, Ill., 1986), takes a somewhat broader view, while Nadav Safran, *Israel: The Embattled Ally* (Cambridge, Mass.,
1978), looks at the relationship from Israel's perspective.

Necessary to a fuller appreciation of the Israeli perspective is a knowl-
edge of the history of Israel and its antecedents. Abba Eban, *My People: A
History of the Jews* (New York, 1968), and Paul Johnson, *A History of the
Jews* (New York, 1987), are sweeping. Walter Z. Laquer, *A History of Zionism*
(New York, 1972); Martin Gilbert, *Exile and Return: The Struggle for a Jewish Homeland* (Philadelphia, 1978); and Shlomo Avineri, *The Making of Modern Zionism* (New York, 1986), examine the movement that gave birth to the
Jewish state. Noah Lucas, *The Modern History of Israel* (New York, 1975),
and Howard M. Sachar, *A History of Israel* (New York, 1976), deal with the
state that Zionism produced. Specialized works include Leonard Stein, *The
Balfour Declaration* (London, 1961), and Michael Brecher, *Decisions in Israel's Foreign Policy* (New Haven, Conn., 1975). Walter Laquer and Barry
Rubin, eds., *The Israel-Arab Reader* (New York, 1984), provides a spectrum
of opinions on Israel's relations with its neighbors.

The study of American relations with the Arabs should start with the
three aforementioned surveys by Polk, Badeau, and Stookey. Several works
treat American relations with particular Arab countries. Egypt has received
the greatest attention. H. W. Brands, *The Specter of Neutralism: The United
States and the Emergence of the Third World, 1947–1960* (New York, 1989),
gives a succinct overview of American relations with Egypt during the 1950s.
Gail E. Meyer, *Egypt and the United States: The Formative Years* (Ruther-
ford, N.J., 1980); Geoffrey Aronson, *From Sideshow to Center Stage: U.S.
Policy toward Egypt, 1946–1956* (Boulder, Col., 1986); and Peter L. Hahn,
The United States, Great Britain, and Egypt, 1945–1956 (Chapel Hill, N.C.,
1991), cover the same ground at greater length. William J. Burns, *Economic
Aid and American Policy toward Egypt, 1955–1981* (Albany, N.Y., 1985), con-
centrates on dollar diplomacy in the direction of the Nile.

To understand the Arab background to the developments of the last half-
century in the Middle East, the reader should consult works dealing with the
history of the Arabs. William R. Polk, *The Arab World* (Cambridge, Mass.,
1980), gives the big picture, starting early and describing the roots of modern
Arab culture and society, as well as politics. So do Jacques Berque, *The Arabs*
(trans. Jean Stewart: London, 1964), and Bernard Lewis, *The Arabs in History* (New York, 1976). Fouad Ajami, *The Arab Predicament: Arab Political
Thought and Practice since 1967* (New York, 1982), describes the intellectual

and cultural milieu of the contemporary Arab world. Bernard Lewis, *The Cambridge History of Islam* (Cambridge, England, 1978), and Robin Wright, *Sacred Rage: The Crusade of Modern Islam* (New York, 1985), cover more than the Arabs, but say much about what makes them the way they are.

More directly pertinent to recent developments are Jon Kimche, *The Second Arab Awakening* (London, 1970); Hisham Sharabi, *Nationalism and Revolution in the Arab World* (Princeton, 1966); Malcolm H. Kerr, *The Arab Cold War: Gamal Abd al-Nasir and His Rivals, 1958–1970* (London, 1971); Tawfig Y. Hasou, *The Struggle for the Arab World: Egypt's Nasser and the Arab League* (London, 1985); and A. I. Dawisha, *The Arab Radicals* (New York, 1986).

As these titles suggest, Egypt and Nasser figure centrally in most treatments of postwar Arab politics. Other titles acknowledging and demonstrating this fact are Anthony Nutting, *Nasser* (New York, 1972); Jean Lacouture, *Nasser* (trans. Daniel Hofstadter: New York, 1973); Raymond William Baker, *Egypt's Uncertain Revolution under Nasser and Sadat* (Cambridge, Mass., 1978); P. J. Vatikiotis, *Nasser and His Generation* (New York, 1978); and John Waterbury, *The Egypt of Nasser and Sadat* (Princeton, N.J., 1983).

Studies of Arab countries besides Egypt include A. L. Tibawi, *A Modern History of Syria, including Lebanon and Palestine* (New York, 1970); John Devlin, *Syria: Modern State in an Ancient Land* (Boulder, Col., 1983); Tim Niblock, *Iraq: The Contemporary State* (New York, 1982); Phebe Marr, *The Modern History of Iraq* (Boulder, Col., 1985); Nadav Safran, *Saudi Arabia: The Ceaseless Search for Security* (Cambridge, Mass., 1985); and David C. Gordon, *Lebanon: The Fragmented Nation* (Stanford, Cal., 1980). At the time of its writing, the subtitle of Dana Schmidt's *Yemen: The Unknown War* (New York, 1968), was apt; but this book and two subsequent ones—Edgar O'Ballance, *The War in the Yemen* (Hamden, Conn., 1971); and Christopher J. McMullen, *Resolution of the Yemen Crisis, 1963* (Washington, 1980)—narrowed the knowledge gap.

Until the 1980s, almost no one paid much heed to American relations with Libya. But since the rise of Qaddafi as the *bête noire* of U.S. antiterrorist policy, Libya has received more attention—although, in terms of books, still not a whole lot. Three books are useful: Edward P. Haley, *Qaddafi and the United States since 1969* (New York, 1984); Mahmoud G. El-Warfally, *Imagery and Ideology in U.S. Policy toward Libya* (Pittsburgh, 1988); and Brian L. Davis, *Qaddafi, Terrorism, and the Origins of the U.S. Attack on Libya* (New York, 1990).

No single issue of Middle Eastern affairs has proved more vexing than that of the Palestinians. In proportion to the vexation has been the output of literature on the subject. Readers might get their bearings with Charles D. Smith, *Palestine and the Arab-Israeli Conflict* (New York, 1988). Pamela Ann Smith, *Palestine and the Palestinians, 1876–1983* (London, 1984), tells much of the same story. Barry Rubin, *The Arab States and the Palestine*

Conflict (Syracuse, 1981), deals with the origins of the Palestine question to the 1950s; J. C. Hurewitz, *The Struggle for Palestine* (New York, 1968), carries the story into the 1960s. Edward W. Said, a well-known Palestinian-American, unapologetically delivers an apologia for the Palestinians in *The Question of Palestine* (New York, 1979). The Palestinian shadow government is the subject of Helena Cobban, *The Palestine Liberation Organization* (New York, 1984); Alain Gresh, *The PLO: The Struggle Within* (trans. A. M. Berrett: London, 1985); Neil C. Livingstone and David Halevy, *Inside the PLO* (New York, 1990); and Rashid Kalidi, *Under Siege: P.L.O. Decision-making During the 1982 War* (New York, 1986). William W. Harris, *Taking Root: Israeli Settlements in the West Bank, the Golan, and the Gaza-Sinai, 1967–1980* (New York, 1980), treats the issue of the settlements in the occupied territories.

3. IRAN, TURKEY, CYPRUS

Iran formed something of a backwater in the study of American foreign relations until the Iranian revolution in the late 1970s. Barry Rubin, *Paved with Good Intentions: The American Experience and Iran* (New York, 1980), and James A. Bill, *The Eagle and the Lion: The Tragedy of American-Iranian Relations* (New Haven, Conn., 1988), are the best surveys of U.S.-Iranian relations, with Rubin being stronger on the U.S. side of the picture, Bill being better on the Iranian side. Richard W. Cottam, *Iran and the United States* (Pittsburgh, 1988) is also useful. Mark Hamilton Lytle, *The Origins of the Iranian-American Alliance* (New York, 1987), focuses on the 1940s and 1950s. Gary Sick, *All Fall Down: America's Tragic Encounter with Iran* (New York, 1985), concentrates on the period of the Iranian revolution. Slow-going but authoritative is the *Report of the Congressional Committee Investigating the Iran-Contra Affair* (Washington, 1987). Theodore Draper pulls together a broader range of evidence in *A Very Thin Line: The Iran-Contra Affairs* (New York, 1991). Gary Sick discusses the possibility of a deal between the Reagan campaign team and the Iranian government in *October Surprise* (New York, 1991).

For background on the events in Iran, see Richard W. Cottam, *Nationalism in Iran* (Pittsburgh, 1979); Amin Saikal, *The Rise and Fall of the Shah* (Princeton, N.J., 1980); George Lenczowski, *Iran under the Pahlavis* (Stanford, Cal., 1978); Sepehr Zabih, *The Mossadegh Era* (Chicago, 1982); Farhad Diba, *Mohammad Mossadegh* (London, 1986); and Rouhollah K. Ramazani, *Iran's Foreign Policy* (Charlottesville, Va., 1975). The Iranian revolution is covered in Marvin Zonis, *Majestic Failure: The Fall of the Shah* (Chicago, 1991), and Mehran Kamrava, *Revolution in Iran* (London, 1990).

The literature on U.S. relations with Turkey has been even thinner than that on U.S. relations with Iran. The starting point is George S. Harris, *Troubled Alliance: Turkish-American Problems in Historical Perspective, 1945–1971* (Washington, 1972). For background on this region of long memories, consult Lawrence Evans, *United States Policy and the Partition of Turkey, 1914–1925* (Baltimore, 1965), and Feroz Ahmad, *The Turkish Experiment in Democracy, 1950–1975* (Boulder, Co., 1977), which contains a sizable amount of material on U.S.-Turkish affairs.

Policy toward Turkey was connected closely with policy toward Greece, especially during the early Cold War and regarding Cyprus. Best on the era of the Truman Doctrine are Lawrence S. Wittner, *American Intervention in Greece, 1943–1949* (New York, 1982), strongly critical of U.S. policy; and Howard Jones, *"A New Kind of War": America's Global Strategy and the Truman Doctrine in Greece* (New York, 1989). Laurence Stern, *The Wrong Horse: The Politics of Intervention and the Failure of U.S. Diplomacy* (New York, 1977), covers more recent ground, including the Cyprus crises of the 1960s and 1970s. For more on Cyprus, try Christopher Hitchens, *Cyprus* (London, 1984); Polyvios G. Polyviou, *Cyprus* (Washington, 1975); and Theodore A. Couloumbis and Sallie M. Hicks, eds., *U.S. Foreign Policy toward Greece and Cyprus* (Washington, 1975).

4. PARTICULAR EVENTS AND SPECIAL TOPICS

The Iran crisis of 1945–46 had ramifications for world affairs that went far beyond its effects in the Middle East. The best book on the subject is Bruce R. Kuniholm, *The Origins of the Cold War in the Near East: Great Power Conflict and Diplomacy in Iran, Turkey, and Greece* (Princeton, N.J., 1980). Kuniholm also documents U.S. decision making regarding the Turkish Straits affair and the Truman Doctrine. George Lenczowski, *Russia and the West in Iran, 1918–1948* (Ithaca, N.Y., 1949), gives more background on the Iran crisis. On the straits issue, see also Harry N. Howard, *Turkey, the Straits, and U.S. Policy* (Baltimore, 1974).

No single event in the recent history of the Middle East has generated more bitter debate than the Suez crisis of 1956, which has produced, it sometimes seemed, enough ink to float a ship through the canal. The most readable book on American actions during the crisis, with much material on other countries, is Donald Neff, *Warriors at Suez: Eisenhower Takes America into the Middle East* (New York, 1981). Earlier volumes that still hold up well are Herman Finer, *Dulles over Suez* (Chicago, 1964); Kennett Love, *Suez: The Twice-Fought War* (New York, 1969); and Anthony Nutting, *No End of a Lesson* (New York, 1967), an insider's account. Wm. Roger Louis and Roger Owen, eds., *Suez 1956* (Oxford, England, 1989), and Selwyn Ilan Troen and

Moshe Shemesh, eds., *The Suez-Sinai Crisis 1956* (New York, 1990), are recent reassessments.

The several Arab-Israeli wars have produced a sizable literature. A sampling includes Netanel Lorch, *The Edge of the Sword: Israel's War of Independence, 1947–1949* (New York, 1961); Larry Collins and Dominique Lapierre, *O Jerusalem!* (New York, 1972), on the Palestine War; Donald Neff, *Warriors for Jerusalem: The Six Days that Changed the Middle East* (New York, 1984), and Eric Hammel, *Six Days in June* (New York, 1992), on the June War of 1967; Michael Howard and Robert Hunter, *Israel and the Arab World: The Crisis of 1967* (London, 1967); Michael Brecher, *Decisions in Crisis: Israel 1967 and 1973* (Berkeley, 1979); Ibrahim Abu-Lughod, ed., *The Arab-Israeli Confrontation of June 1967: An Arab Perspective* (Evanston, Ill., 1970); Edgar O'Ballance, *No Victor, No Vanquished: The Yom Kippur War* (San Rafael, Cal., 1978); Lawrence Whetten, *The Canal War (1967 to 1974)* (Cambridge, Mass., 1974); and Ze'ev Schiff and Ehud Ya'ari, *Israel's Lebanon War* (New York, 1984). On the attack on the U.S.S. *Liberty* in the June War, see James M. Ennes, *Assault on the Liberty* (New York, 1979). Martin Gilbert, *The Arab-Israeli Conflict: Its History in Maps* (New York, 1975), supplies cartographical orientation.

The Gulf war of 1991 is too recent to have spawned many solid book-length studies. The best is Lawrence Freedman and Efraim Karsh, *The Gulf Conflict 1990–1991* (Princeton, N.J., 1992). For background, see Judith Miller and Laurie Mylroie, *Saddam Hussein and the Crisis in the Gulf* (New York, 1990), and Elaine Sciolino, *The Outlaw State: Saddam Hussein's Quest for Power and the Gulf Crisis* (New York, 1991). Bob Woodward, *The Commanders* (New York, 1991), elucidates decision making in Washington, as does Roger Hilsman, *George Bush vs. Saddam Hussein* (Novato, Cal., 1992).

On the ever-interesting topic of oil, by far the most compelling and comprehensive work is Daniel Yergin, *The Prize* (New York, 1990). Leonard Mosley, *Power Play: Oil in the Middle East* (New York, 1973), is gossipy and fun, if less authoritative. Anthony Sampson, *The Seven Sisters: The Great Oil Companies and the World They Shaped* (New York, 1976), is more authoritative than Mosley but less fun. Stephen H. Longrigg, *Oil in the Middle East* (London, 1968), is more authoritative than either but less fun than both. Also worthy of mention are Gerald D. Nash, *United States Oil Policy, 1890–1964* (Pittsburgh, 1968); Robert Engler, *The Brotherhood of Oil* (Chicago, 1976); John M. Blair, *The Control of Oil* (New York, 1977); Aaron David Miller, *Search for Security: Saudi-Arabian Oil and American Foreign Policy, 1939–1949* (Chapel Hill, N.C., 1980); Michael B. Stoff, *Oil, War, and American Security: The Search for a National Policy on Foreign Oil, 1941–1947* (New Haven, Conn., 1980); and David S. Painter, *Oil and the American Century* (Baltimore, 1986).

The oil countries of the Middle East have used their petroleum revenues to buy many things they don't make themselves. Weapons usually top the shopping lists. On arms and arms control, try Jon D. Glassman, *Arms for the Arabs: The Soviet Union and War in the Middle East* (Baltimore, 1975); Anthony Sampson, *The Arms Bazaar* (New York, 1977); Aaron S. Klieman, *Israel's Global Reach: Arms Sales as Diplomacy* (Washington, 1985); and Paul Jabber, *Not by War Alone: Security and Arms Control in the Middle East* (Berkeley, 1981).

5. THE MIDDLE EAST IN WORLD CONTEXT

The Middle East wasn't a problem for American policy makers only—far from it. The global connections to the region were much of what made U.S. Middle East policy so difficult. Readers interested in learning about these global connections can consult, first of all, some general works: Bernard Lewis, *The Middle East and the West* (New York, 1968); George C. Lenczowski, *The Middle East in World Affairs* (Ithaca, N.Y., 1980); and William R. Polk, *The Elusive Peace: The Middle East in the Twentieth Century* (London, 1979).

The international developments that helped produce the postwar Middle East are traced in Howard M. Sachar, *Europe Leaves the Middle East, 1936–1954* (New York, 1972), and Barry Rubin, *The Great Powers in the Middle East, 1941–1949* (London, 1979). Elizabeth Monroe, *Britain's Moment in the Middle East, 1914–1971* (London, 1981), is the best brief account of British activities in the region; Wm. Roger Louis, *The British Empire in the Middle East, 1945–1951* (Oxford, England, 1984), is the best non-brief account. Wm. Roger Louis and Robert W. Stookey, eds., *The End of the Palestine Mandate* (Austin, Tex., 1986), brings together the work of several authors and several national viewpoints. Michael Cohen, *Palestine and the Great Powers, 1945–48* (Princeton, 1982), covers the same subject by himself. Bruce Kuniholm, *The Origins of the Cold War in the Near East,* relies mostly on American sources but also elucidates what the other great powers were up to at the end of World War II.

Soviet activities in the Middle East have interested many authors, not to mention American leaders and those of other countries. Pertinent titles include Oles M. Smolansky, *The Soviet Union and the Arab East under Khrushchev* (Lewisburg, Pa., 1974); Galia Golan, *Yom Kippur and After: The Soviet Union and the Middle East Crisis* (Cambridge, England, 1977), and *The Soviet Union and the Palestine Liberation Organization* (New York, 1980); Yaacov Ro'i, ed., *The Limits to Power: Soviet Policy in the Middle East* (London, 1979); Alvin Z. Rubinstein, *Red Star on the Nile: The Soviet-Egyptian Relationship Since the June War* (Princeton, N.J., 1977); Karen Dawisha, *Soviet Foreign Policy Towards Egypt* (London, 1979); and Mohammed

Heikal, *Sphinx and Commissar: The Rise and Fall of Soviet Influence in the Arab World* (London, 1978). Soviet activities also show up in two works that include much other material as well: Donald Neff, *Warriors for Jerusalem*, and Lawrence Whetten, *The Canal War*. For an assortment of viewpoints, try Paul Marantz and Blema S. Steinberg, eds., *Superpower Involvement in the Middle East* (Boulder, Col., 1985).

6. FIRSTHAND ACCOUNTS

Diplomats and statesmen (and the occasional stateswoman) can claim precious little success in solving the disputes that have wracked the Middle East during the last half-century. Their excuses for their failures fill many volumes of memoirs. On the American side, those with the most to say about the Middle East include, first of all, presidents: Harry S. Truman, *Memoirs* (Garden City, N.Y., 1955–56); Dwight D. Eisenhower, *The White House Years* (Garden City, N.Y., 1963–1965); Lyndon Baines Johnson, *The Vantage Point* (New York, 1971); Richard M. Nixon, *The Memoirs of Richard Nixon* (New York, 1978); Gerald R. Ford, *A Time to Heal* (New York, 1979); Jimmy Carter, *Keeping Faith* (New York, 1982); and Ronald Reagan, *An American Life* (New York, 1990). Next come secretaries of state: Dean G. Acheson, *Present at the Creation* (New York, 1969); Dean Rusk, *As I Saw It* (New York, 1990); Henry A. Kissinger, *White House Years* (Boston, 1979), and *Years of Upheaval*, (Boston, 1982); Cyrus Vance, *Hard Choices* (New York, 1983); and Alexander M. Haig, *Caveat* (New York, 1984). A secretary of defense follows: Caspar W. Weinberger, *Fighting for Peace* (New York, 1990); succeeded by lesser functionaries: Bartley C. Crum (of the Anglo-American Committee on Palestine), *Behind the Silken Curtain* (New York, 1947); James G. McDonald (first American ambassador to Israel), *My Mission to Israel* (New York, 1951); Robert Murphy (undersecretary of state and Eisenhower's all-around troubleshooter), *Diplomat among Warriors* (Garden City, N.Y., 1964); Vernon Walters (a man of many tongues who guided the less fluent through numerous negotiating sessions), *Silent Missions* (New York, 1978); George Ball, *The Past Has Another Pattern* (New York, 1982); Zbigniew K. Brzezinski, *Power and Principle* (New York, 1983); John S. Badeau (U.S. ambassador to Israel during the 1960s, among other posts), *The Middle East Remembered* (Washington, 1983); William H. Sullivan, *Mission to Iran* (New York, 1981); and Gen. H. Norman Schwarzkopf, *It Doesn't Take a Hero* (New York, 1992).

The spies have the most interesting stories, although it is difficult to check their assertions. Kermit Roosevelt was the CIA's top official for the Middle East before he wrote *Countercoup: The Struggle for the Control of Iran* (New York, 1979). Miles Copeland and Wilbur Crane Eveland were disillusioned lower-downs; Copeland authored *The Game of Nations: The*

Amorality of Power Politics (New York, 1969), while Eveland penned *Ropes of Sand: America's Failure in the Middle East* (London, 1980).

Officials of other countries have been somewhat less loquacious, or perhaps their literary agents haven't pushed so hard for publishing contracts. Israelis who have lifted the veil, more or less, include Chaim Weizmann, *Trial and Error* (New York, 1966); Shimon Peres, *David's Sling* (London, 1970); David Ben-Gurion, *My Talks with Arab Leaders* (New York, 1973); Golda Meir, *My Life* (New York, 1975); Moshe Dayan, *The Story of My Life* (New York, 1976); Abba Eban, *An Autobiography* (New York, 1977), and *Personal Witness* (New York, 1991); Menachem Begin, *The Revolt* (trans. Samuel Katz: New York, 1978 ed.), about Begin's years with the Zionist underground; Yitzhak Rabin, *The Rabin Memoirs* (Boston, 1979); and Ezer Weizmann, *The Battle for Peace* (New York, 1981).

Egyptians have been the most talkative of the Arabs. See Gamal Abdel Nasser, *Philosophy of the Revolution* (Washington, 1955); Anwar El Sadat, *Revolt on the Nile* (London, 1957) and *In Search of Identity: An Autobiography* (New York, 1978); Mohammed H. Heikal (journalist and confidant of Nasser and Sadat), *Nasser: The Cairo Documents* (London, 1972), *The Road to Ramadan* (New York, 1975), and *Cutting the Lion's Tail: Suez through Egyptian Eyes* (New York, 1987). King Hussein of Jordan says something but not much surprising in *Uneasy Lies the Head* (New York, 1962).

Iranian memoirs include Shah Mohammed Reza Pahlavi, *Mission for My Country* (New York, 1961), and *Answer to History* (New York, 1980); and Muhammad Mussadiq (Mossadeq), *Mussadiq's Memoirs* (London, 1988), published posthumously.

British officials who have told tales of interest for U.S. relations with the Middle East include Richard Crossman (of the Anglo-American Committee), *Palestine Mission* (London, 1947); Anthony Eden, *Full Circle* (Boston, 1960); Harold Macmillan, *Riding the Storm* (New York, 1971); and C. M. Woodhouse (Britain's answer to Kermit Roosevelt), *Something Ventured* (London, 1982). John B. Glubb, author of *A Soldier with the Arabs* (London, 1957), was the British commander of Jordan's army through the mid-1950s.

Nikita Khrushchev's two volumes of memoirs, *Khrushchev Remembers* (trans. Strobe Talbott; Boston, 1970–74), give the Soviet leader's side of the story.

Index